POSTCARD HISTORY SERIES

Wicomico County and Delmar

POSTCARD HISTORY SERIES

Wicomico County and Delmar

John E. Jacob

ARCADIA PUBLISHING

ISBN 978-0-7385-0000-3

Published by Arcadia Publishing
Charleston, South Carolina

Printed in the United States of America

For all general information contact Arcadia Publishing at:
Telephone 843-853-2070
Fax 843-853-0044
E-mail sales@arcadiapublishing.com
For customer service and orders:
Toll-Free 1-888-313-2665

Visit us on the Internet at www.arcadiapublishing.com

Contents

ACKNOWLEDGMENTS

I owe a debt of gratitude that I will be hard pressed to repay to Retta W. Mills. Not only has she typed my manuscript, she has suggested corrections, and has also dug up facts and cards for me on the story of Delmar, her hometown.

I also owe my heartfelt thanks to Charles M. Truitt for sharing his expertise and for putting together a conference on Delmar lore and legend.

I wish to thank J. Howard Adkins for his help and suggestions in the Mardela area, and Mrs. Dorothy Graham for sharing her knowledge of Tyaskin with me.

And thanks to Oswald Wilkerson for his generosity in sharing his cards of Hebron.

And my thanks and gratitude to James Jackson, who has loaned me so many cards.

And my appreciation for cards loaned by Gene Wharton, Walter Sullivan, Richard Carter, Robert S. Withey, Daniel E. Withey, Sylvia Taylor, and Betty Webster.

And the list would not be complete without saying thank you to Rebecca Miller and Corinne S. Lescallette of the Edward H. Nabb Research Center for Delmarva History and Culture at Salisbury State University for pictures loaned.

And to Herman Wheatley for sharing his knowledge of Sharptown.

And last but not least to my wife, Diane, so long suffering and patient, but firm when she feels firmness is in order.

Unless otherwise noted, the postcards presented in this book are from the collection of the author.

INTRODUCTION

Wicomico's history as a county began in 1867 with a referendum. The County was created by the Constitutional Convention, subject to a referendum that required a victory in each part of the two counties from which it was created, Somerset and Worcester.

This vote was most fortunate; the campaign for or against the new county was non-partisan, non-political, non-Union or Confederate. It was a vote for progress or the status quo. Fortunately, progress won, and its proponents never looked back.

After the referendum was won, a new election was required with voters electing new officers for a six-year term. These officers had an imposing task; the new county had not as much as a mule, a schoolhouse, a courthouse, a ledger, or a piece of chalk. They could not borrow their start up money from the bank; there was no bank in the county.

Teamwork was required, and it materialized. Deficit financing was organized, and new taxes were imposed and collected. Space for county offices was leased, oyster shells for county roads were bought, and teachers were hired and paid. And partisanship was submerged in the need to cooperate.

Business leaders and elected officials learned how to get along with each other, and that spirit of cooperation has never been lost. As it faces a new century, Wicomico has excellent schools, a prosperous economy, and a population at peace with itself.

We have the sense that Wicomico has come a long way in the years since its formation; and with the feeling of having solved so many problems already, we can face the future with confidence.

One

Both Sides of the Mason-Dixon Line

Why, in a history of Wicomico County, do we include a part of Delaware? Delmar is a town too big for one state, and since part is in Wicomico we include it all.

Delmar straddles the Mason-Dixon Line and is legally two towns. Having single water and sewer systems, one police force, one town hall, and separate parks, Delmar has but one history. Delmar was born in 1859 when the Delaware railroad reached the state line and stopped in an open field. Marylanders organized a line to continue it to Somers Cove (now Crisfield). The railroads merged, and the new railroad, the New York, Philadelphia and Norfolk, extended its line to Cape Charles and beyond by ferry. The railroad crews changed at Delmar, and a repair yard and train yard was established here.

Elijah Freeny built the first house, on Railroad Avenue and formed a partnership with a future governor of Maryland, Elihu Jackson, to open a store, and Jackson became the first postmaster.

Two banks were organized in Delmar, one on each side of the state line. Two separate schools were also organized here, but subsequently merged, with the elementary school in Maryland and the high school in Delaware. Today it is a prosperous community of over three thousand souls sharing churches and schools, as well as municipal services.

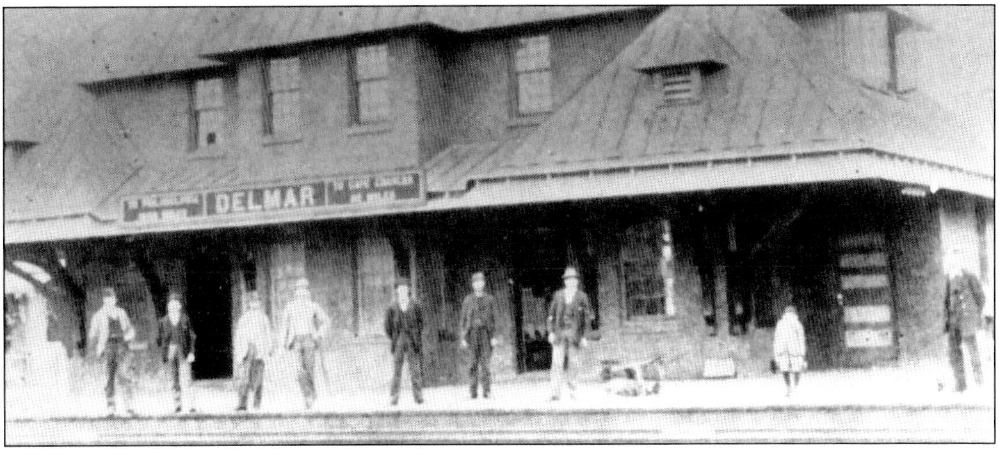

New Railroad Station. The first railroad station burned to the ground in the fire of 1892. When the new one was completed in July 1893, it was built of brick and described as follows: "one story with a sharp pitched roof and dormer windows, the former in shape resembling a farmer's broad brimmed Malaga hat, after a seasons wear more than anything else one can compare it to, it is not suited to so low a building." The sign says Delmar, with "to Philadelphia" on the north and "to Cape Charles" on the south. (Collection of the late Hilda Fowler.)

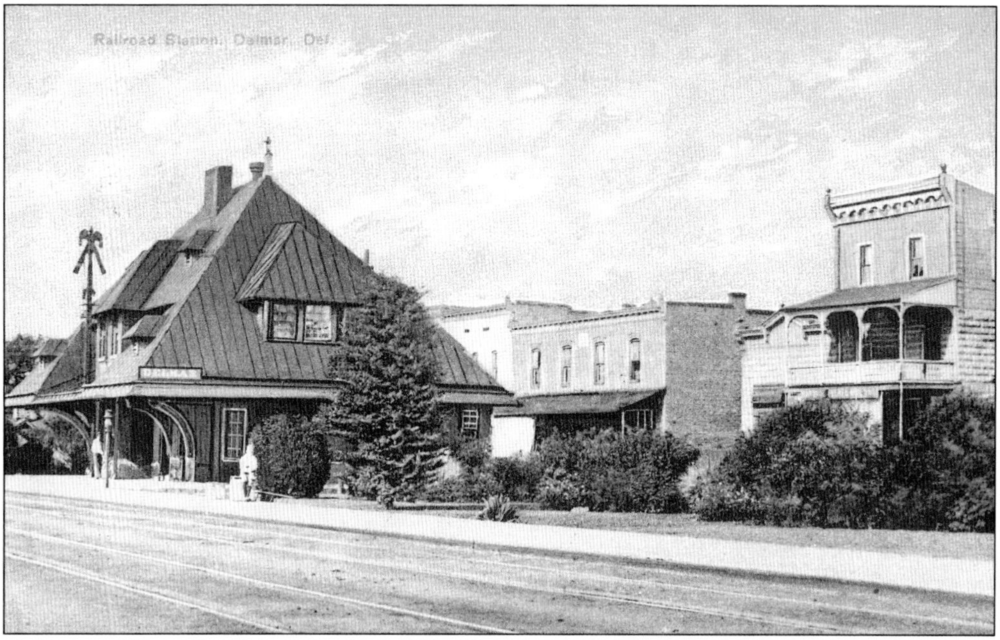

RAILROAD STATION. The original roof of soldered metal with vertical seams is clearly visible, along with the buildings on the right. Telephone was available to the station, but there were no electric poles. The station was torn down in 1957 after a fire on the second floor, and the ticket agent moved to the freight office.

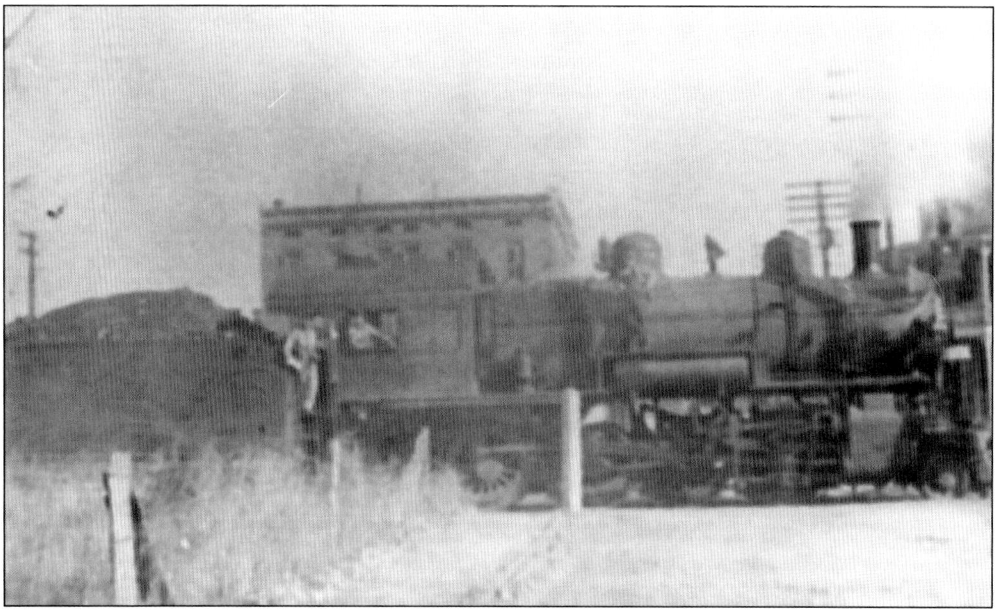

H6-STYLE LOCOMOTIVE. This picture is of a locomotive crossing State Street. The locomotive is an H6, which came into use about 1906. The hotel and the Center can be seen beyond the locomotive. (Collection of the late Hilda Fowler.)

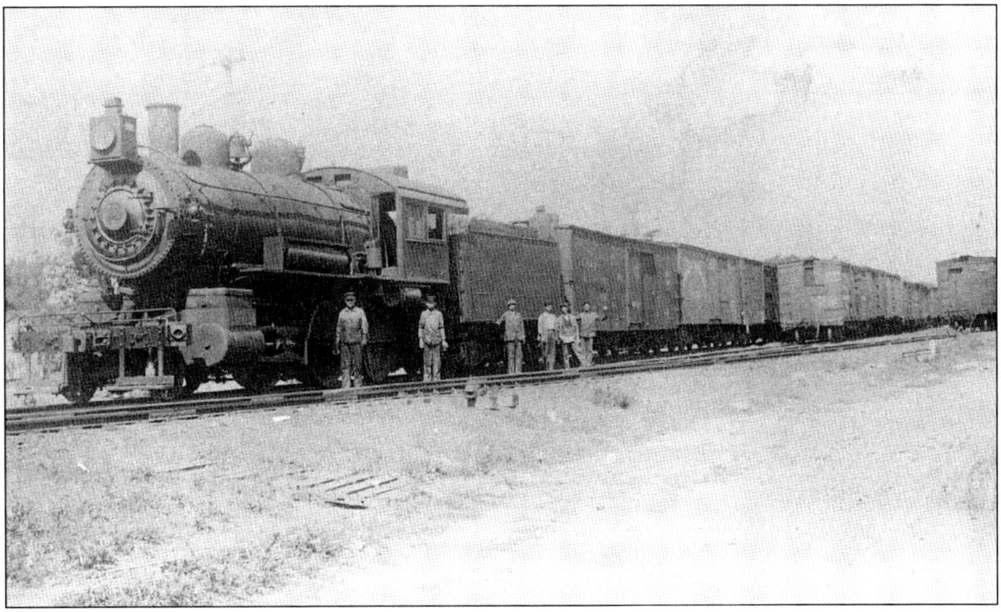

Locomotive. This E3-style locomotive is shown hooked to a number of freight cars. The E3 came into use after 1900 and remained in use for about 20 years. This picture was taken in the freight yards; note the three separate tracks. (Collection of the late Hilda Fowler.)

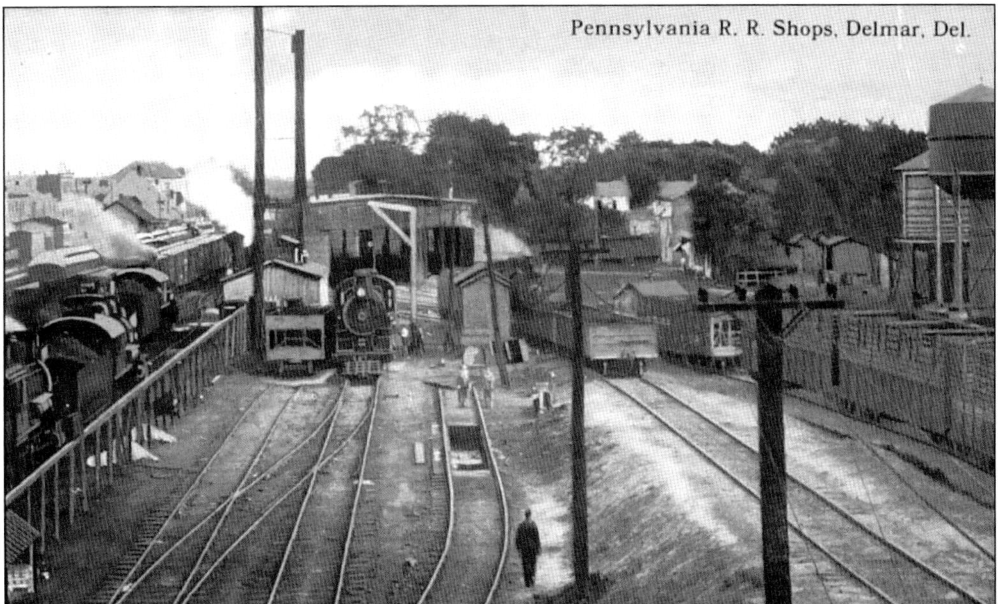

Pennsylvania Railroad Shops, Delmar, Delaware. The open shed-like building at left rear was used for servicing the locomotives and for making inspections and minor repairs. The track in the center was used to back the locomotive up to be refueled with coal. Ashes were dumped into the pit shown in the center of the picture and the coal cars on the inclined track were shoved forward alongside the empty coal car of the engine and then tipped to fill it. A look at the man in the foreground will give some idea of the height of the incline. The locomotive headed toward the camera is the type known as H8.

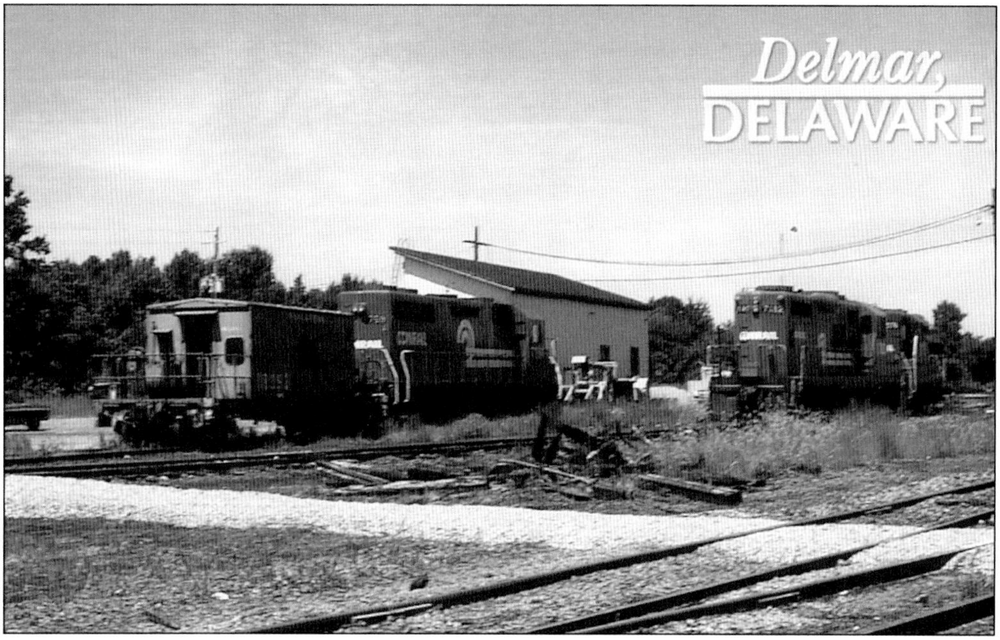

Delmar, Delaware. This more modern postcard is from 1979. It shows one GP-387759 and one PC N9-E cabin, along with two CR GP-10's, outside the Delmar engine house. (Photograph by Daniel Withey.)

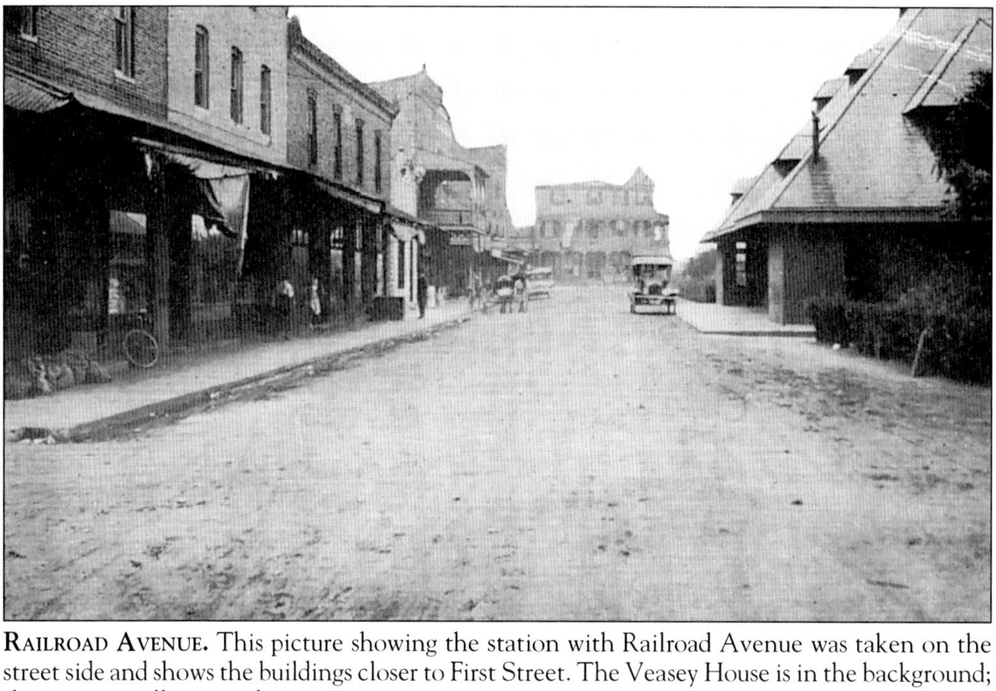

Railroad Avenue. This picture showing the station with Railroad Avenue was taken on the street side and shows the buildings closer to First Street. The Veasey House is in the background; the street is still unpaved.

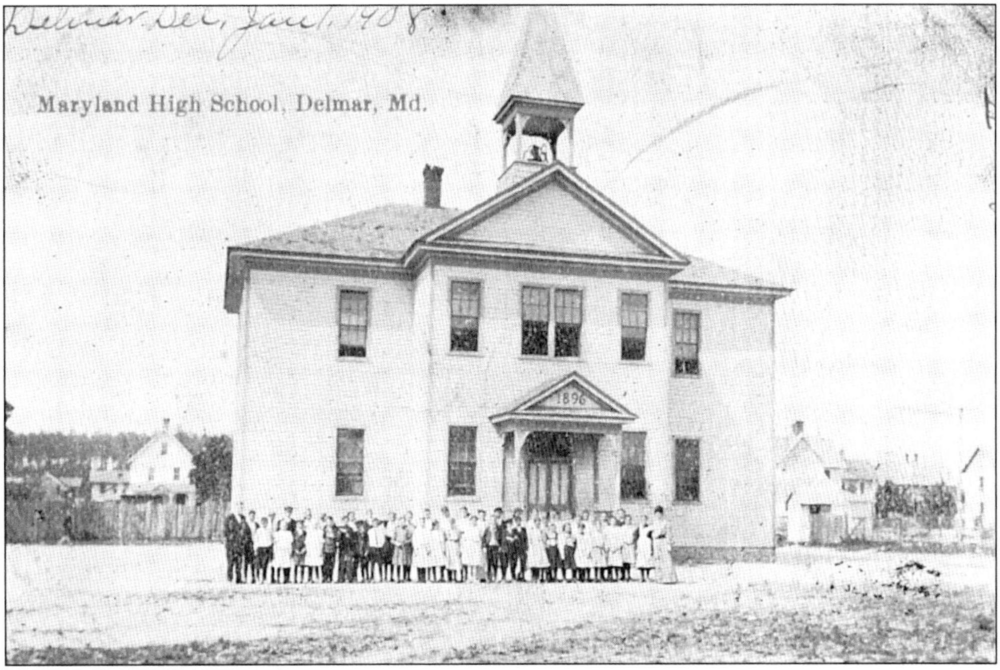

MARYLAND HIGH SCHOOL. This school was located where the Catholic church now stands. At this time the school was for all grades. It was built in 1896. This picture was made later and the card mailed on January 1, 1908. It is a Byrd of Salisbury card. In 1914 the school had an enrollment of 267, 39 of which were in high school. The school was overcrowded and grades one and two were moved to the Masonic Temple. In 1919 a new brick school was planned.

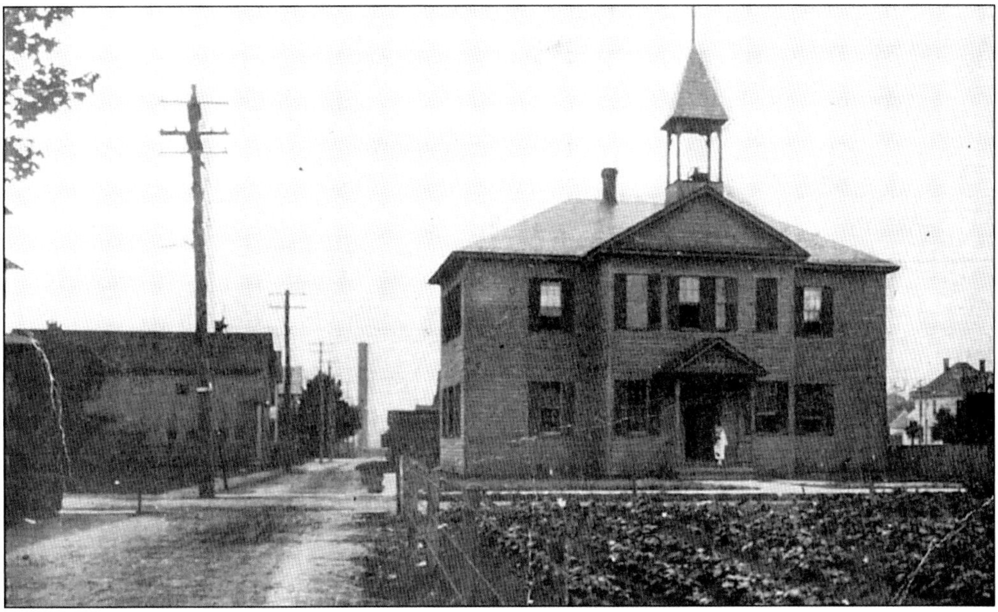

THE DELAWARE HIGH SCHOOL. It was located at First and Grove Streets and obviously had nothing across the street from it. The building was built in 1902, and there is a picture in the Delmar library of its first graduating class, of six girls, with Willard Deputy, the principal. It served until 1919 when a new school was built.

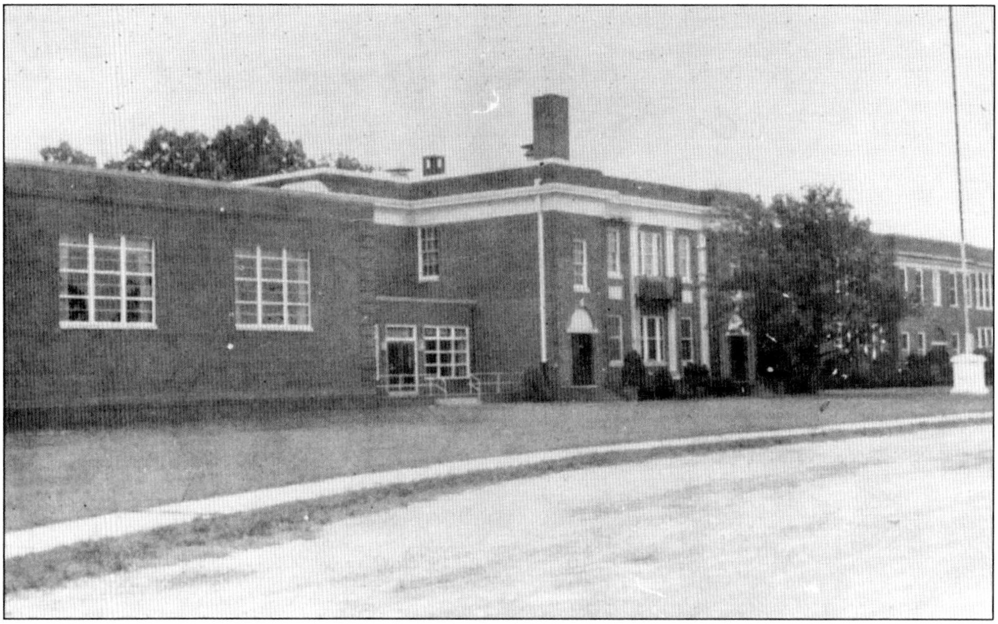

The Maryland Elementary School. The central section of the Maryland Elementary School was built in 1920, and in 1923 only grades seven to 11 went here. Now the enlarged school teaches only the elementary grades, and high school students go to school at the Delaware High School. (Collection of Gene Wharton.)

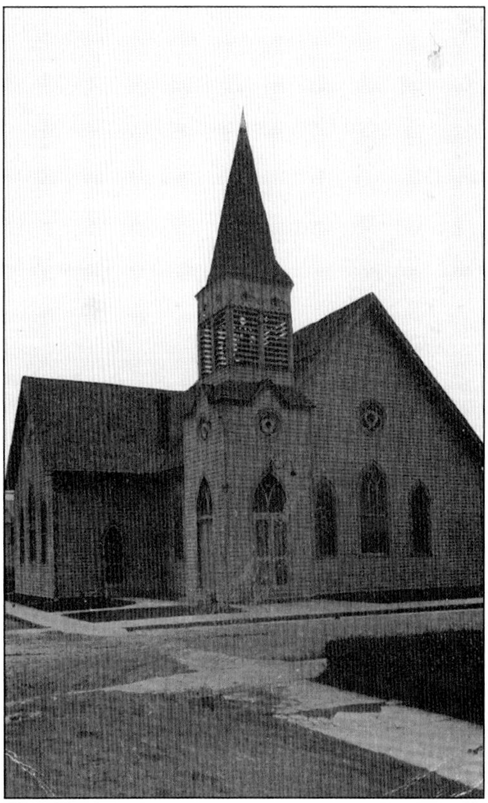

M.E. Church, Delmar, Delaware. The first religious service held in Delmar was conducted by Rev. Joseph Cook, a M.E. Clergyman, on Wednesday, September 4, 1867. He came to Delmar at the invitation of Thomas Asbury Nelson and preached on the front lawn of the home of M.M. Hill.

Soon afterward a plank church, 19 by 30 feet, was built and lasted for five years. In 1872 $1,000 was subscribed for a new church to be built in Delaware on the land of Elijah Freeny. It was finished and dedicated on November 30, 1872. The first church bell didn't satisfy the congregation and they traded it back on a new one with a mellower tone. This original structure was destroyed by fire in 1892, and the church shown was built anew in 1893, with a tower and steeple.

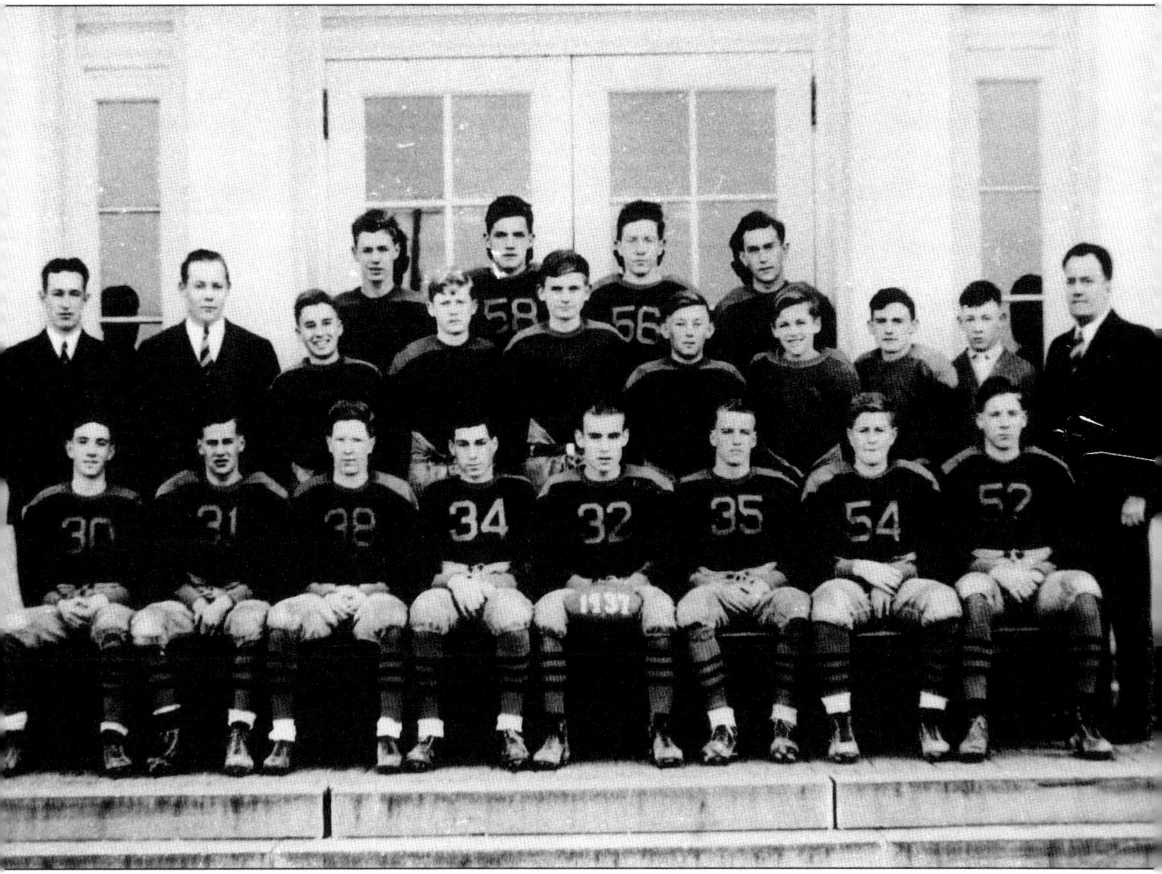

1937 Delmar High Football Team. It is rare to find a group picture of a football team on a postcard, particularly as late as 1937. It can only bespeak great pride in the team, which ended the year with an enviable record.

Pictured from left to right are the following: (first row) Billy Hearn, Ray Wilkinson, Lenwood LeCates, Roy Aydelott, Vaughn Lockerman, Bobby Kelly, Oliver Cook, and Donald Dickerson; (second row) Coach Mitchell, Walter Sullivan, John Sample, Andrew Conaway, Jack Whitney, Howard Davis, Glen Hastings, Ward Baker, Randolph Cooper, and the principal, Harold Whiteside; (third row) Dallas (Skeeter) Ellis, Joseph Dickerson, Charles Rider, and William Beach. (Collection of Walter Sullivan.)

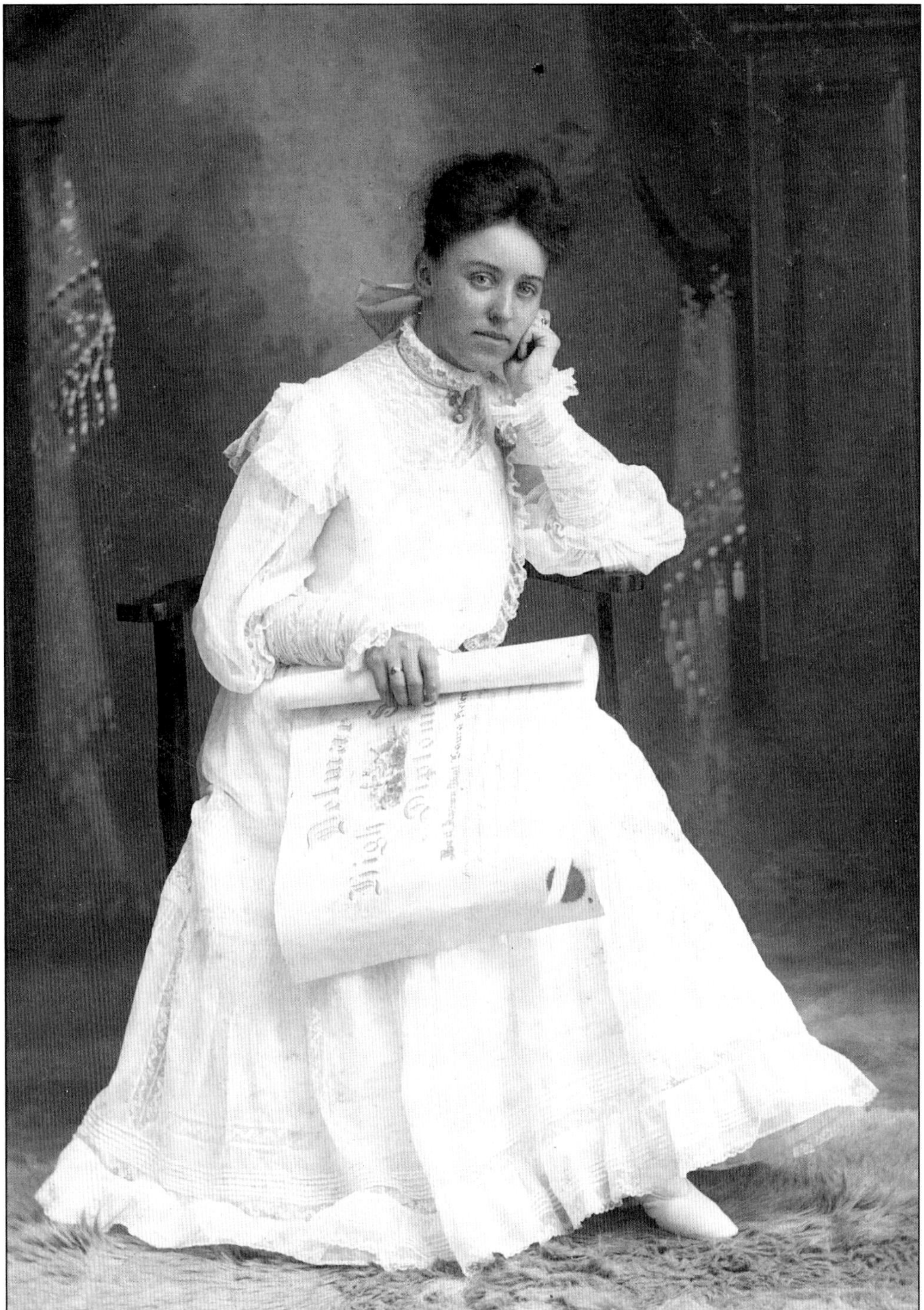

A Sweet Girl Graduate. This is the graduation picture of Helen Lowe, who graduated from Delmar High School in about 1903. She is wearing her white graduation dress and has a partially unrolled diploma from Delmar High School in her hand. In 1903 there were probably not more than eight in the graduating class.

M.P. CHURCH, DELMAR, DELAWARE. A Methodist Protestant congregation was formed in Delmar in 1889. A church was built on West Church Street beyond the Baptist church, and the first services were held on November 30, 1889. After phenomenal growth in membership, a new church was built in 1893 on the north side of State Street, this time beyond the M.E. Church, also completed in November. (Collection of E. Pusey.)

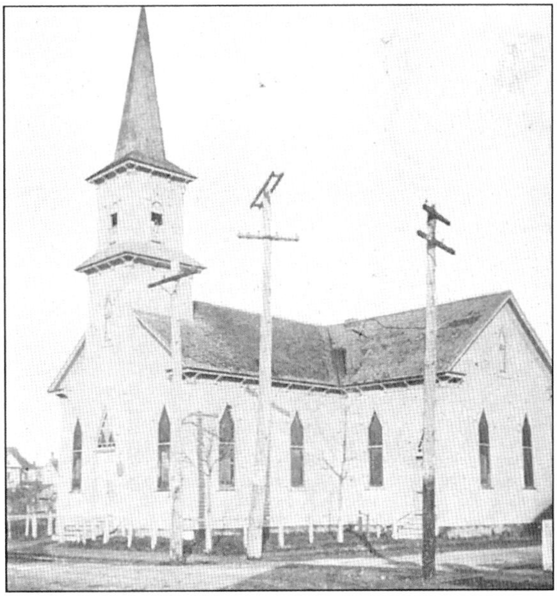

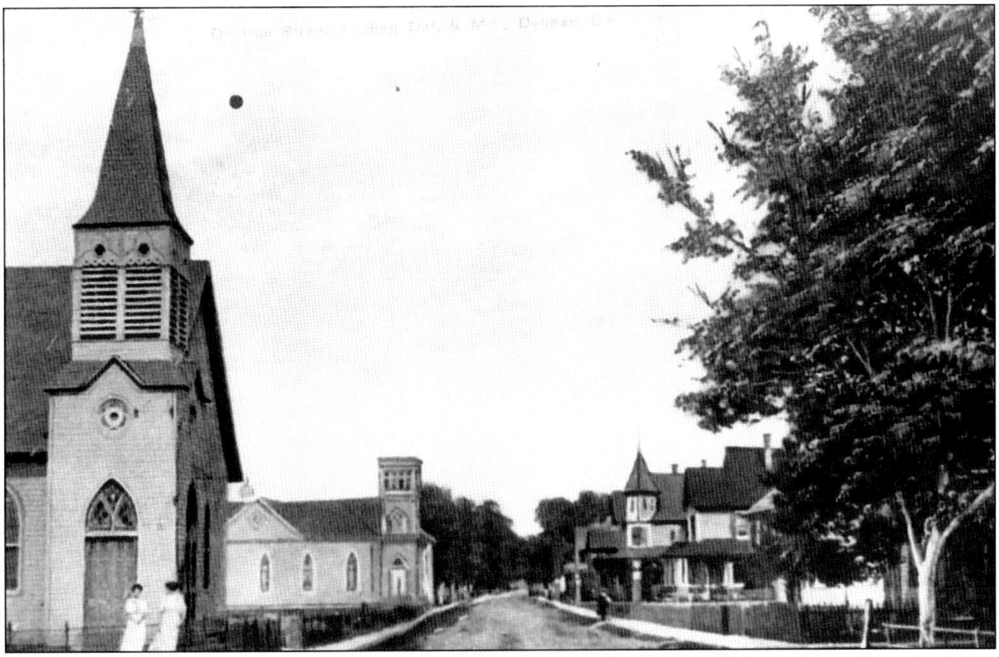

DIVISION STREET DIVIDING DELAWARE AND MARYLAND. This postcard shows how close the M.E. and the M.P. Churches were to each other so that when union came between the two branches of Methodism, it became sensible in Delmar to have a single congregation and a single church. When the two congregations merged in 1964, the members selected St. Stephen's Methodist Church of Delmar as the name of the united congregation.

The former M.E. Church had the larger sanctuary, so regular services were continued in it. Since then the former M.P. Church has been sold and the former M.E. Church building completely remodeled, a work done with grace and beauty, but not yet recorded on postcard. The closest house across the street in Maryland belonged to Bert Elliott. The next one with the tower belonged to Joseph Hastings. (Collection of A. Frank Holloway.)

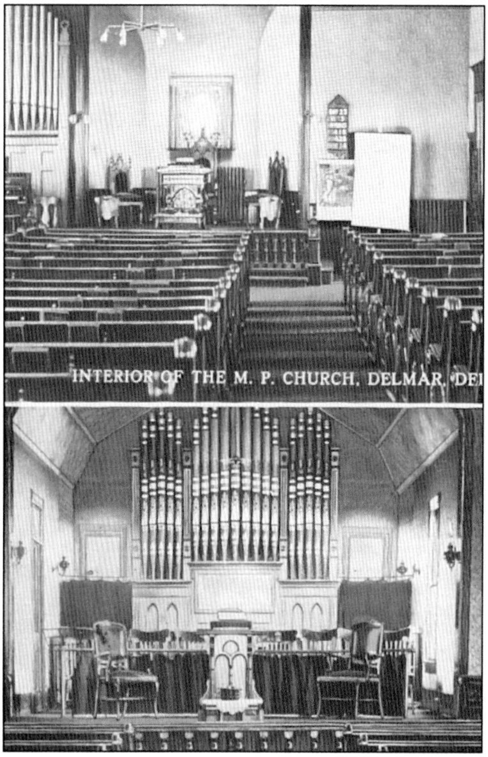

INTERIORS OF THE M.P. AND M.E. CHURCHES. A forerunner of the eventual union of the M.P. and M.E. Churches was the printing of the pictures of the interiors of both churches on one postcard. Heat and electricity had been installed in the M.P. Church, as was its pipe organ by the time this picture was taken. The pipe organ was not installed until May 1907 so the M.P. interior picture was after this date. The pipe organ in the M.E. Church was dedicated on January 19, 1899, and it seems to be flanked by oil lamps with globes, so this picture may pre-date the other by several years.

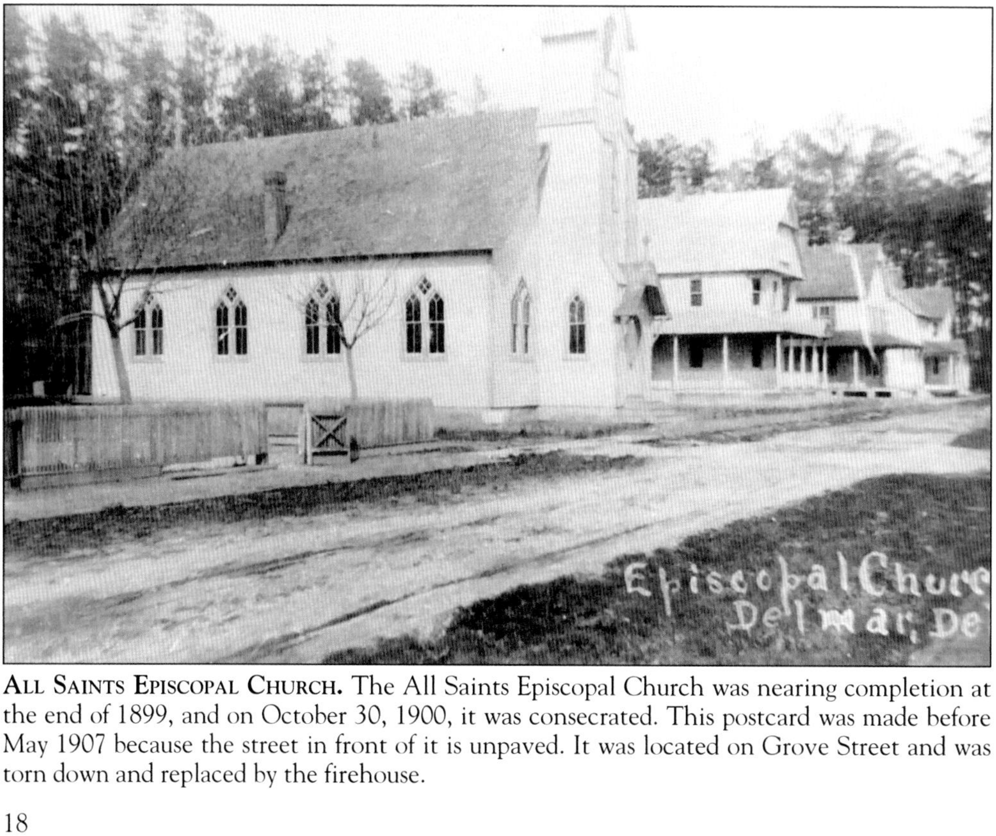

ALL SAINTS EPISCOPAL CHURCH. The All Saints Episcopal Church was nearing completion at the end of 1899, and on October 30, 1900, it was consecrated. This postcard was made before May 1907 because the street in front of it is unpaved. It was located on Grove Street and was torn down and replaced by the firehouse.

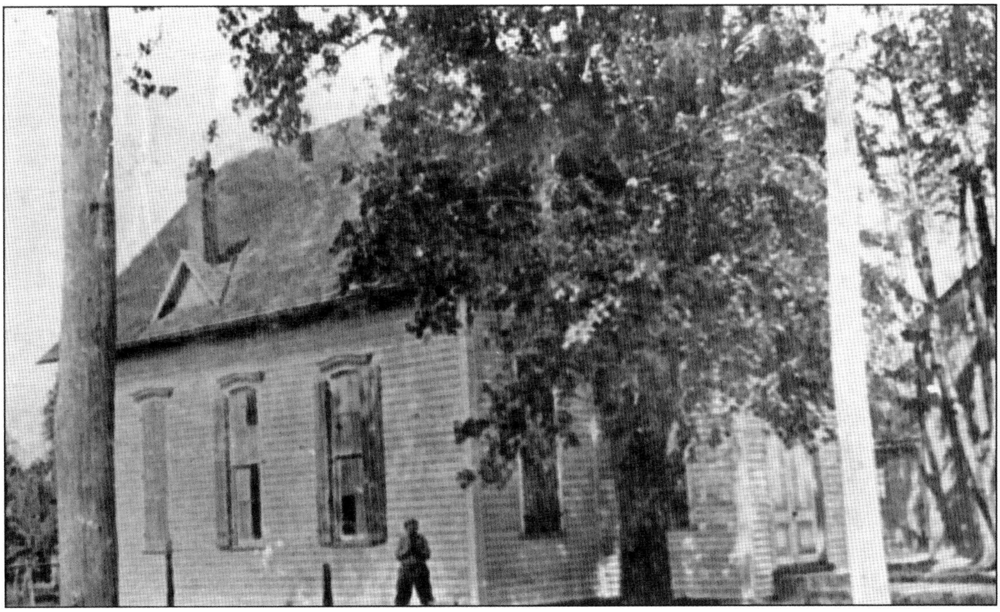

First Baptist Church of Delmar. The first meeting of the church was held in the schoolhouse on May 6, 1883, with John T. Craig, Sunday school missionary of the American Baptist Publication Society, in the chair. Twenty-two people formed the initial congregation, and they chose J.T. Craig as temporary pastor. In the summer of 1883, a lot on State Street was purchased and a building built and dedicated on November 27, 1883.

The church continued to grow under succeeding pastors, and the congregation began a search for a different site for a new, enlarged, and modern church. After more than two decades, a new site was secured at Bi-State Boulevard and Walnut Street. A new building was erected and dedicated on Easter Sunday, 1964 after which the original building shown here was disposed of. (Collection of the late Hilda Fowler.)

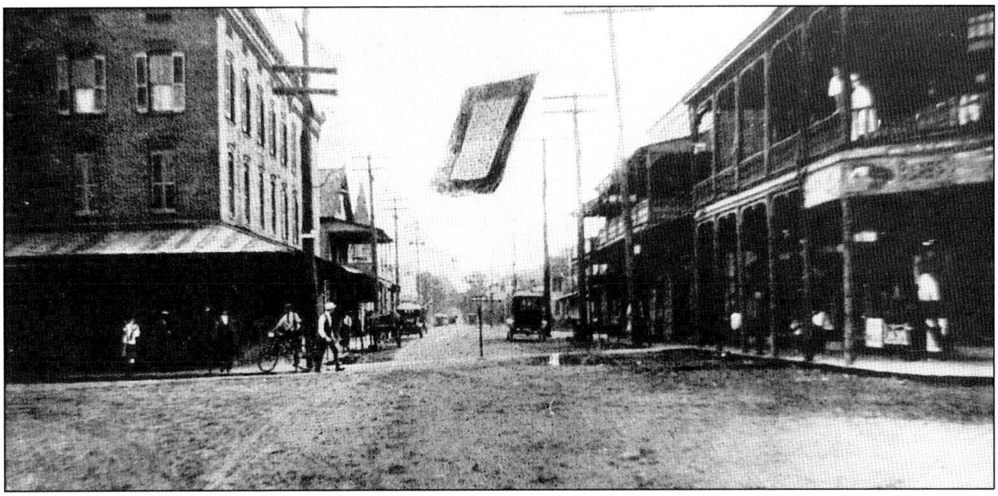

State Street Looking East. This postcard scene was taken after a rain that caused water to cover the streets. The Veasey House is on the right with Whielan's Drug Store behind it. On the Delaware side is the Center. Hearn and Smith Jewelers are in the corner with Doda Hearn's Men Clothing store behind it, and next is the Stone Hotel. The picture was probably made about 1905. (Collection of the late Hilda Fowler.)

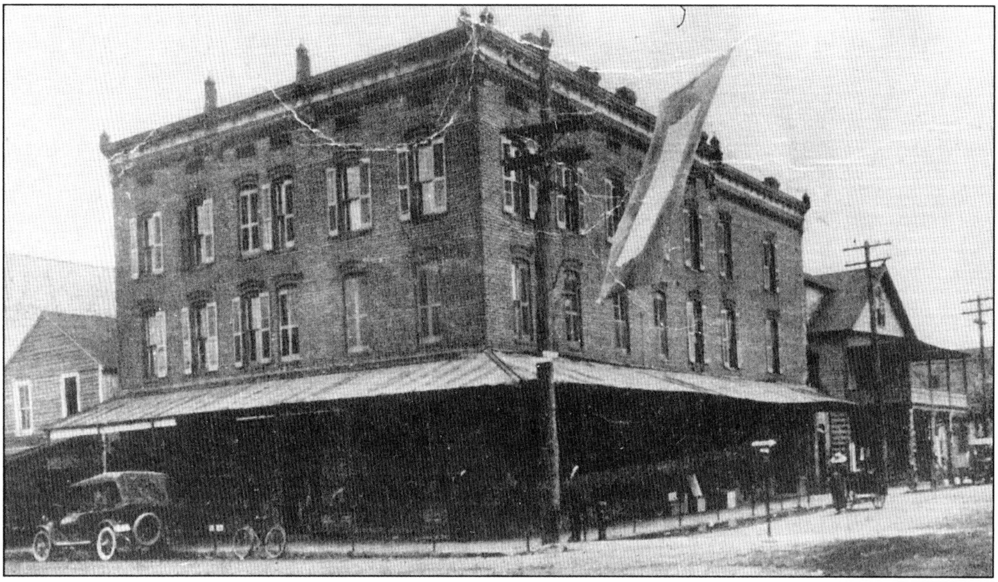

The Center. The same banner flies in the middle of the street, but the street itself is dry. The white streaks on the left are probably rolled up canvas, and the pole in the center of State Street is for traffic regulation. An arrow on the pole is directing southbound traffic on Railroad Avenue to make a left turn to go around it. (Collection of E. Pusey.)

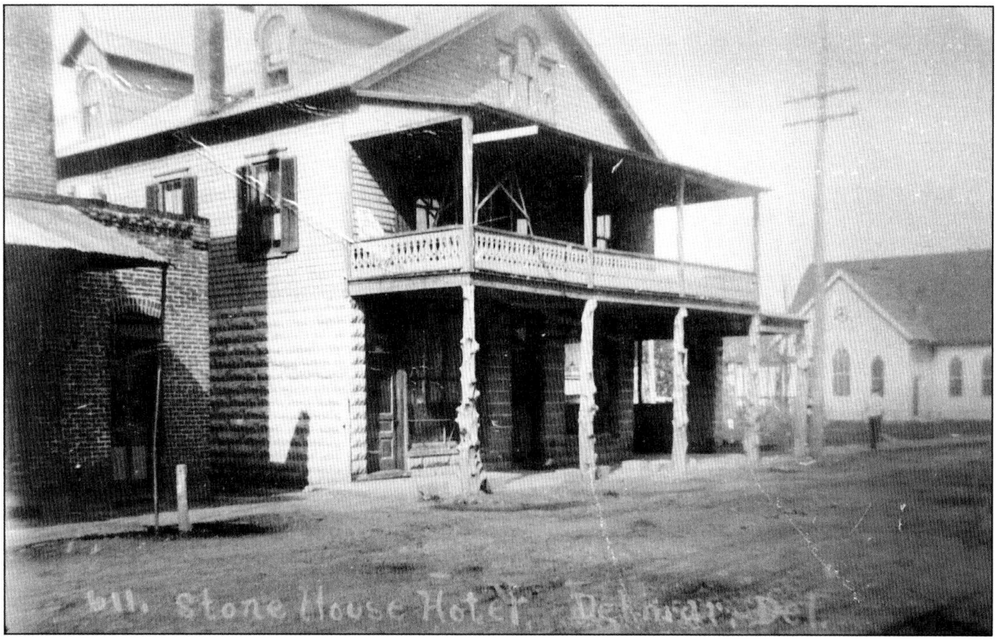

Stone House Hotel. The Stone House Hotel was built on the Delaware side of State Street after the Maryland side went "dry" in 1904 as the result of a local option referendum. It was owned by Dorey Veasey, who operated it for the bar until the Delaware side of town also went "dry." Mr. Veasey still rented rooms after he could no longer sell liquor. This building has also been used as a shirt factory and was the post office for many years. The building is still standing. The Methodist Episcopal Church is shown at right, and there was a barbershop in the building on the left. (Collection of E. Pusey.)

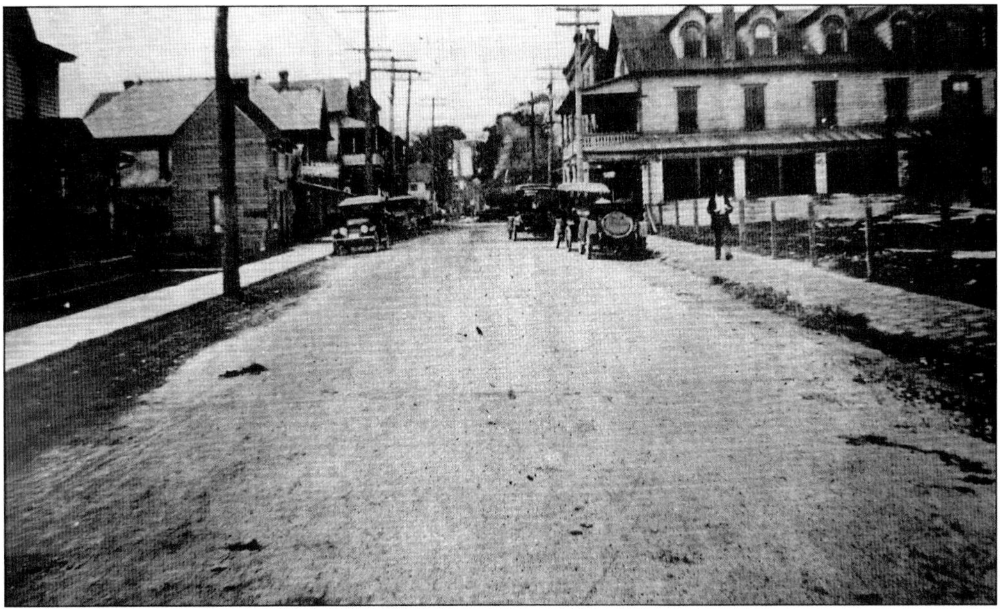

State Street Looking West. On the Delaware side (right) was the Stone House Hotel. On the Maryland side (left) was the shoe repair store of Greensbury White, the seafood shop of Archlaus Elliott, the Bank of Delmar, and Sewell Whielen's Drugstore with the porch upstairs. Note the northbound train crossing the street in the background. (Collection of E. Pusey.)

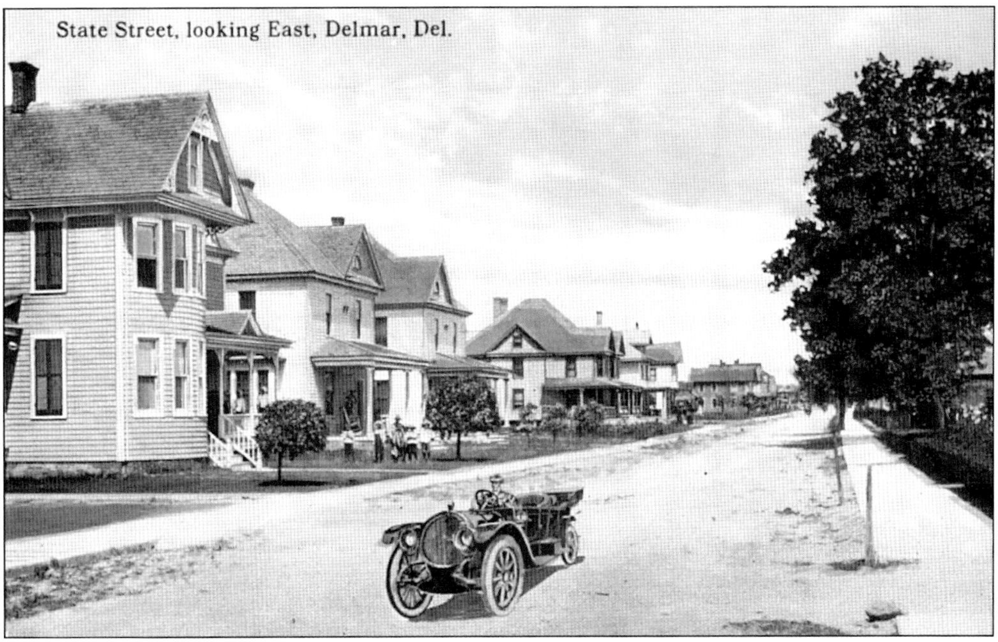

State Street Looking East. Everything is real but the automobile. This cut-and-paste scene is looking east at Sixth Street. The first house on the left is that of the preacher, Frank Falconer. The fourth house is that of John Henry Sturgis, and then Ira Hearne's. The last building on the left has since burned. On the right side, the house of Burt Lecates is barely visible.

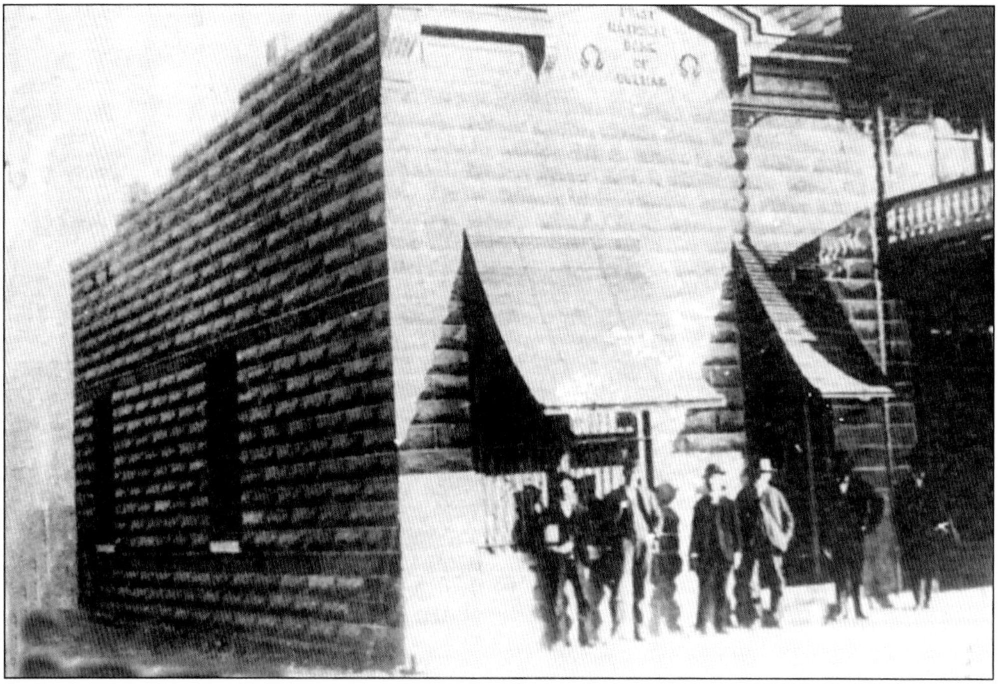

First National Bank of Delmar. The First National Bank of Delmar opened its doors for business the week of April 21, 1904. The building was erected by the firm of Slemons and Bounds and was built of concrete and cement blocks. It had initial capital of $30,000. S. Ker Slemons and W.W. Ellis were the president and cashier respectively, and at the end of the first year their surplus was $11,000.

The bank voluntarily closed in 1938 under the presidency of Samuel Culver. Arthur W. Ellis was cashier, Leo B. Hearn was assistant cashier, and Amy Culver Waller was the bookkeeper. Ellis went to work for the Bank of Delmar. No money was lost by any stockholder. The building is now a barbershop. (Collection of the late Hilda Fowler.)

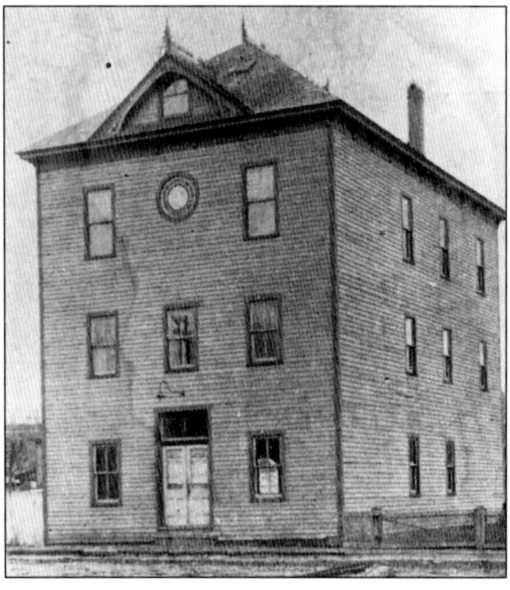

Masonic Temple, Delmar. The Masonic Temple on East Railroad Avenue was built in 1901. In 1917–18 it was used by the Delmar, Maryland School for additional classroom space for the first and second grades. The Masons built a new temple in 1925 and sold the old building to the Delmar Moose Lodge. Eventually the Moose Lodge disintegrated and the Delmar Bank got title to it. The bank and the Town of Delmar swapped land, and the town got the building that was torn down to make space for town use. (Collection of the late Hilda Fowler.)

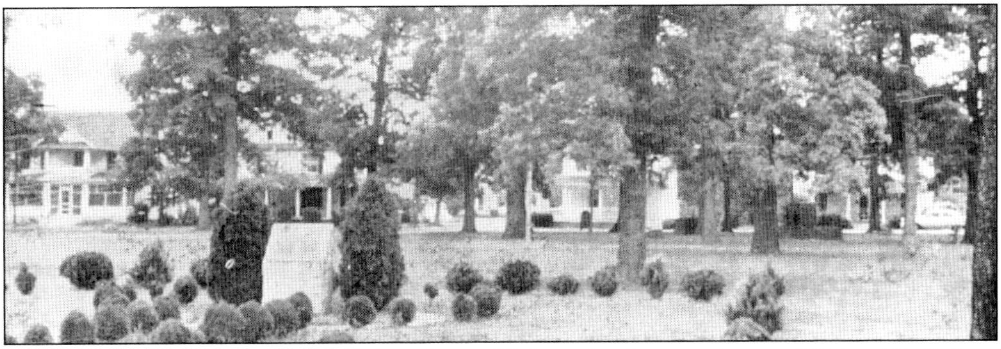

The Delmar Park. In 1940 the Delmar Lions Club, under the presidency of Richard E. Cullen, purchased from George Sparrow three-fourths of what is now the Delmar Park for $2,000. The Lions were unincorporated and broke so Mr. Cullen's father loaned them the $2,000 at 1 percent interest and took title in his name. Later they discovered that Mrs. Minnie Melson, from whom Sparrow had purchased the property, still owned land they needed. This they purchased for $1,100, and Frank Collins advanced the money for this purchase on the same terms.

The land was swampy with a ditch through the center. The Lions members hauled about five hundred loads of fill dirt into the park area after they had gotten the Delaware Highway Department to remove the stumps, which it did without charge. Later the property was conveyed to the two Delmar municipalities, which, after World War II, took over the park's care and maintenance. Today the park sports nearly 3 acres of playground and a picnic pavilion. (Collection of the late Hilda Fowler.)

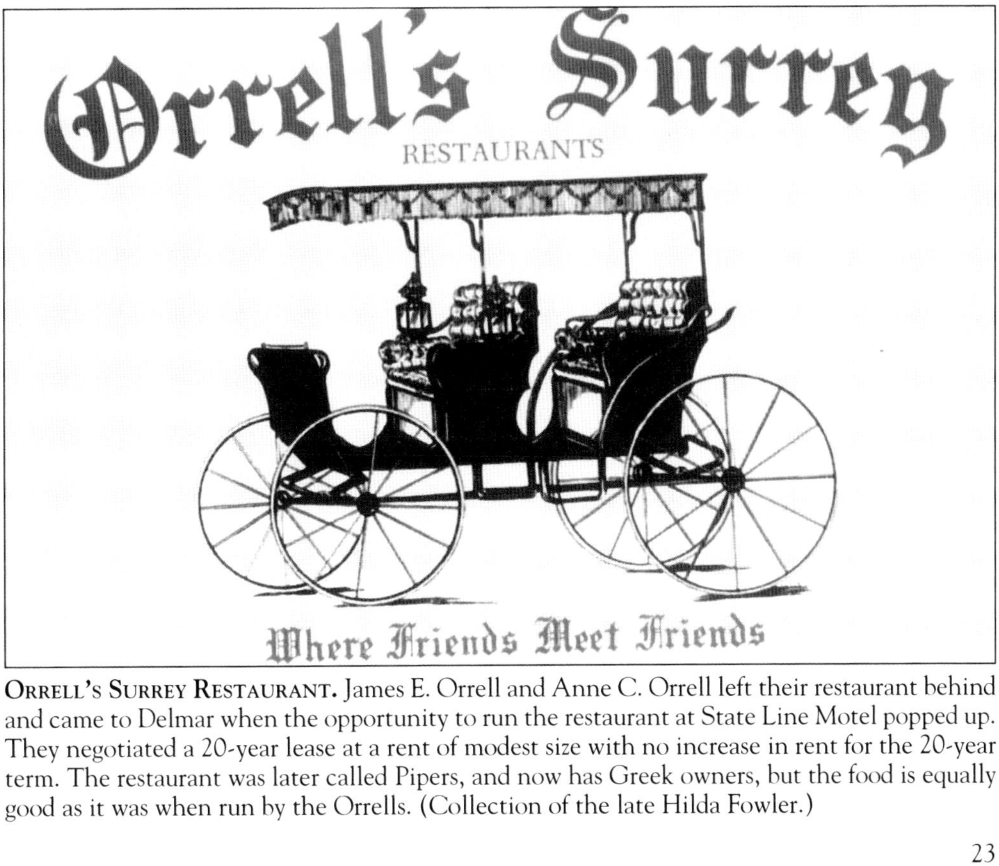

Orrell's Surrey Restaurant. James E. Orrell and Anne C. Orrell left their restaurant behind and came to Delmar when the opportunity to run the restaurant at State Line Motel popped up. They negotiated a 20-year lease at a rent of modest size with no increase in rent for the 20-year term. The restaurant was later called Pipers, and now has Greek owners, but the food is equally good as it was when run by the Orrells. (Collection of the late Hilda Fowler.)

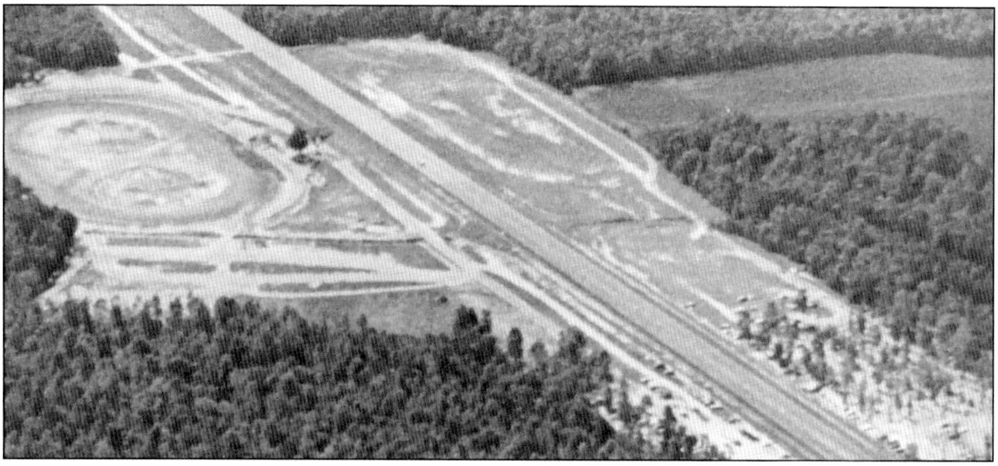

Delmar U.S. 13 Dragway and Delaware International Speedway. William J. Cathell started the U.S. 13 Dragway in August 1963 after careful evaluation of the demand. As he said, "Lots of boys liked to race and had to go to the other side of Baltimore to do it." The racing complex contains 131 acres of land north of Delmar on Route 13. It began with a drag strip, and a speedway was added in 1965, which operates as Delaware International Speedway to avoid confusion between the two types of racing. It has developed over the years and in 1989 was ranked eighth on the list of Delaware tourist attractions, with 103,000 people coming through the gate.

It has installed the most sophisticated timing facilities available, and printed tickets are handed to each contestant at the conclusion of his performance. The bleachers at the Speedway seat 5,000 spectators, and 2,000 seats are available at the Dragway, plus spaces for parked cars. It is still very successful and popular. (Collection of the late Hilda Fowler.)

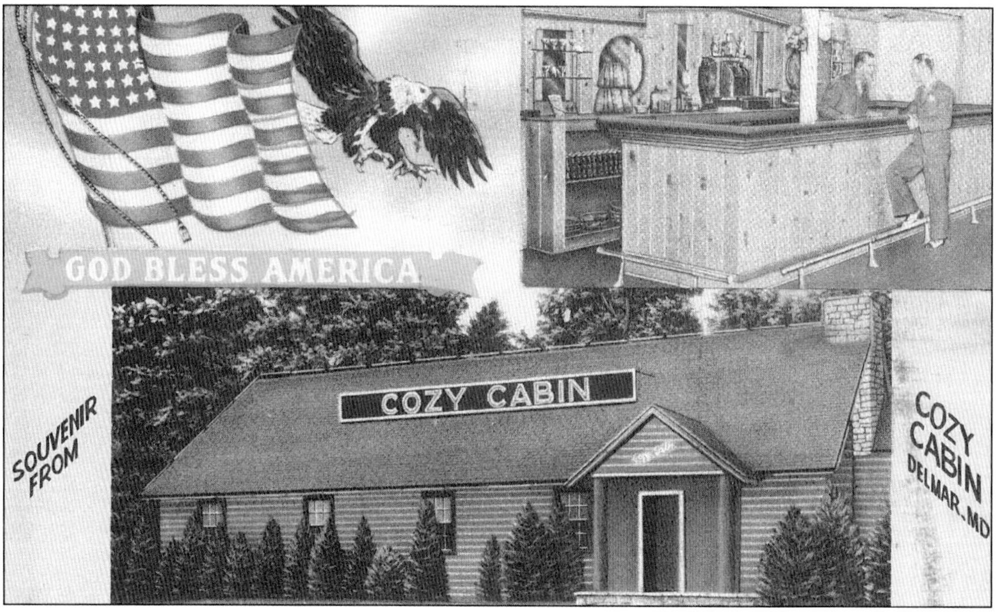

The Cozy Cabin. This night club was located on the West Side of Bi-State Boulevard. It was built and operated by Claude E. Calhoun and reached the height of its popularity in the late 1930s and early 1940s. Calhoun sold the business, and two young Salisbury businessmen operated it. It burned and a residence was built on the site.

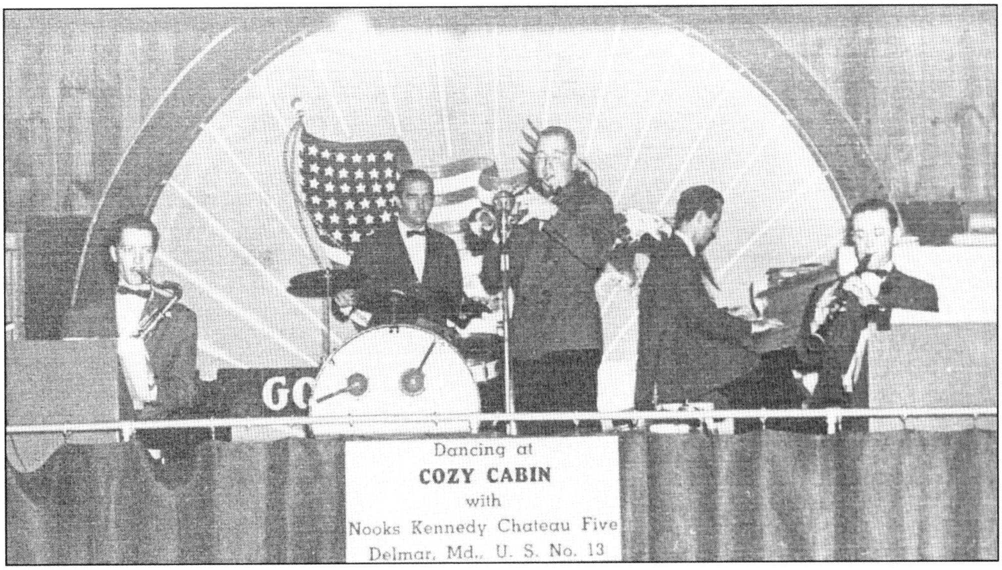

Nooks Kennedy and His Band. This is the band that played at the Cozy Cabin. They played on a regular basis for Mr. Calhoun.

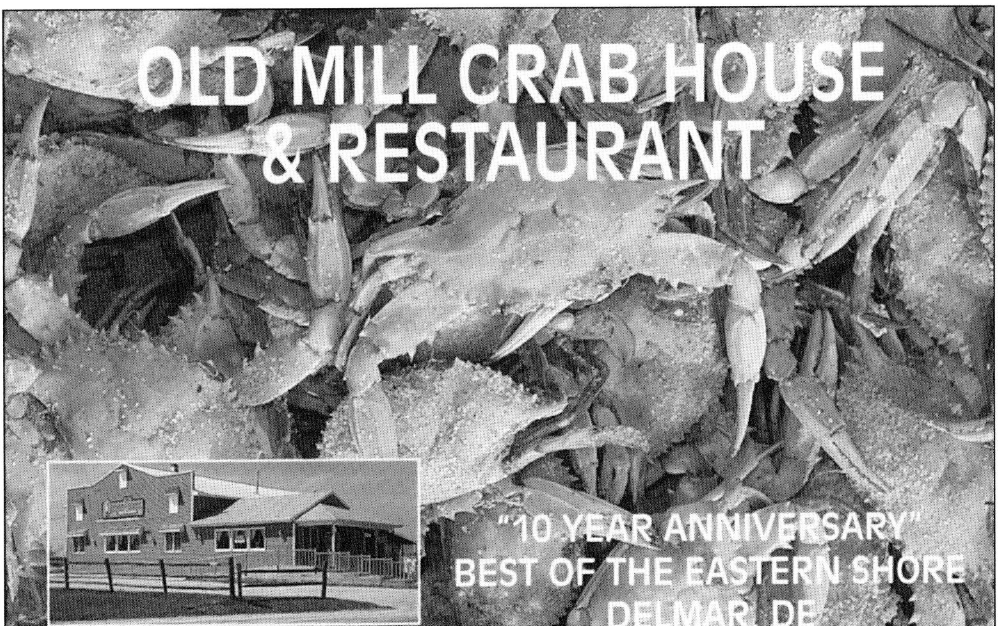

Old Mill Crab House and Restaurant. Robert Kowalski started his restaurant in 1983, and its 10th anniversary was in 1993. It is located where Route 54 meets Waller Road. They serve all you can eat steamed crabs, fried chicken, hush puppies, corn on the cob, clam strips, and popcorn shrimp. (Collection of Retta W. Mills.)

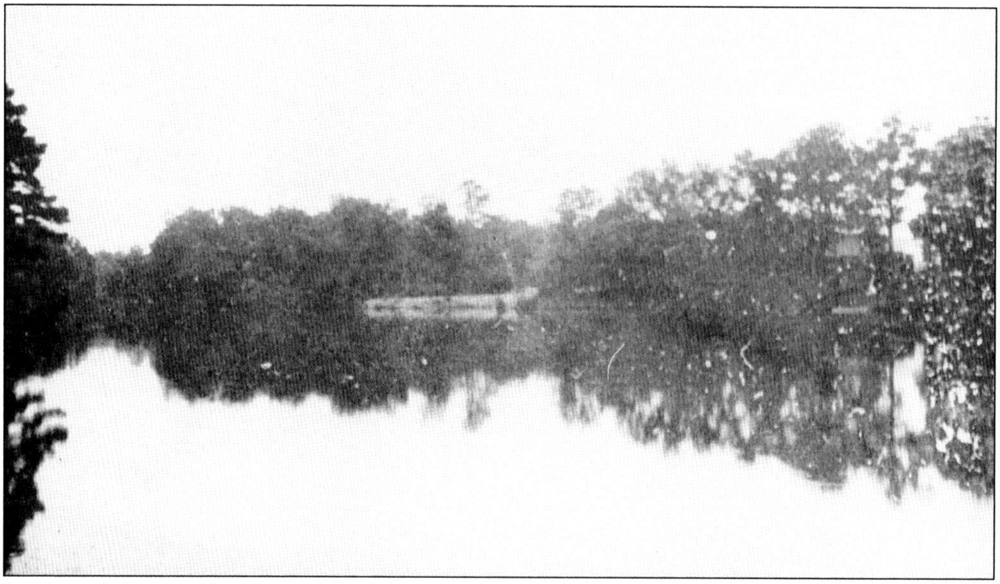

LEONARD'S LAKE. This view of the lake was taken from the bridge over U.S. 13 before the area was fully developed. The Maryland tourist information center and a public park are now on the west side, and the land on the east side is now the site of several housing developments.

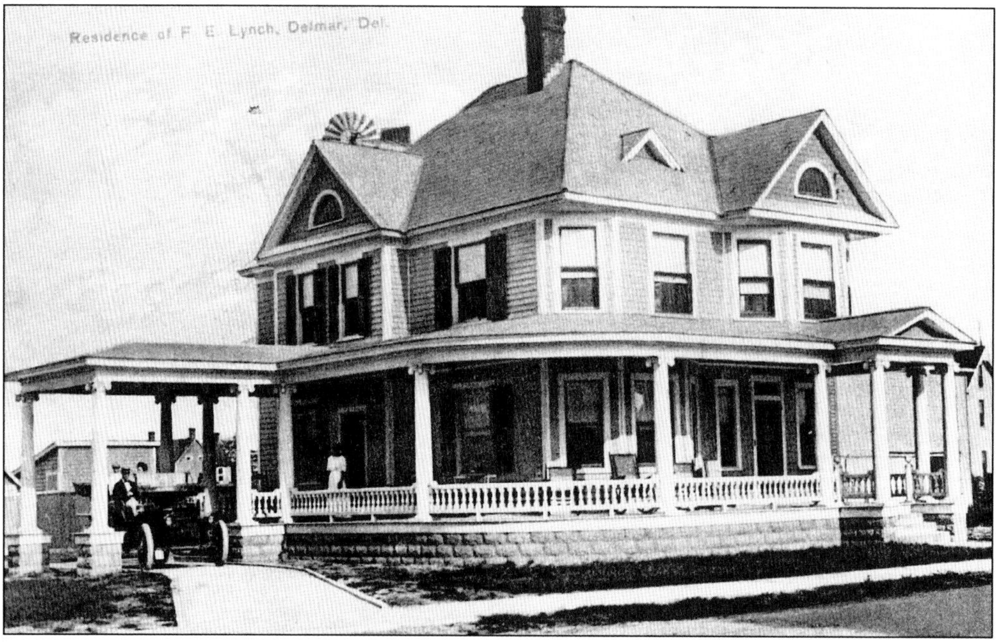

RESIDENCE OF FRANK E. LYNCH. Frank E. Lynch was a farm owner, a businessman, and a speculator. It is rumored that he made a killing in General Motors stock. This picture shows Mr. Lynch in his automobile and Mrs. Lynch on the front porch. She was the choir director of St. Stephens Church for more than 50 years when she was elevated to the status of choir director emeritus. The house was at the northeast corner of North Second Street and Delaware Avenue. It has been torn down and is now the site of Chancellor Care Center. Mr. Lynch set his son Frank up in the first filling station in Delmar, located on the Maryland side of State Street at the corner of First. (Collection of the late Hilda Fowler.)

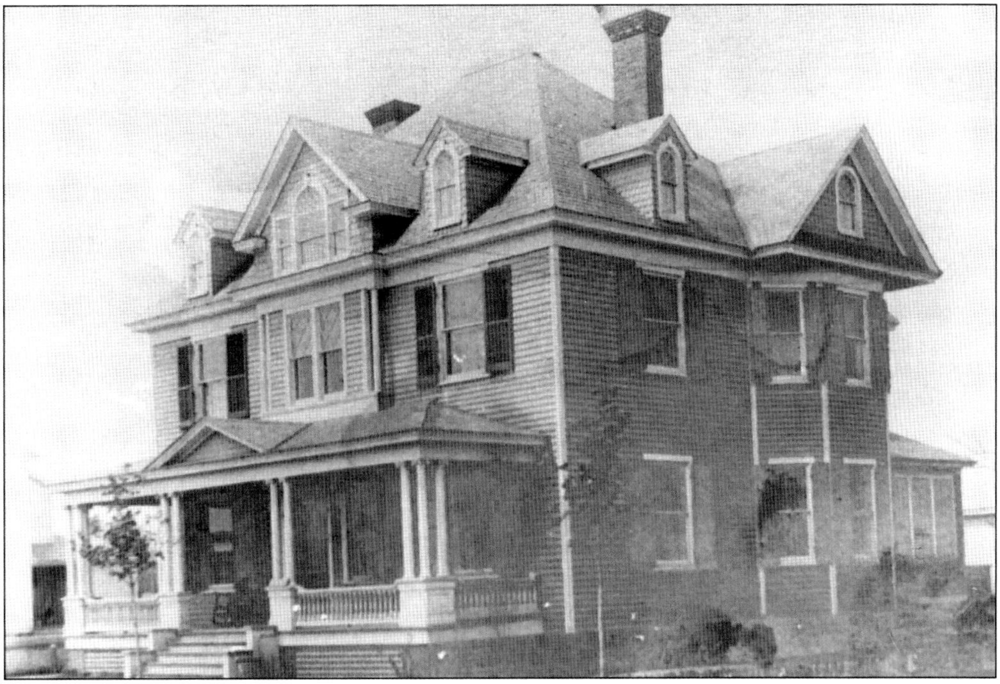

Dr. James Brayshaw House. This was the home of Dr. James Brayshaw. Located on Jewel Street, the second house west of North Second Street, the house is still there. (Collection of the late Hilda Fowler.)

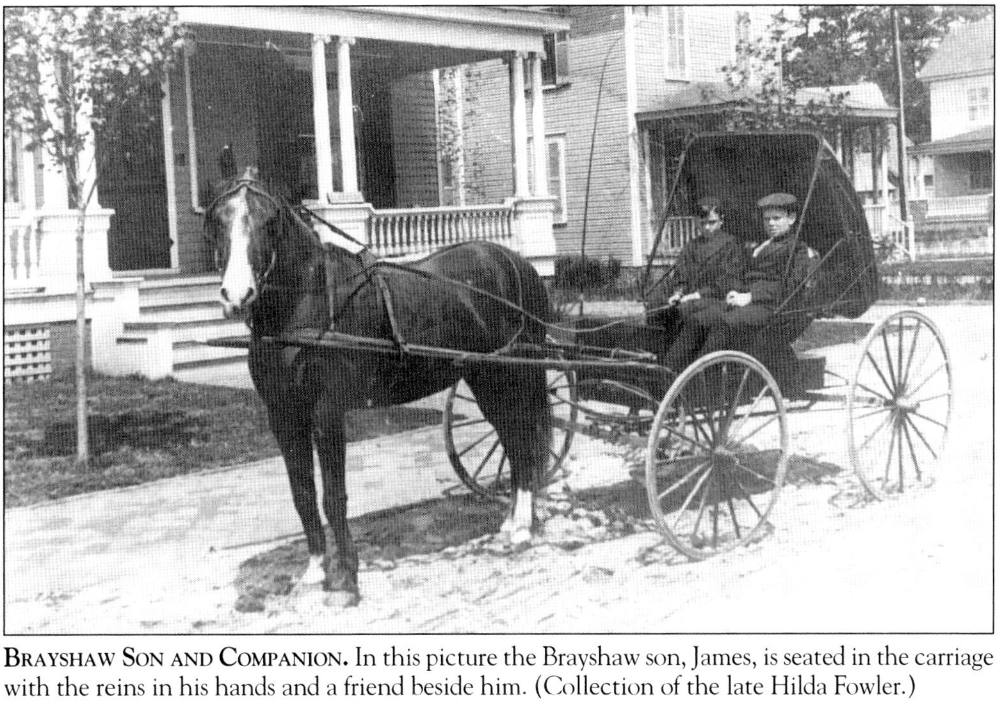

Brayshaw Son and Companion. In this picture the Brayshaw son, James, is seated in the carriage with the reins in his hands and a friend beside him. (Collection of the late Hilda Fowler.)

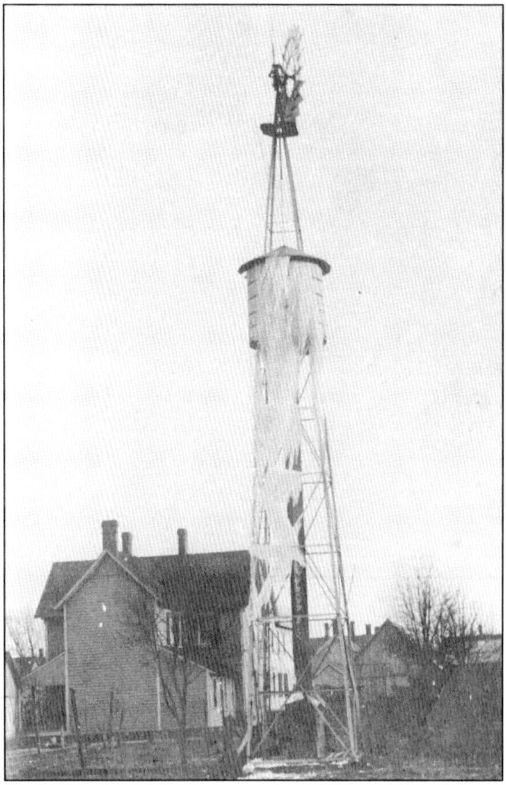

Delmar Windmill. This picture dates from about 1905. A private water company furnished water to Delmar in 1905, and the private wells and windmills became obsolete. This picture was taken in winter when the overflow from the tank had frozen while cascading down the side of the tank along the metal struts toward the ground. A lit lantern was set in the pit under the windmill on cold winter nights to keep the well from freezing, but the overflow on this one was subject to the extreme temperature. The house shown is still there. It was the Loderman house and is located next to the corner at Grove and Seventh Streets. The windmill was sold to a farmer, dismantled, and carried away after the water system was installed. (Collection of Walter Sullivan.)

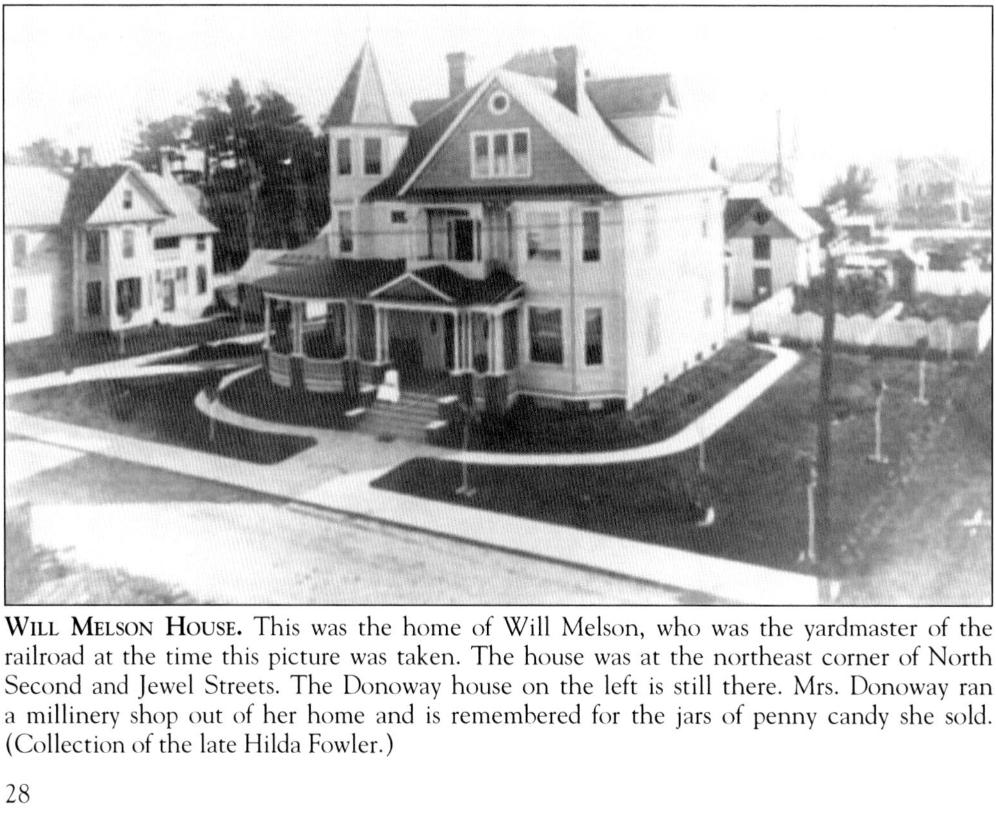

Will Melson House. This was the home of Will Melson, who was the yardmaster of the railroad at the time this picture was taken. The house was at the northeast corner of North Second and Jewel Streets. The Donoway house on the left is still there. Mrs. Donoway ran a millinery shop out of her home and is remembered for the jars of penny candy she sold. (Collection of the late Hilda Fowler.)

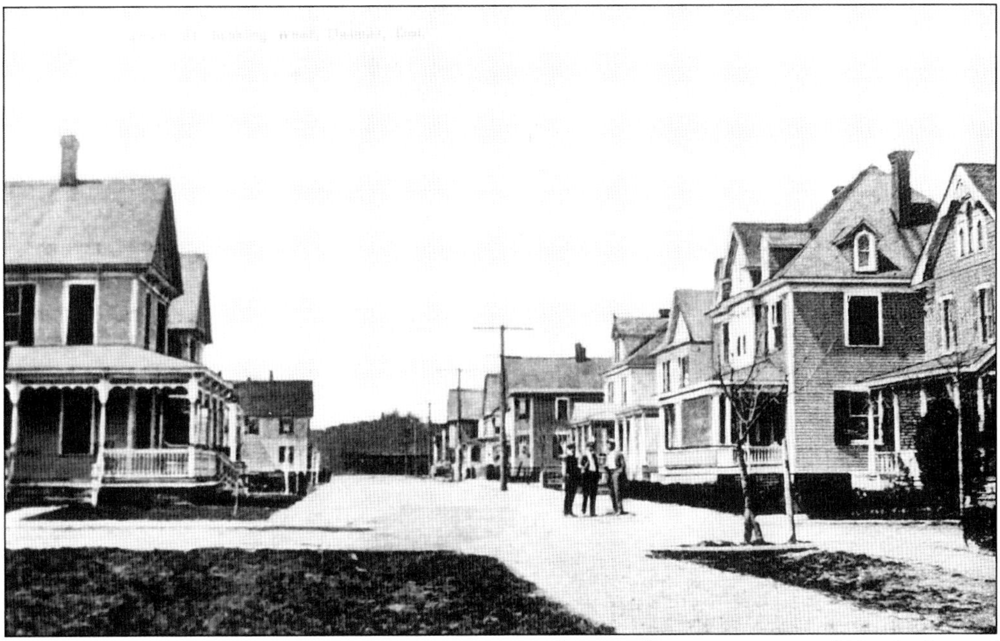

JEWEL STREET LOOKING WEST. This picture was taken at the intersection of North Second Street. On the left is the house of Frances and Alton Truitt, and on the right is the Brayshaw house. A freight car can be seen at the intersection with Railroad Avenue. (Collection of Walter Sullivan.)

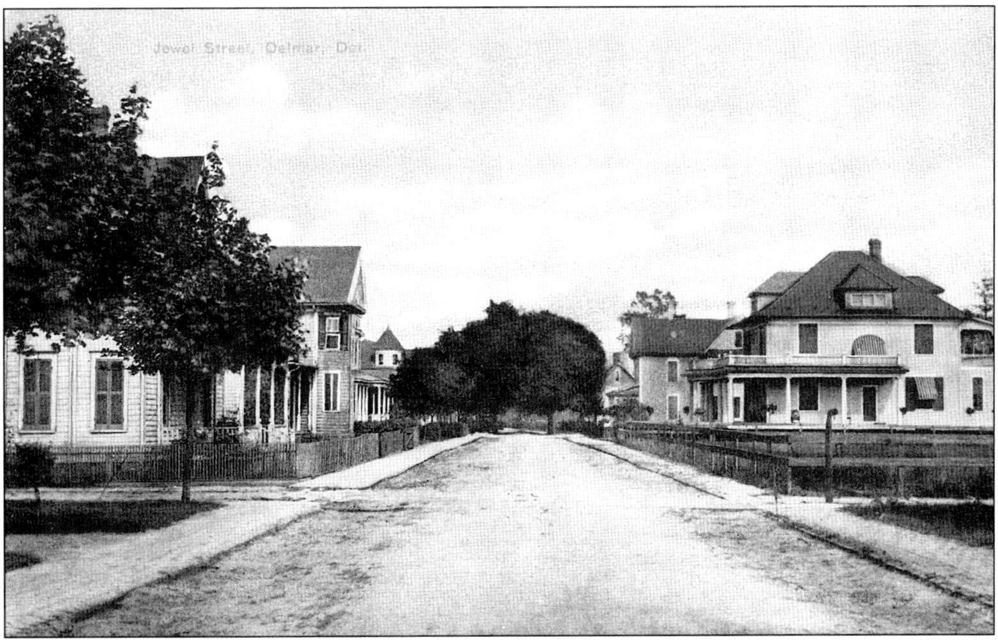

JEWEL STREET. This view was taken at the intersection of Jewel and First Streets. The house on the right is pictured on the card with the Lynch home as the house of Irving Culver, who was the mayor of Delmar at that time.

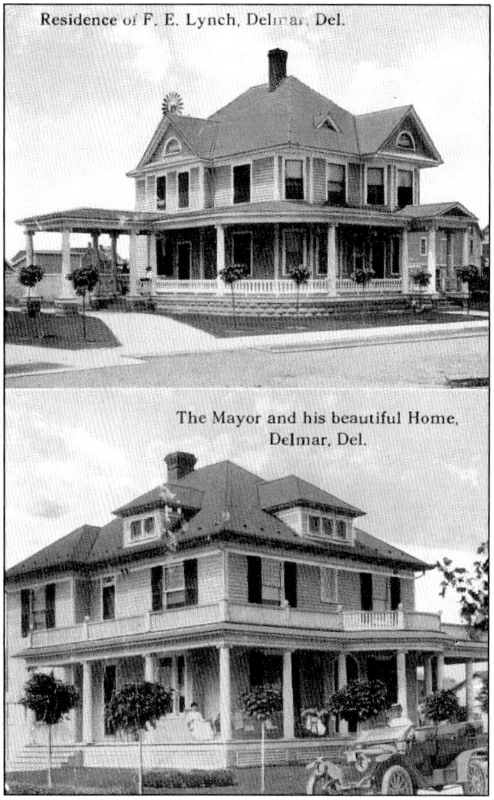

RESIDENCE OF F.E. LYNCH AND THE MAYOR OF DELMAR. Pictured here is the Lynch home (at top) and the mayor's home (at bottom). This view was taken from the opposite side of the mayor's house, which burned about 1930. (Collection of Delmar Public Library.)

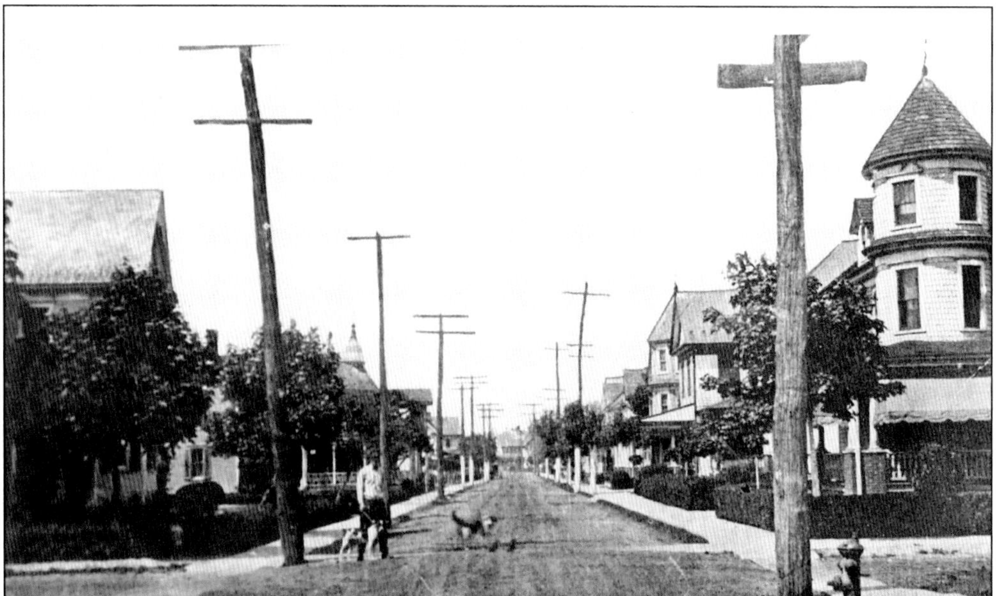

SECOND STREET LOOKING NORTH. This view shows how rough the early electric poles were. Note that all of them are on the street side of the sidewalks. The picture was taken after the water system was installed, but before the street was paved. (Collection of Walter Sullivan.)

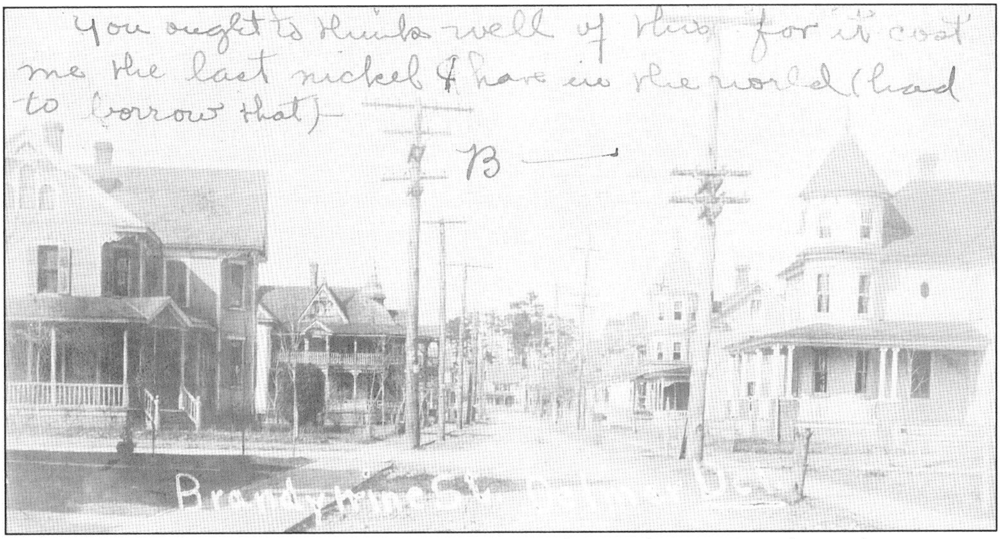

Brandywine Street. This shows the original name of Second Street. It is almost the same view as in the preceding picture except that the man and his dog are missing. Also missing is the fireplug. The second house on the left can be seen clearly with its second-floor porch.

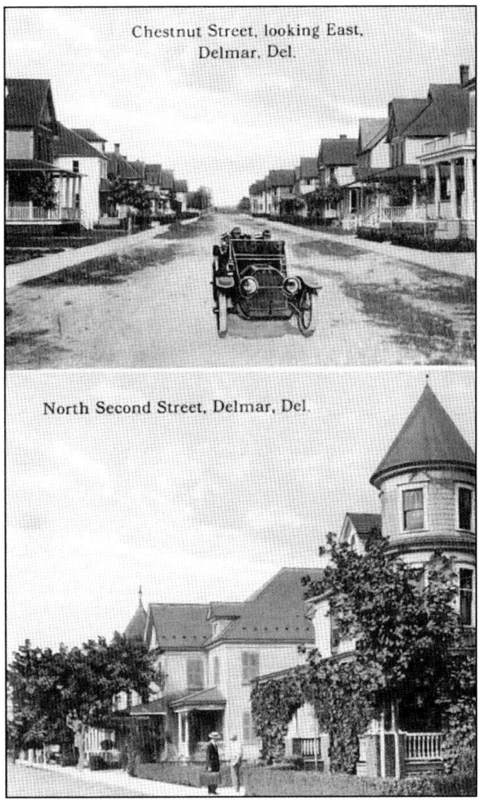

Chestnut Street Looking East and North Second Street. On these pictures of Chestnut and North Second Streets in Delmar, poles and fireplugs are noticeably absent. The car on the Chestnut Street picture is a paste on, and grass grows in the street bed.

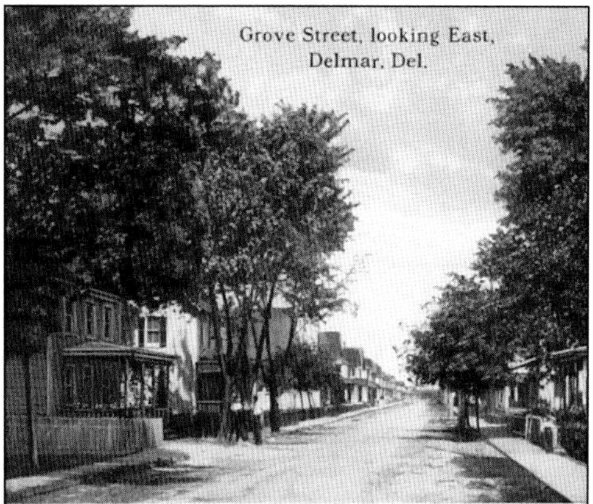

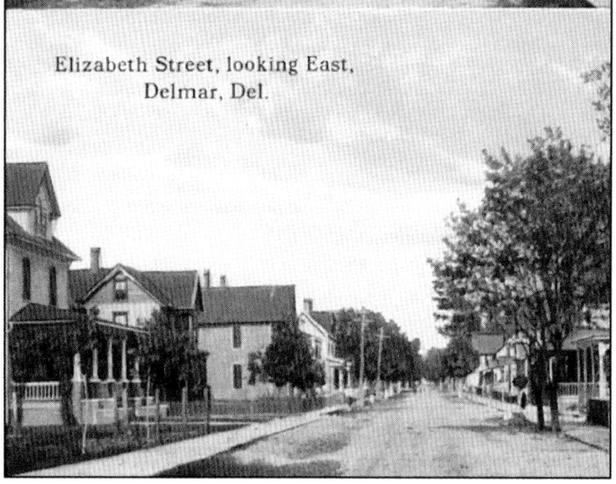

GROVE STREET LOOKING EAST AND ELIZABETH STREET LOOKING EAST. This continues the one Maryland and one Delaware view on each postcard. There are two telephone poles on the lower picture, none on the upper. The street is unpaved on both.

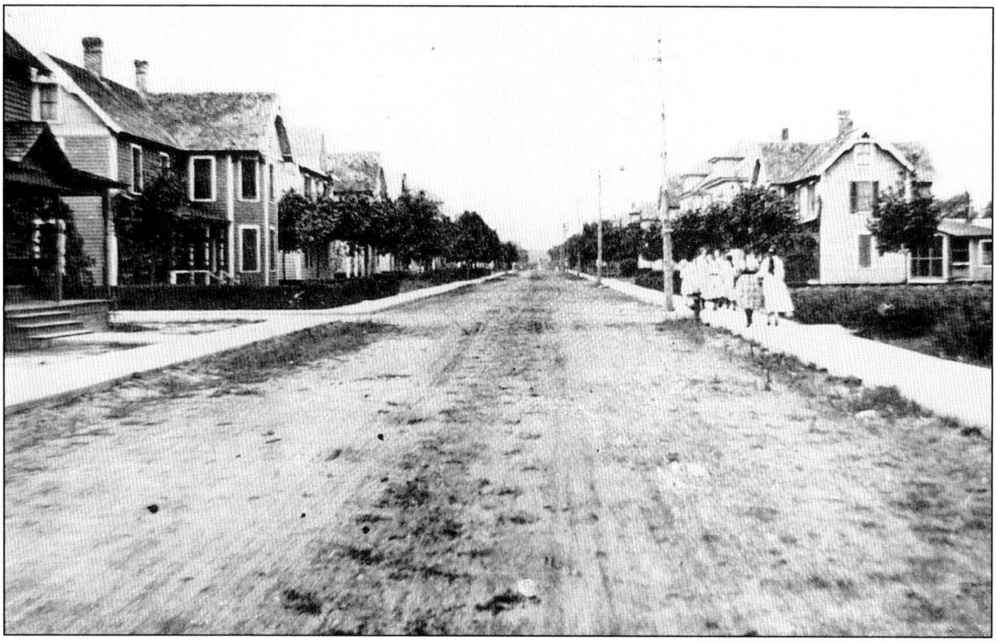

CHESTNUT STREET. This picture dates from about 1910. The scene is at Third Street looking west. The house on the left is that of Rue Hastings with the house of Hubert German behind it. The house on the right belonged to W.H. Willis, principal of the Maryland School. (Collection of E. Pusey.)

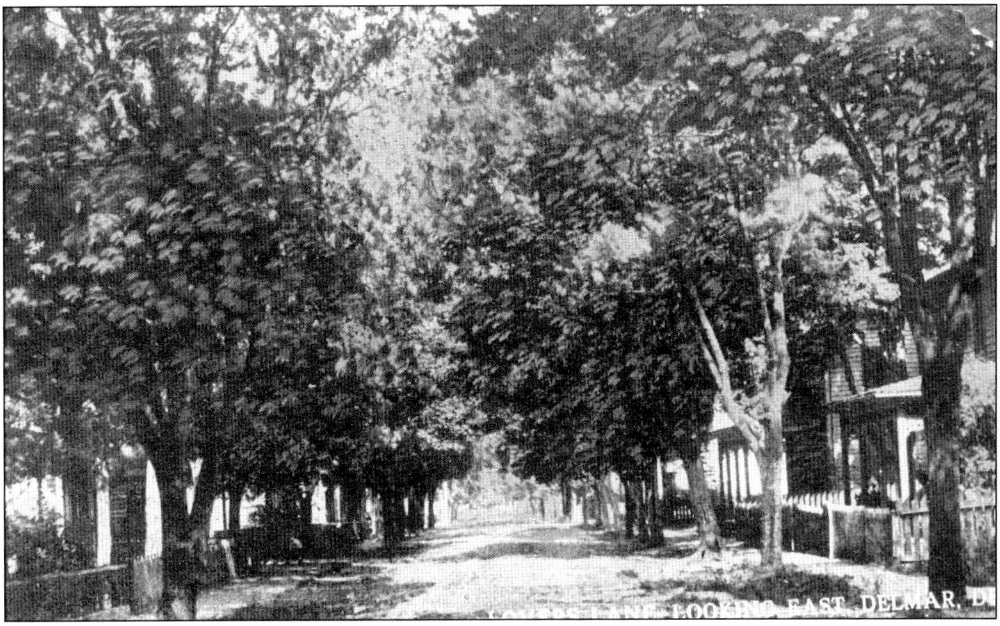

Top: Lovers Lane Looking East. On the East Street picture (bottom), on the left where the porch is close to the street, the house is that of George Barr, road foreman of engines, and the third house on the right is that of Elijah Melson.

It is my belief that these two pictures were made of the same street. The two houses on the right, one barely seen in the East Street picture, appear to be the same. One was taken in summer and the other in winter, and there is a few years difference between them. (Top photo, collection of Helene Ulman Shortall; bottom, collection of the late Hilda Fowler.)

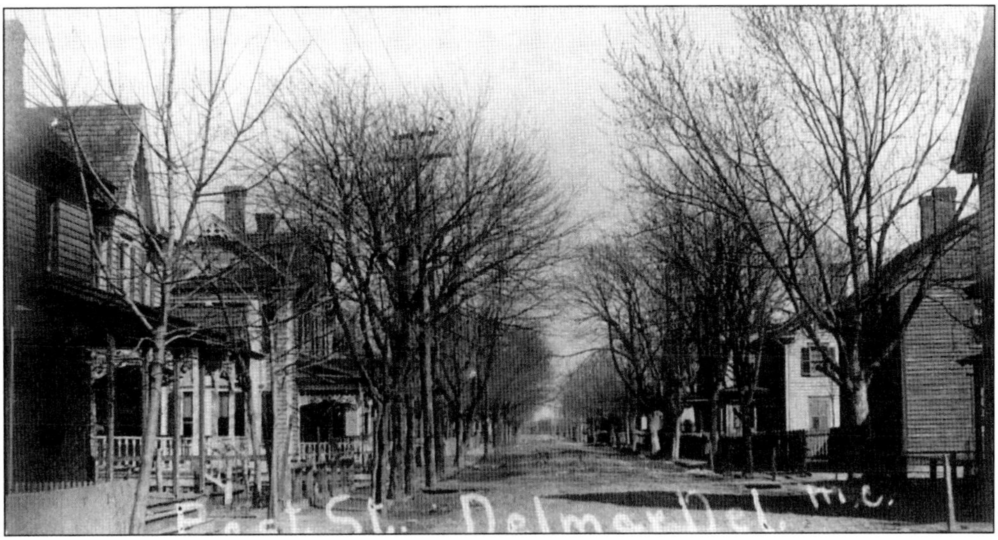

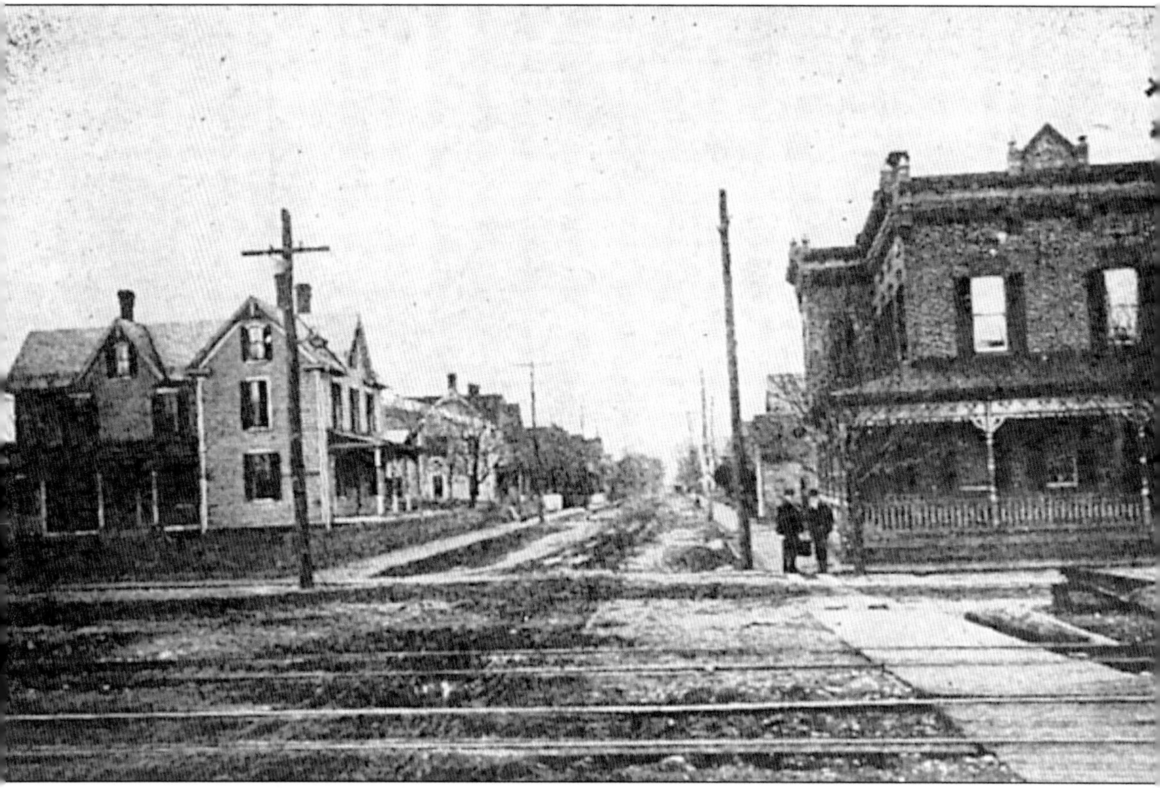

EAST STREET. This picture shows the "Brick Block" on the right side, which is still there. On the left side is where the town hall is presently located. The large wooden house, which was the former office of Dr. Sohler, has been torn down and is a part of the parking lot for the town hall. (Collection of James Jackson.)

Two

Getting to the Point

Sharptown is probably named for Governor Sharp, the next to the last proprietary governor of Maryland. In the days when its shipyard was in operation, when the lumber mill was running, and the shirt factories were humming it was a busy town. Sharptown is now the home of one of the most active and energetic volunteer fire companies in the county, and its firemen's carnival is a real drawing card.

San or Santo Domingo was established about 1820. The first names identified with the community were Dutton, Wright, Brown, Dashiell, and Anthony. All of these were free, black citizens and landowners. A school was established in the 1860s. Today it is a peaceable, home-loving community but it is all black, and proud of it.

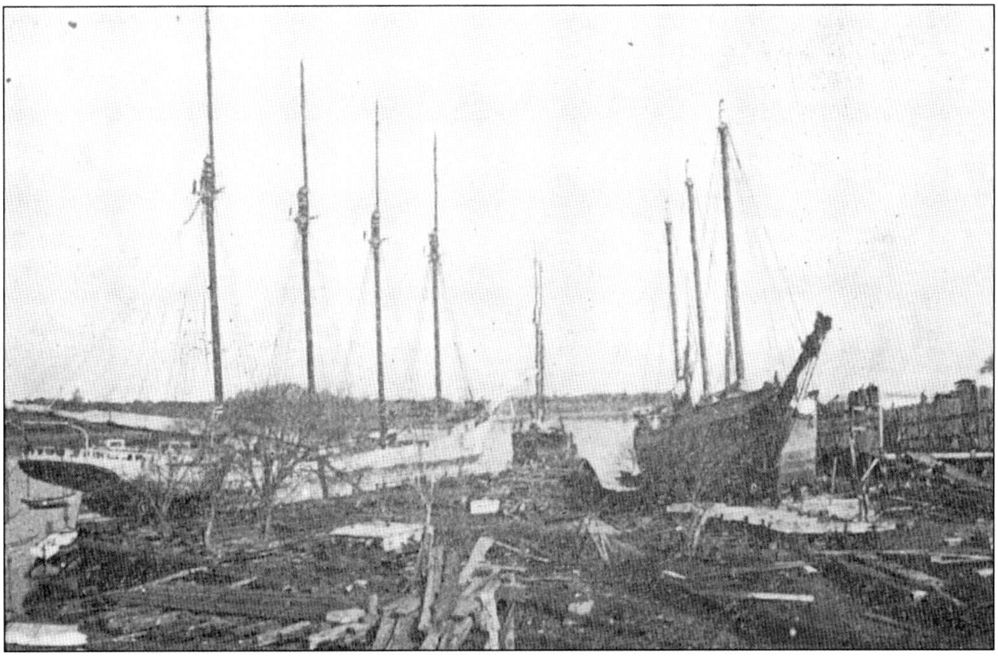

Sharptown Marine Railway. The Sharptown Marine Railway was incorporated in 1899 for $15,000 by S.J. Cooper, merchant; W.H. Knowles, hardware dealer; J.D. Marvil of A.W. Robinson and Company, basket manufacturers; B.P. Gravenor, sailmaker; T.J. Sauerhoff, shipbuilder; James Robinson, retired; and William J. Jackson, a retired sea captain. The Elzey Brothers moved their original business to Sharptown in 1860 from Quantico. Sauerhoff was the manager. The yard built vessels as large as 1,200 tons and was quite successful at first. During World War I the yard built vessels for the Navy but after that the shipyard fell on hard times. The Eastern Shore Shipbuilding Company had taken it over by that time, and on May 15, 1919, that company was sold. (Collection of the late Hilda Fowler.)

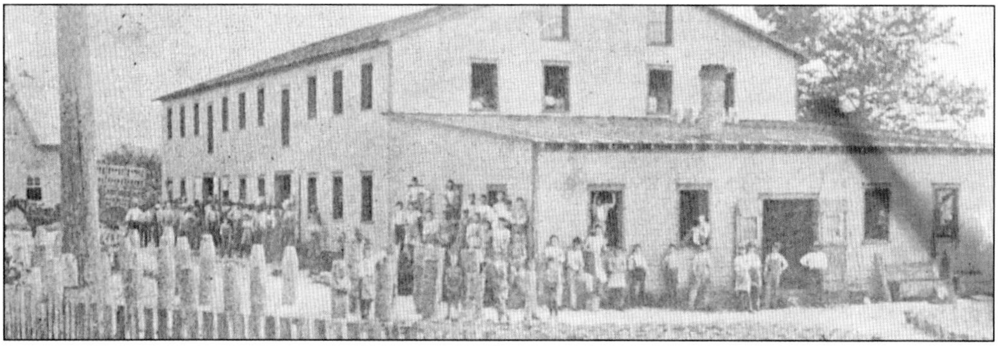

Plant of the Marvil Packing Company. The Marvil Packing Company was formed when Crane, Hynson, and Valliant of Chestertown; J.D. Marvil and Company of Laurel, Delaware; N. Ward and Company of Laurel, Delaware; and A.W. Robinson and Company of Sharptown agreed to merge their companies. A.W. Robinson became the general manager of the plant, which was one of the principal employers at Sharptown employing about 100 people. It became a subsidiary of Atlas Plywood Company.

On the night of April 7, 1953, in the evening hours, a fire was detected in the plant. Within 15 minutes from the time it was discovered the whole building was on fire. It started from a spark from an overheated bearing in the drying room and was fanned into a blaze. The building was a total loss with damage running more than a quarter million dollars, when a quarter million was a lot of money. The building was not rebuilt. When the building was first built, in grading for the building, the remains of Solomon Robinson were exhumed. They were boxed and reburied low enough not to be disturbed in the future. (Collection of the late Hilda Fowler.)

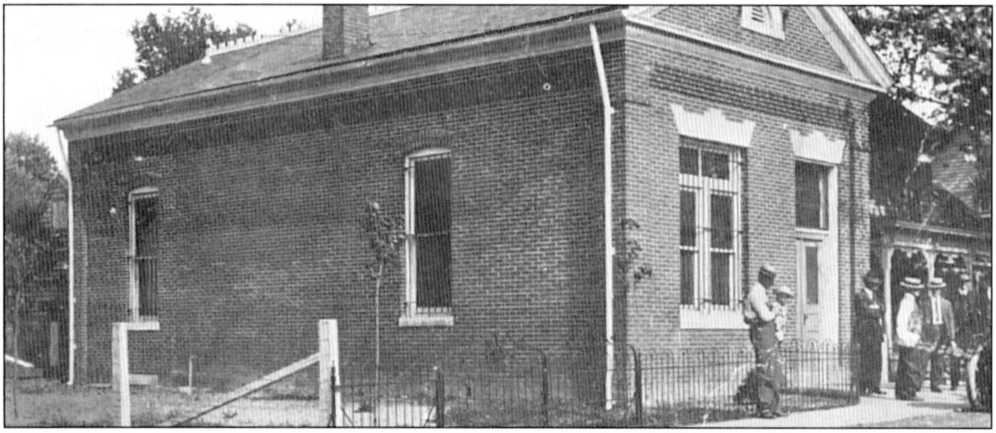

Eastern Shore Trust Company. The bank in Sharptown opened on November 6, 1902, as a branch of the Eastern Shore Trust Company of Cambridge. This building was built on Main Street and was occupied about September 23, 1905. John H. Caulk, the oldest merchant in town in point of experience, was given the honor of making the first deposit. Purnell T. White was cashier; A.W. Robinson was president. The Board was made up of S.J. Cooper, B.P. Gravenor, W.D. Gravenor, J.W. Covington of Sharptown, J.S. Cooper of Columbia, and O.N. Blunett of Riverton.

Pilchard and Furniss of Pocomoke built the building for $3,000. The previous location of the bank had been in the building of S.J. Cooper and Company. The building was enlarged in 1914 when a new vault was put inside and a toilet was added to the first floor. It is now a branch of the Hebron Savings Bank, and the house shown alongside the bank has been torn down. (Collection of James Jackson.)

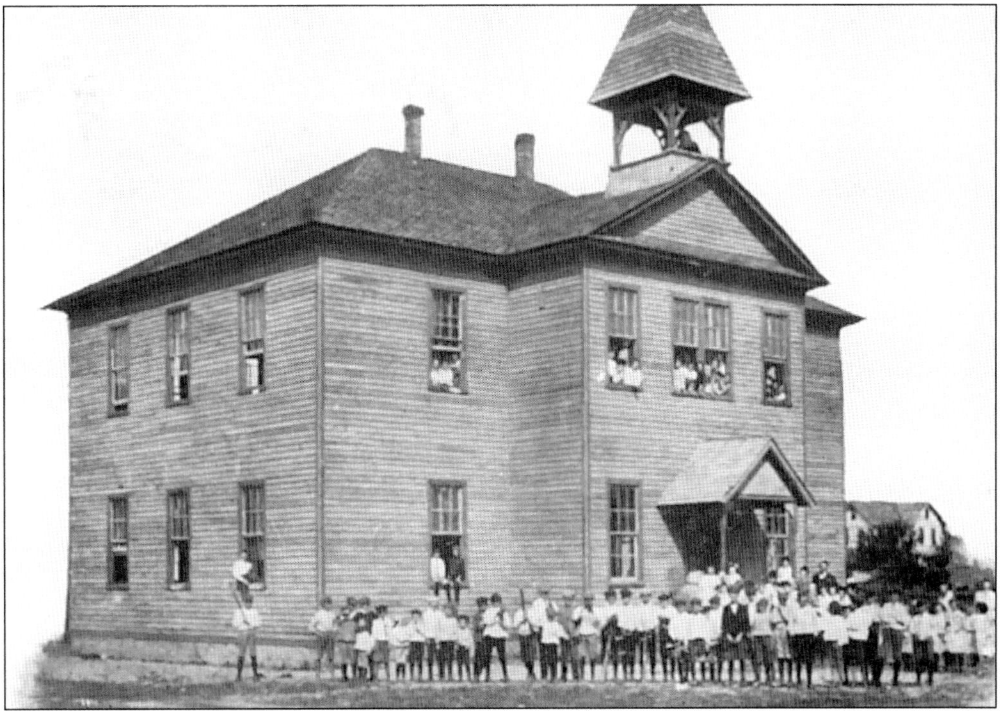

SHARPTOWN HIGH SCHOOL. Sharptown High was built in 1896 with 150 pupils. Professor Gordy, who would later become superintendent of schools in Carlisle, Pennsylvania, was its principal. This card was mailed in 1906, but the school stayed in use until the 1930s.

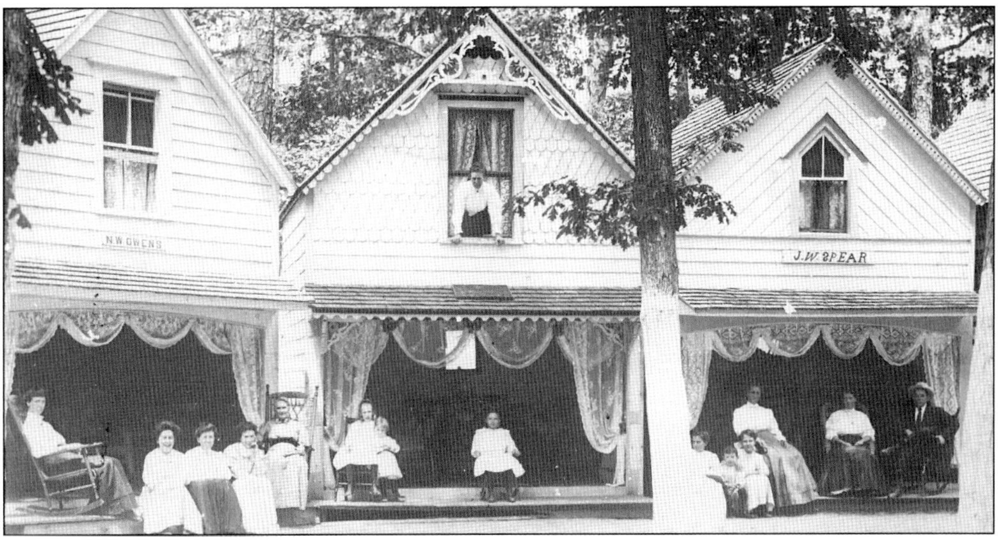

SHARPTOWN CAMP MEETING. This revival camp was located near the Firemen's Carnival grounds. The picture is of the "tents" of Noah W. Owens and J.W. Spear with an unknown tent between them. The tents were individually owned and were built so that you could hear the revival preacher while relaxing in them, or watch the people as they slowly walked past. The "tents" were well built, and when the camp closed after World War I the owners moved them to their homes. The "tents" contained no running water or bathroom facilities, and the netting had to be let down every night to keep out flies and mosquitoes.

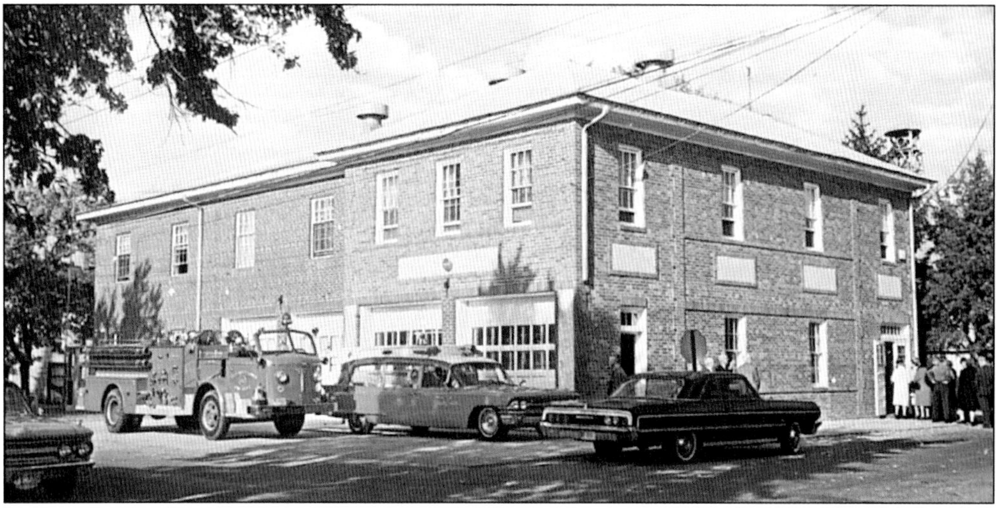

The Old Sharptown Firehouse. The Sharptown Fire Company put out this picture. The language on the back of the card touts its carnival as "one of the most complete and popular carnivals on Delmarva." And the specific use of the card was to advertise its annual Fall Oyster and Chicken 'n Dumpling Dinner on October 29, 1967. The price for adults was $1.75 and the children's dinner was 75¢. There is a line of people at the door indicating that it was made at the annual dinner of the year before.

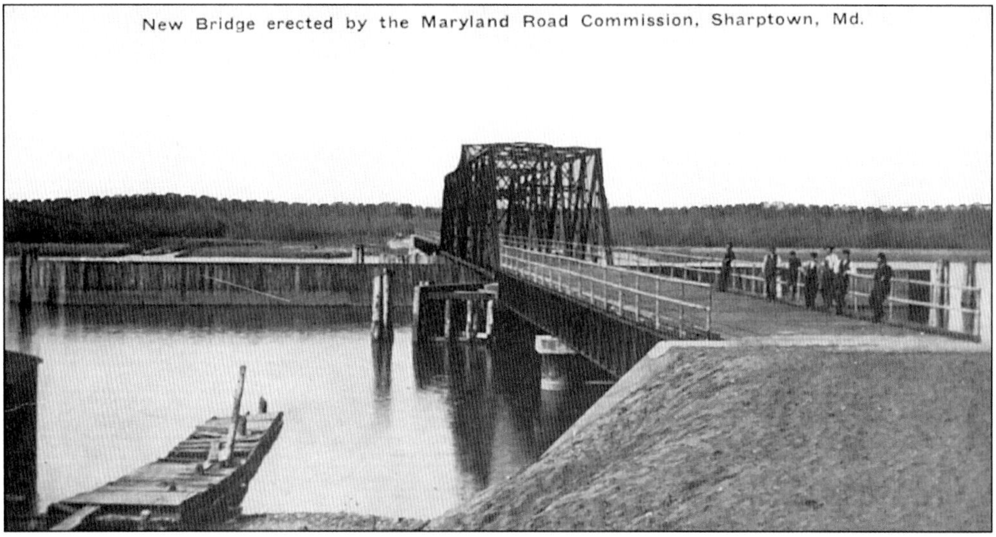

The New Bridge at Sharptown. State Senator Jesse D. Price secured the appropriation for a new bridge in the 1909 session of the legislature. By the time the necessary permit for it had been obtained, the plans drawn, and bidding took place, it was 1911 before the work got started. There were nearly 600 pilings to be driven and the bridge was to be built of steel and concrete. The bridge was completed in the spring of 1913 and opened for traffic, but the approaches to the bridge were on swampy ground and fill was extended 100 feet on each side. Captain Elijah R. Bennett was the first bridge tender.

The present bridge had a more tempestuous beginning. The State of Maryland let the War Department permit run out and a new one had to be obtained. Delaware objected to the level of the bridge and carried the case to the Delaware District Court and won, requiring the bridge level to be raised to its present height.

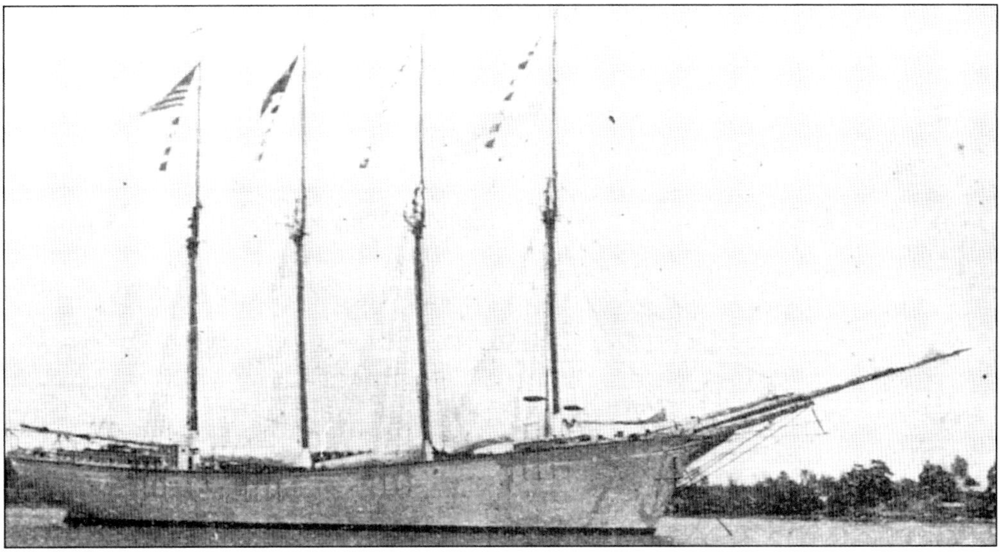

The Schooner *Albert W. Robinson*. The *Albert W. Robinson* was launched at 9:15 a.m. on February 21, 1907. A.W. Robinson, for whom she is named, was the largest owner in the ship. He was also a director of the Sharptown Marine Railway, who built her. The new schooner was 150 feet in length, had a 34-foot beam, and a depth of hold of 12 feet. She was built entirely of native oak and Georgia pine. An up-to-date heating plant would be installed in the vessel by which the staterooms would be heated. She was to be ready to sail in May 1907. Capt. E.G. Bennett's wife, Oyola Bennett, christened her. Mr. Robinson presented the burgee, U.S. flag, the Union Jack, and a complete set of signal flags and gilded trail and quarter boards. She was designed by Thomas Sauerhoff, had a cost of $30,000, and was to be managed by S.J. Cooper and Son. (Collection of the late Hilda Fowler.)

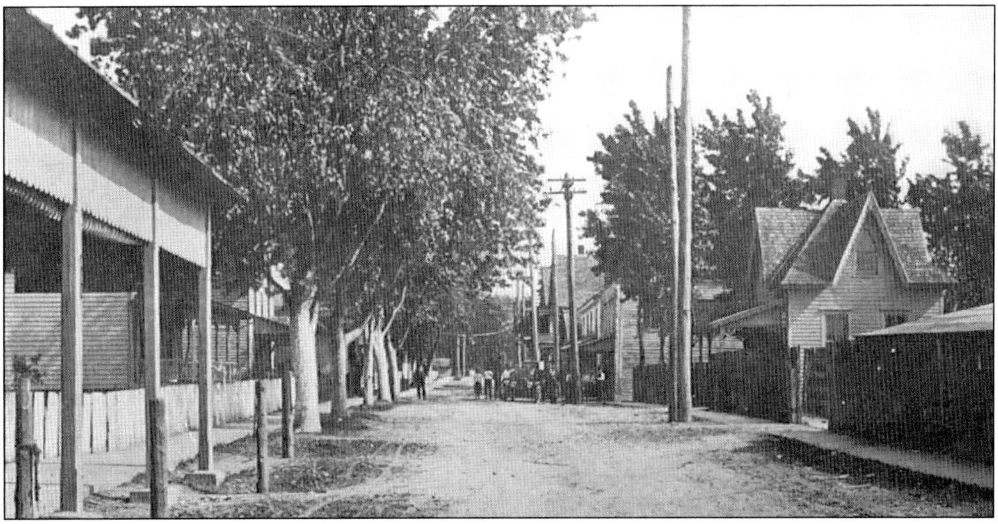

Main Street, Business Section, Sharptown. The building, left foreground, is Cooper's General Store with Mr. Sammy Cooper's house behind it. The whitewashed trees are now gone. In the right foreground is a shed belonging to the Marvil Package Company with their office building behind it. Showard's store is next with the automobile in the street in front of it and the drugstore showing up behind it. The scene is looking east with the Nanticoke River behind the photographer.

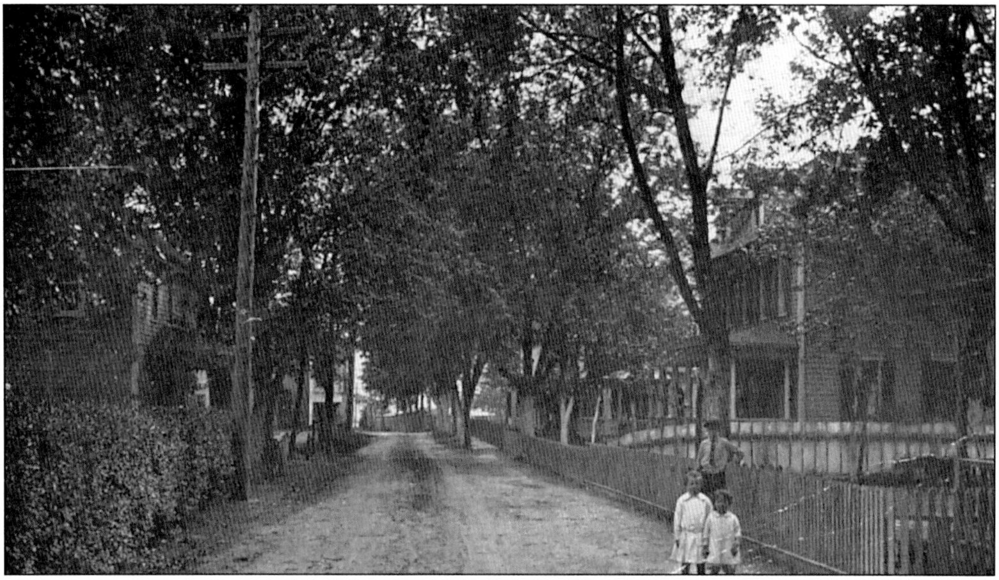

WATER STREET LOOKING WEST. This view is west from Ferry Street and was taken about 1915. The man shown behind the children is Norman D. Smith, whose uniform cap shows his employment by the Nanticoke River steamship line. The house on the right belonged to Smith.

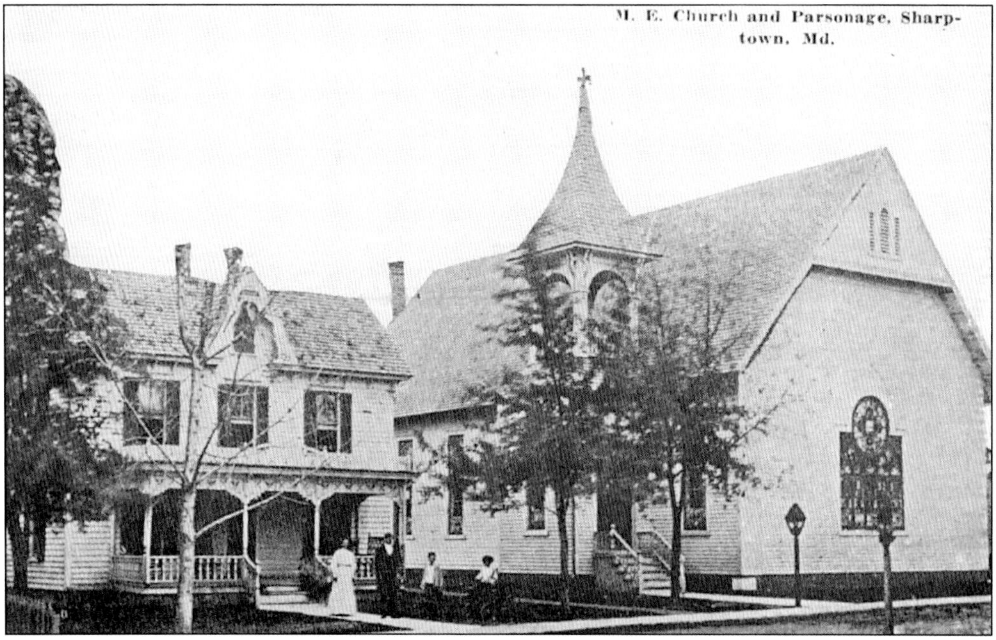

ASBURY METHODIST CHURCH AND PARSONAGE. The church has been brick faced, the large front window elevated, and a new entrance made so access is no longer through the tower. The side window in the tower is still there. The original parsonage is shown with the more modern addition shown on front. Awnings have been placed over the windows on the second floor and the porch has been screened in. The Victorian gingerbread molding on the third floor has been retained from the original parsonage. (Collection of the late Hilda Fowler.)

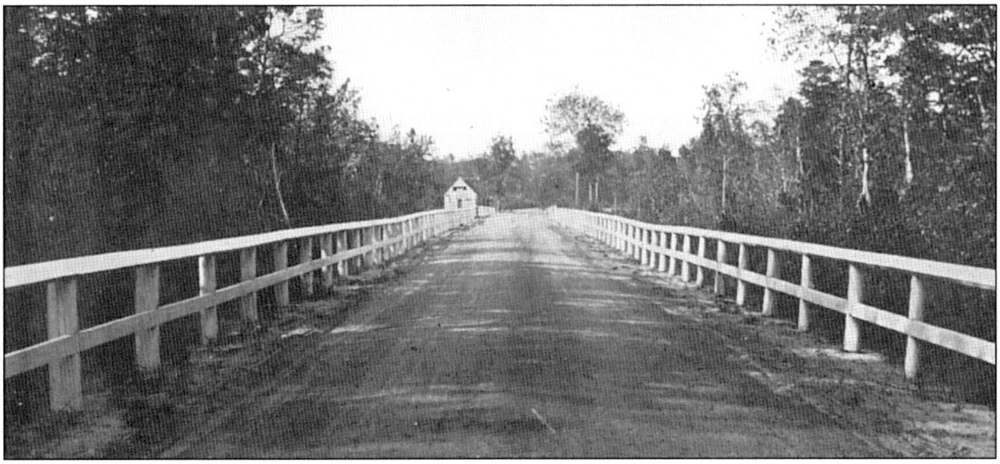

PLUM CREEK DRIVE. This is actually a portion of the road between Sharptown and Riverton where the road crossed Plum Creek. The house on the left was occupied by a family named Eckridge. The white fence has long since been removed and the road widened. The road shown is dirt and may depict a time when it was built across the lower dam over Plum Creek and was part of the old road which made a "U"-shaped drive around the circle, the mill dam forming the base of the "U."

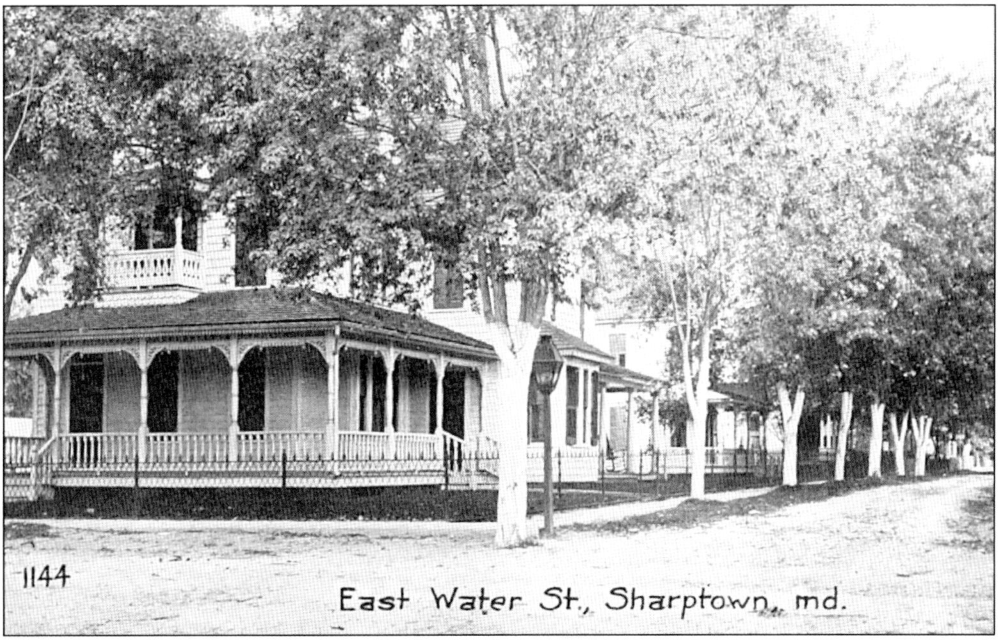

EAST WATER STREET. The house in the foreground was the home of Samuel Cooper, more affectionately known as Mr. Sammy. Later it was home for his daughters, Lena and Mary. His son, S.J. Cooper, lived in the second house. The line of white-washed trees is gone and the street is paved to the sidewalk. A block wall topped by balls at the corners and openings has replaced the iron fence. Asphalt shingles have replaced the roof, and storm windows and doors have been added. The fancy woodwork and balcony are still intact, and the columns are still in place. At the second house the picket fence is gone and asphalt shingles cover the roof, but the house itself has not been changed except for a brick wall on the porch line supporting the columns.

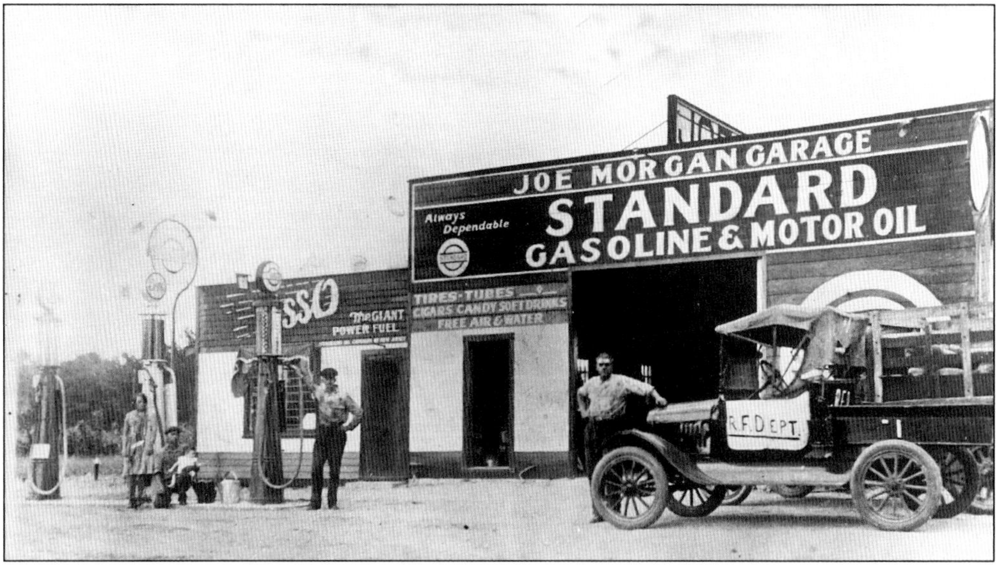

JOE MORGAN GARAGE. This garage was a fixture of the community. The man standing by the Ford truck, which belonged to the Volunteer Fire Company, is James Henry Morgan. Royce Bailey is standing by the first gas pump. Martha Morgan and Joe Morgan are together with the baby, Joanna Morgan. The time is 1931. Note the old gas tanks; one had to pump the gas manually, and each tank held 10 gallons.

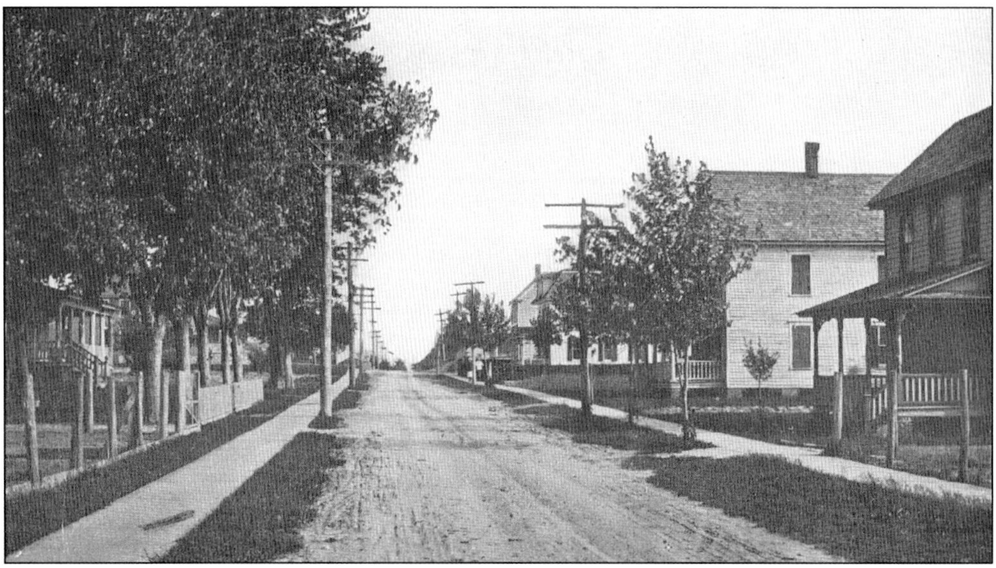

MAIN STREET LOOKING SOUTH. This scene is looking up the slope toward the carnival grounds.

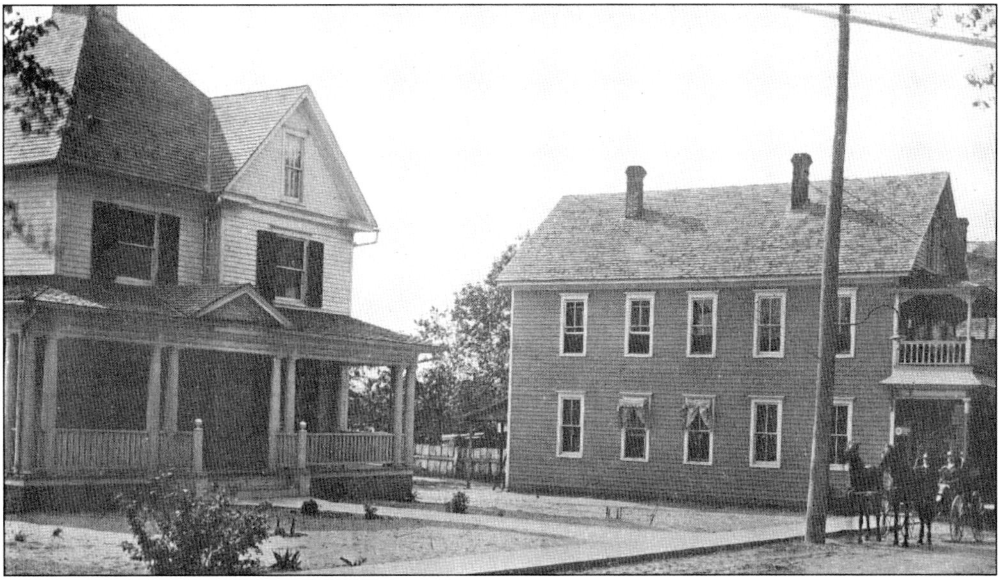

The Dr. C.E. James Drug Store. The house on the left is still there as is the drugstore next to it. Note the laundry drying on a line on the second-floor porch.

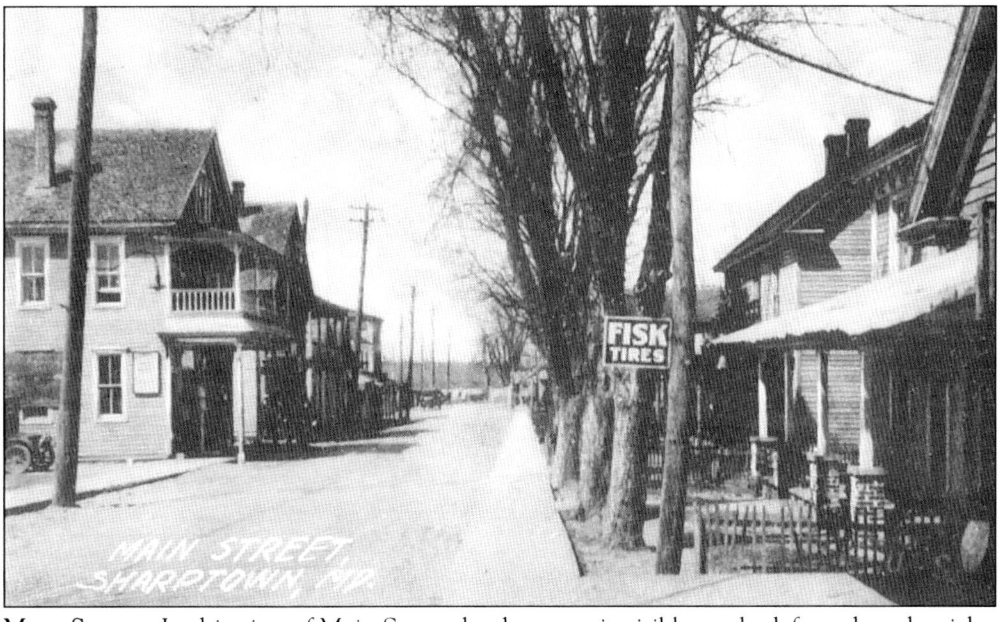

Main Street. In this view of Main Street the drugstore is visible on the left, and on the right, where the Fisk tire sign is shown, is the house of Gus Caulk, who owned a filling station on the lot opposite. One automobile is barely visible on the gas station lot. The second Sharptown telephone exchange was in the second house on the right.

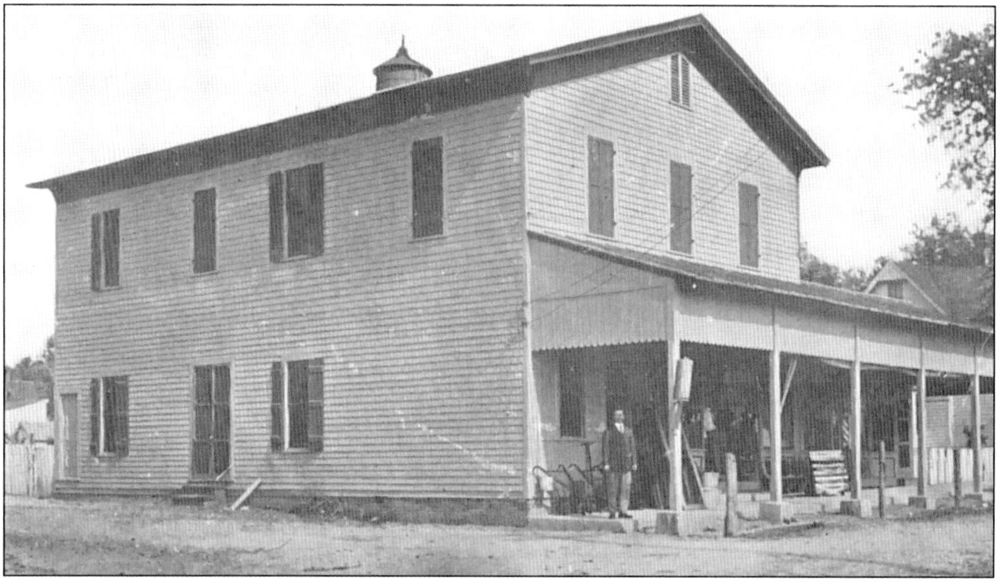

R.H. Phillips and Bros. Store. This is a building that was severely damaged by fire; it burned the front off the store. Three buildings were assembled to replace the damage.

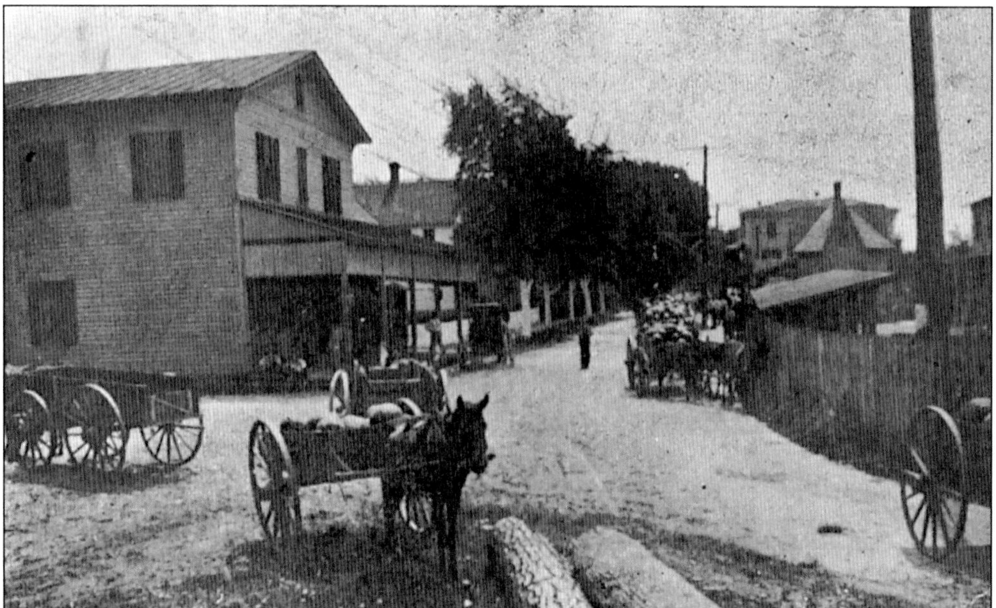

Main Street, Looking South. This is a scene near the dock at the foot of Main Street. The wagons are loaded with watermelons waiting to be transferred to the boat.

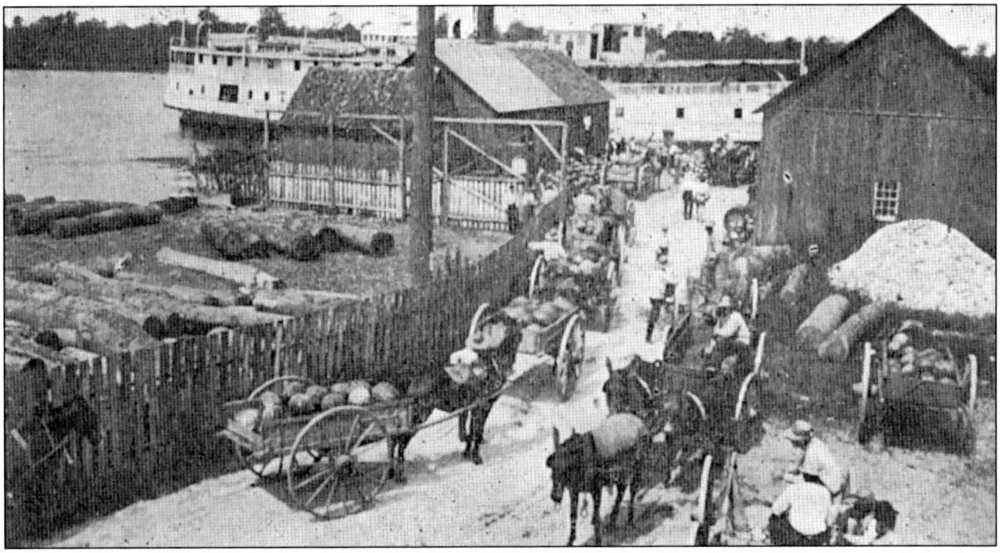

B.C. & A. PIER, SHARPTOWN, MARYLAND. This card shows the steamer *Tangier* at the wharf in Sharptown. The *Tangier* served the Nanticoke River Line about 30 years, terminating her service in 1923. This picture was taken in the summer; the wagons waiting to deliver their loads to the steamer all have watermelons.

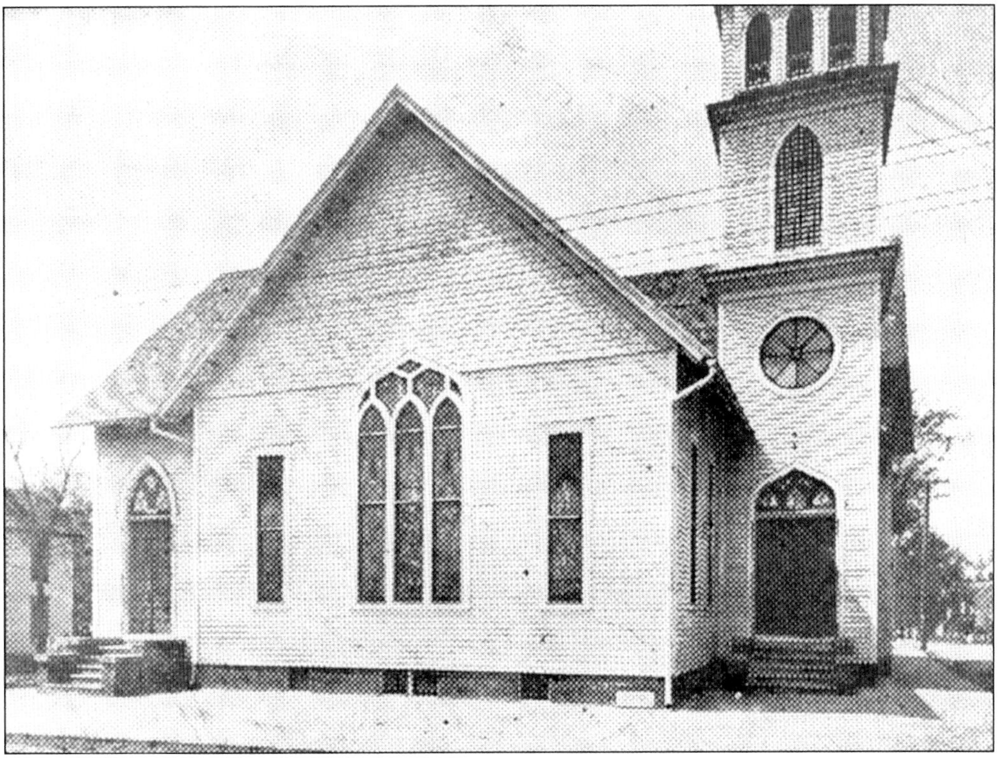

M.P. CHURCH. In 1830 the Methodist Protestants began meetings. In 1831 they held services at Mt. Pleasant Church 4 miles from Sharptown. They built a church at Portsville in 1832. A new church was built in Sharptown in 1885 on a lot at Church and Railway Streets. And again a new church was built in 1916.

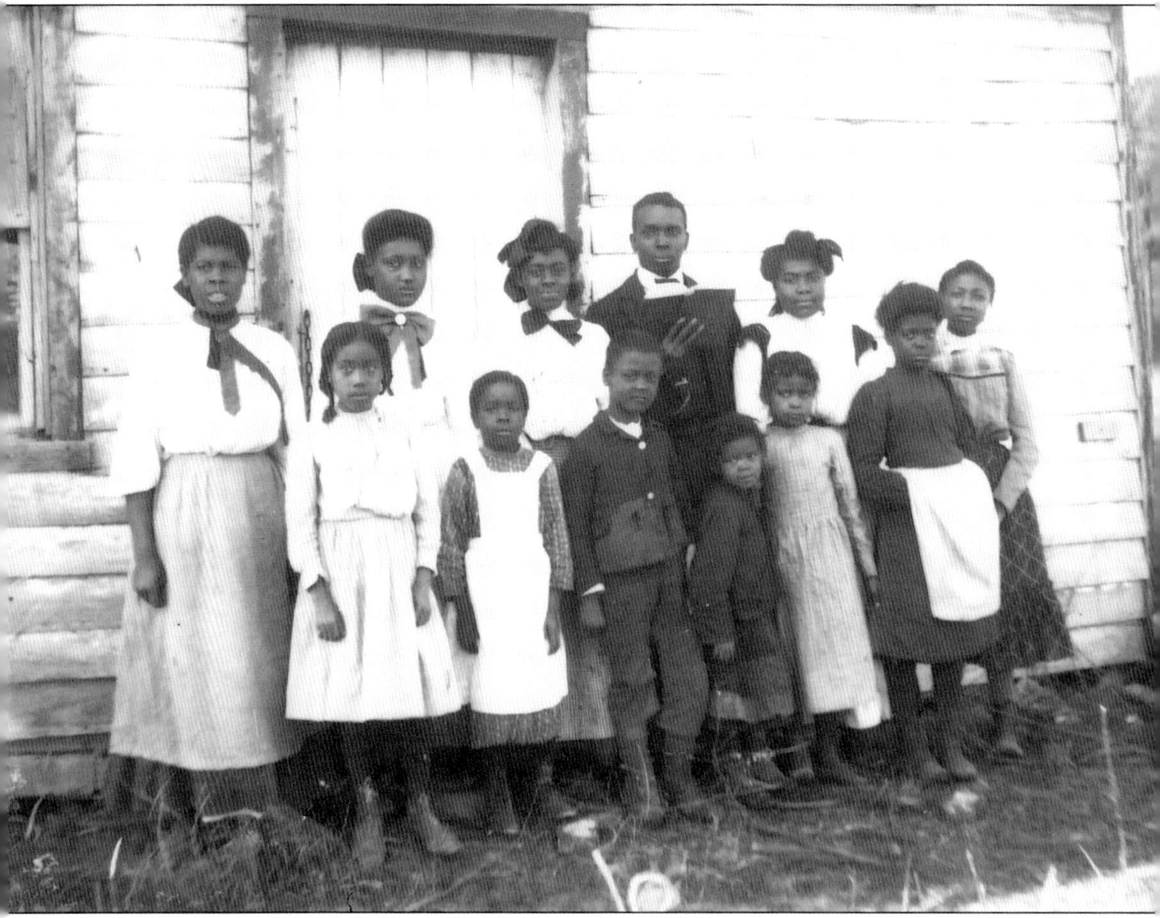

Black Segregated Elementary School. This is probably the school for the San Domingo area. A local photographer took this picture on a glass plate negative. Copies were given to the Nabb Research Center at Salisbury State University, but they are valueless unless identified. Help! (Courtesy of Nabb Research Center at the University.)

Three

MARDELA SPRINGS

Mardela has had many names, including Baron Creek, Barren Creek, and Russum. It consisted of only a few houses when the provincial government designated it as the site for a tobacco warehouse. All tobacco in the area had to be brought to the warehouse where it was inspected and graded. The grower was then given a certificate, which stated the weight of his tobacco and the grade. This certificate could then be used as money and probably accounted for the first store in the town.

By 1840 Mardela had become known as the place for political debate. On the Fourth of July the political parties would each gather here; they would meet separately in the morning where speakers would harangue their adherents. After lunch they would gather for a debate between their two chosen speakers, one for each side. In 1840 Senator Reverdy Johnson spoke for the Whigs, and Dr. Cathell Humphreys orated for the Democrats.

The spring water had been renowned since Indian days when the Nanticokes drank it, and later a hotel was built near the springs. Finally in 1897 two smart men decided to bottle the water and sell it. But they decided that the name Barren Creek Springs wouldn't sell many bottles and renamed the town Mardela Springs.

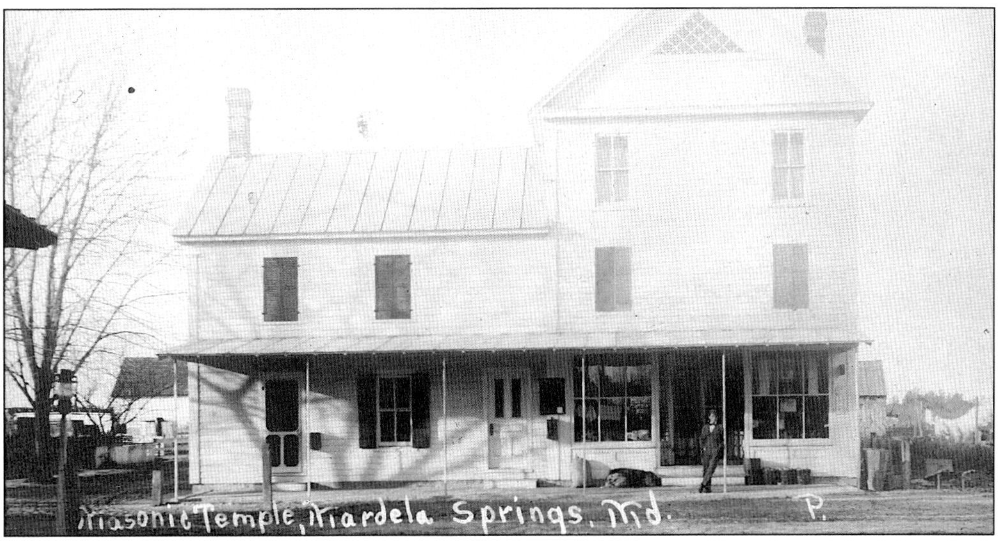

MASONIC TEMPLE. This card shows the building of the Masonic Temple in Mardela, which burned in 1935. The store downstairs was possibly in the possession of John T. Bennett in 1909. The name, Edith Risler, written on the top of the card, was the sender; she was Edith Bratten before her marriage. (Collection of Richard Carter.)

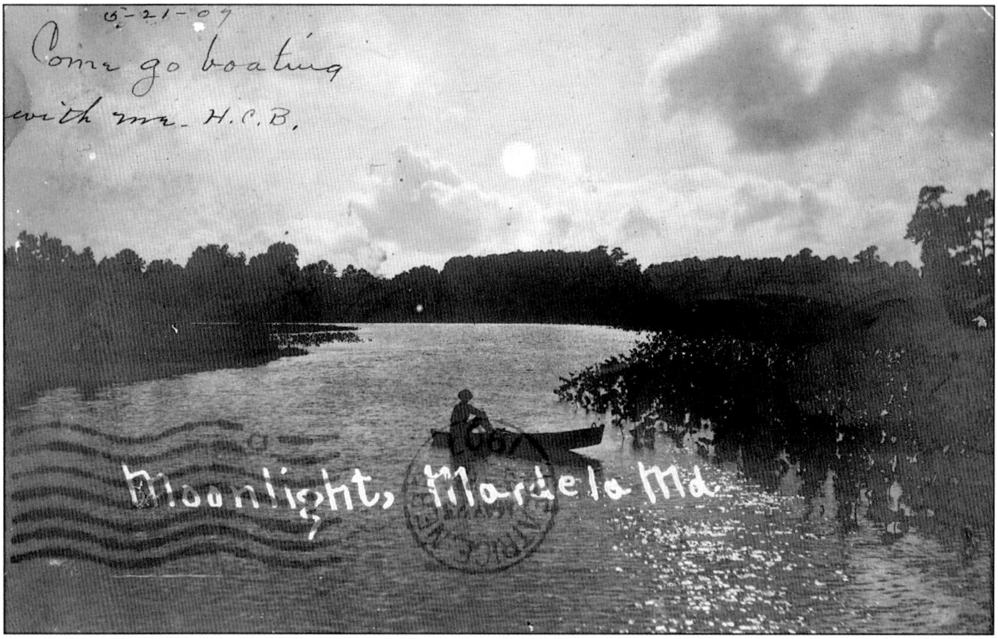

MOONLIGHT MARDELA. This card was designed to promote nostalgia for home. The picture was probably taken above the bridge where Barren Creek is wide.

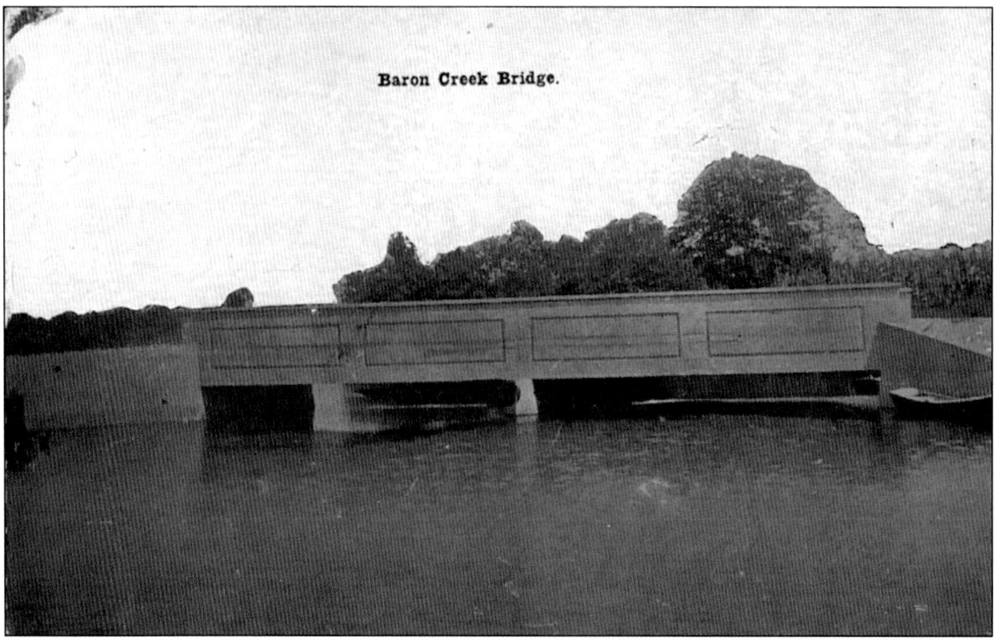

THE BARREN CREEK BRIDGE. This picture was taken when the bridge over the creek had just been built. The bridge was replaced about 1950 and raised to a level above flood stage.

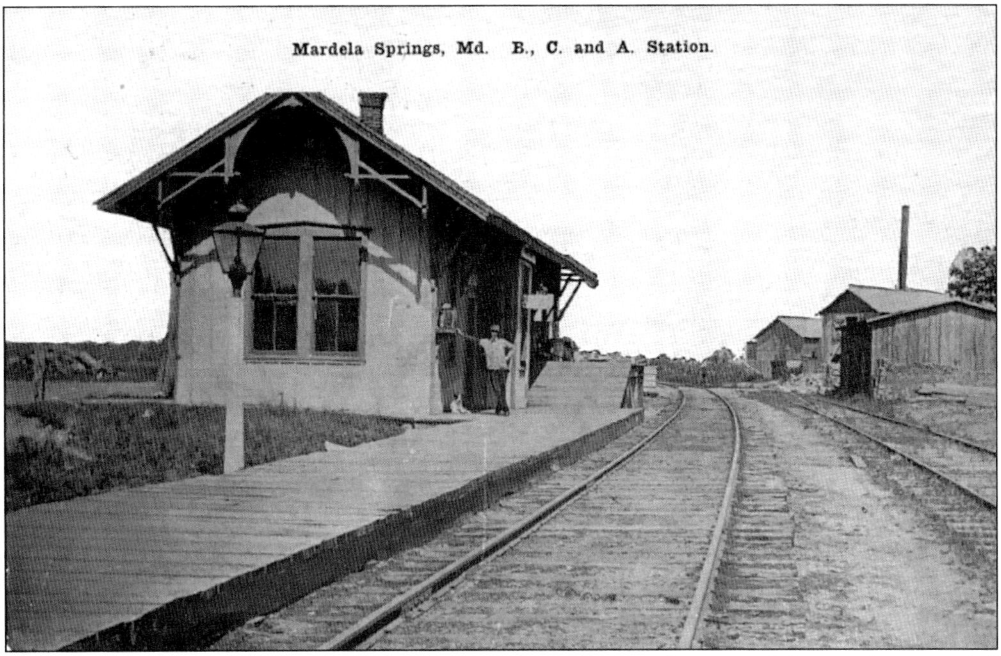

MARDELA SPRINGS, BALTIMORE, CHESAPEAKE AND ATLANTIC STATION. This card was mailed in 1911 when the B.C. & A. Railroad was at the height of its prosperity. The card shows the lumber mills near the tracks and the siding leading to it. (Collection of E. Pusey.)

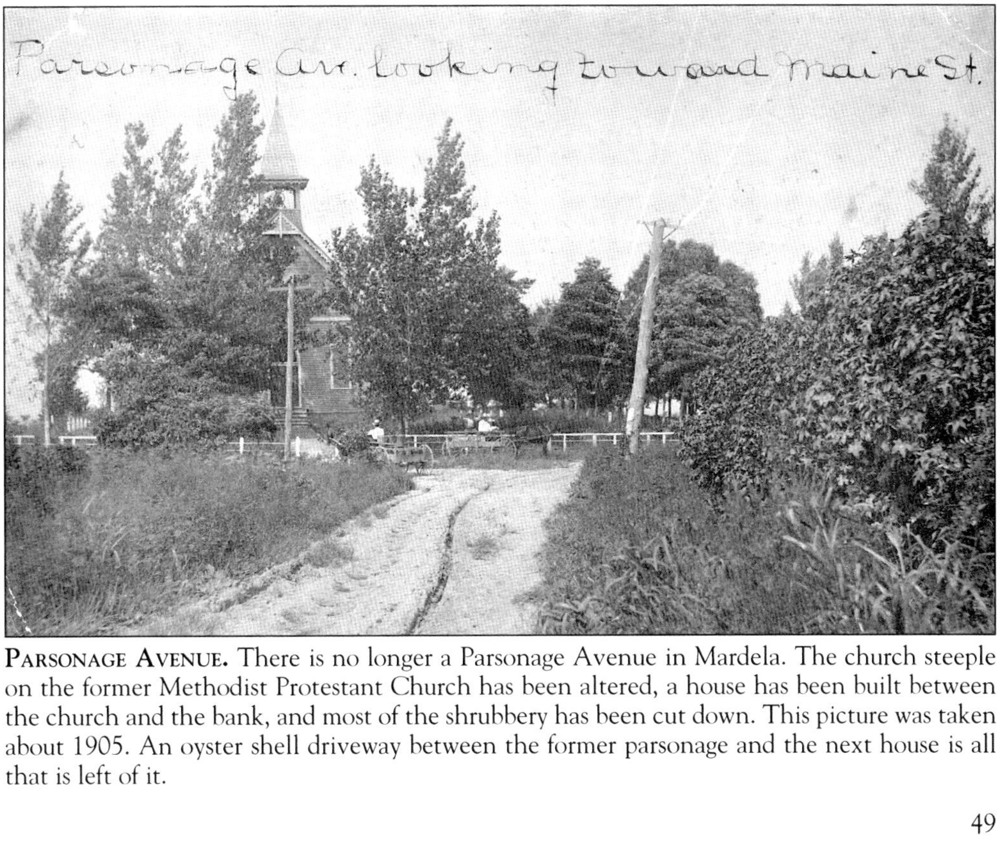

PARSONAGE AVENUE. There is no longer a Parsonage Avenue in Mardela. The church steeple on the former Methodist Protestant Church has been altered, a house has been built between the church and the bank, and most of the shrubbery has been cut down. This picture was taken about 1905. An oyster shell driveway between the former parsonage and the next house is all that is left of it.

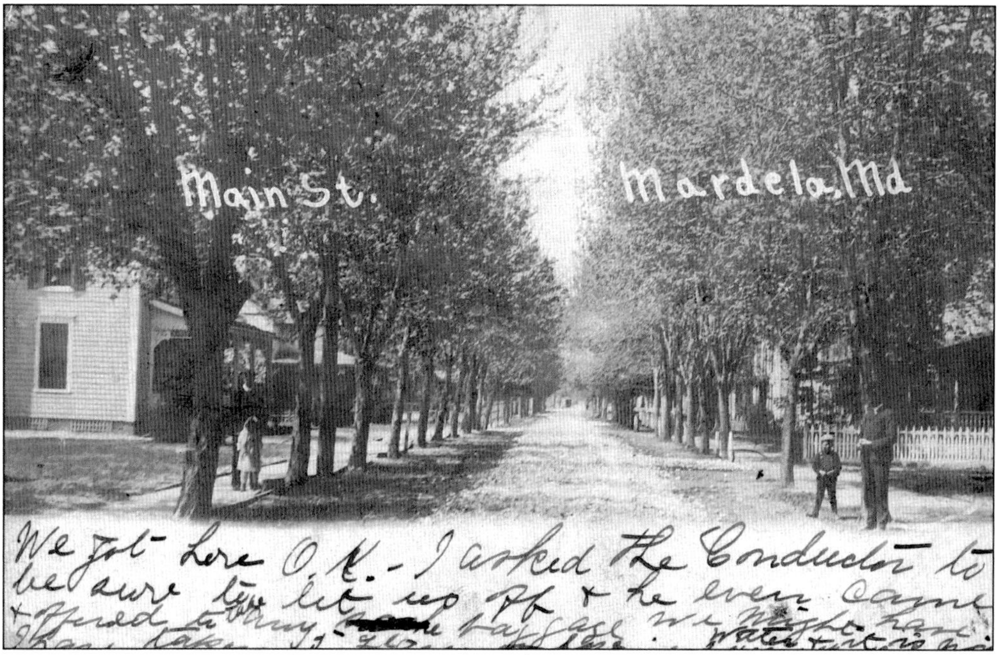

MAIN STREET MARDELA. This is a rare picture. The picket fence and the trees are long gone. The house on the right once was the Harlan Grahams, and the one on the left was where Miss Bessie Bounds lived. (Collection of James Jackson.)

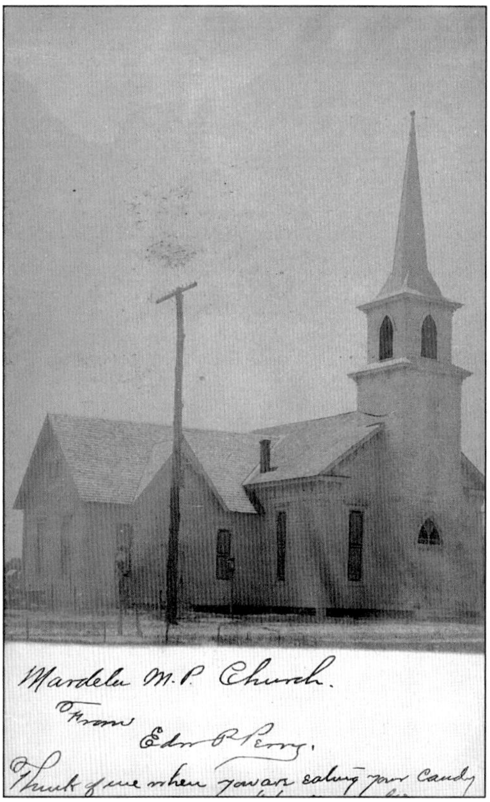

THE METHODIST PROTESTANT CHURCH. This is now the United Methodist Church at Mardela. In 1939 after the union of the two churches this became the Emanuel United Methodist Church, and the M.E. Church was sold. It is descended from the former Methodist Episcopal Protestant chapel that was located on the south side of Barren Creek on the Athol Road. The cornerstone of this church is dated 1871 as the Barren Creek Springs Methodist Protestant Church. In 1906 the Sunday school wing was added, and the Education building was opened in 1963. The two windows in the front of the steeple were closed in order to put up the cross when the building was covered with formstone about 30 years ago. The land on which the church is erected was the gift of Madora Elliott. (Collection of the late Hilda Fowler.)

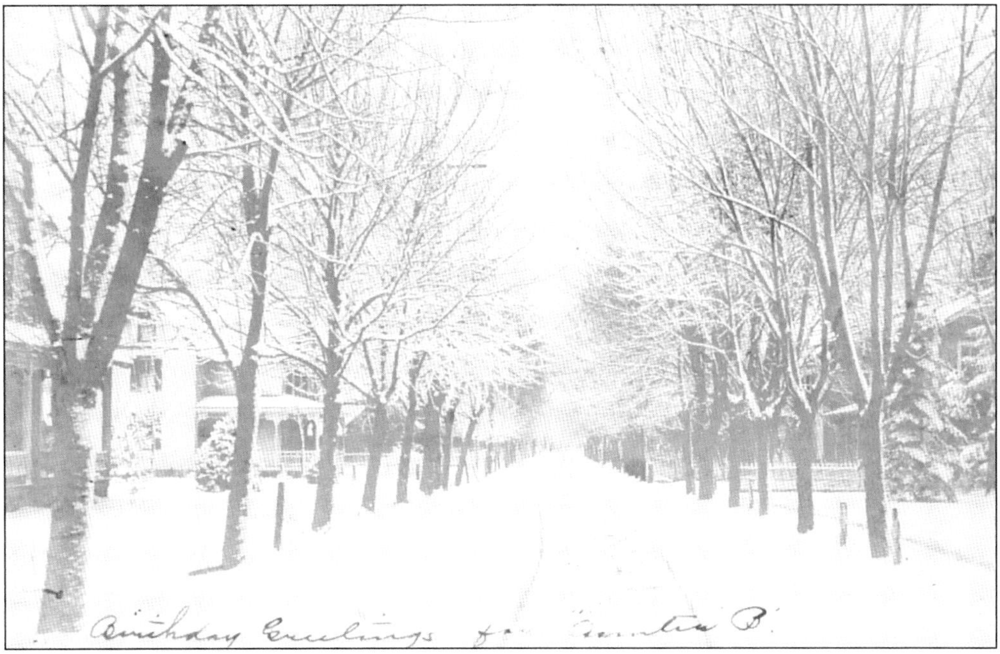

SNOW SCENE, MARDELA SPRINGS, MARYLAND. This picture is blurred by snow but the probability is that the house on the left is the Waller-Gunby house before the addition, and the house across the street is the house with the large corner boards. The picture is looking east along Main Street.

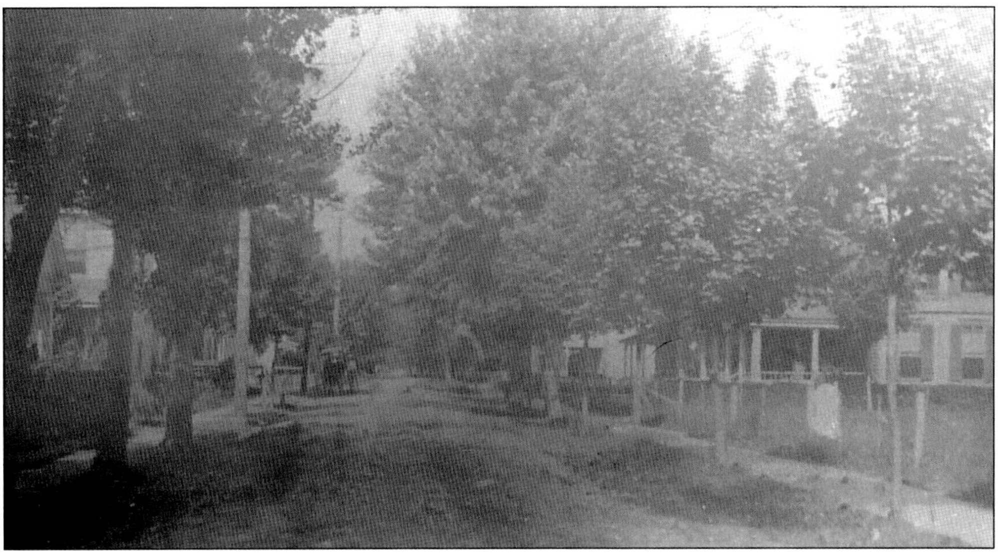

MAIN STREET, MARDELA. This picture was taken from near the Old Railroad looking east. The clue was the Thomas Bounds property, which is the only Main Street house that does not face the street. The porch on both sides, only one of which is visible, with the window over it and the windows facing the street were the clues. The house on the right side has been changed too much for easy identification. The second house with its elaborately milled porch posts is still identifiable. (Collection of the late Hilda Fowler.)

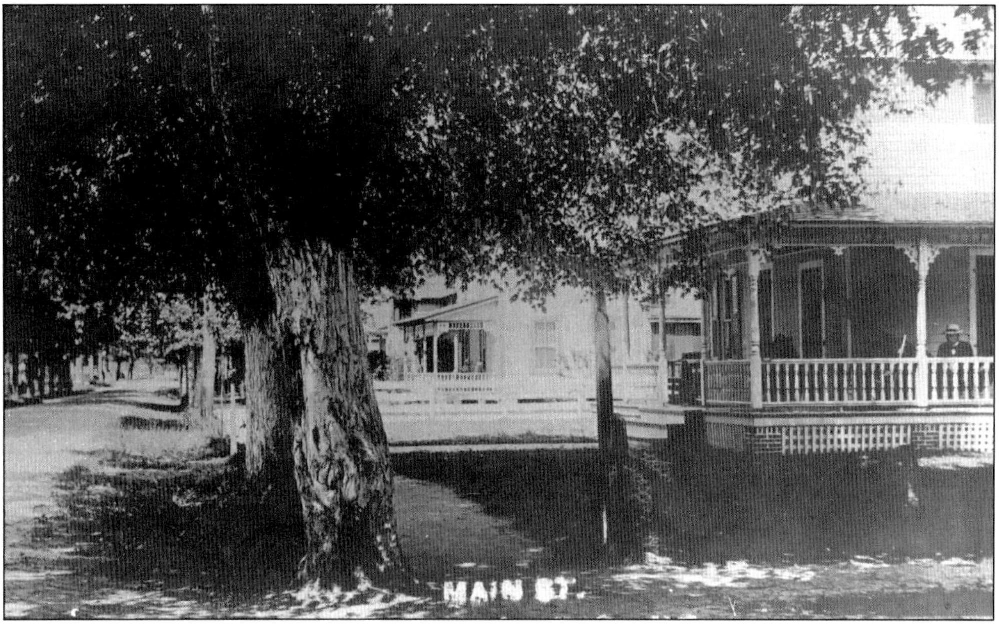

MAIN STREET, MARDELA SPRINGS. The house on the right is located next to the First Baptist Church, and the house behind it would be the lot on which the church is built. The Victorian gingerbread on the house is distinctive, with the little cluster of decoration in the middle of the rest of the woodwork. The brackets around the poles are also a giveaway for Victorian gingerbread. This picture is taken from the east because the porch is "L" shaped only on its western side. (Collection of the late Hilda Fowler.)

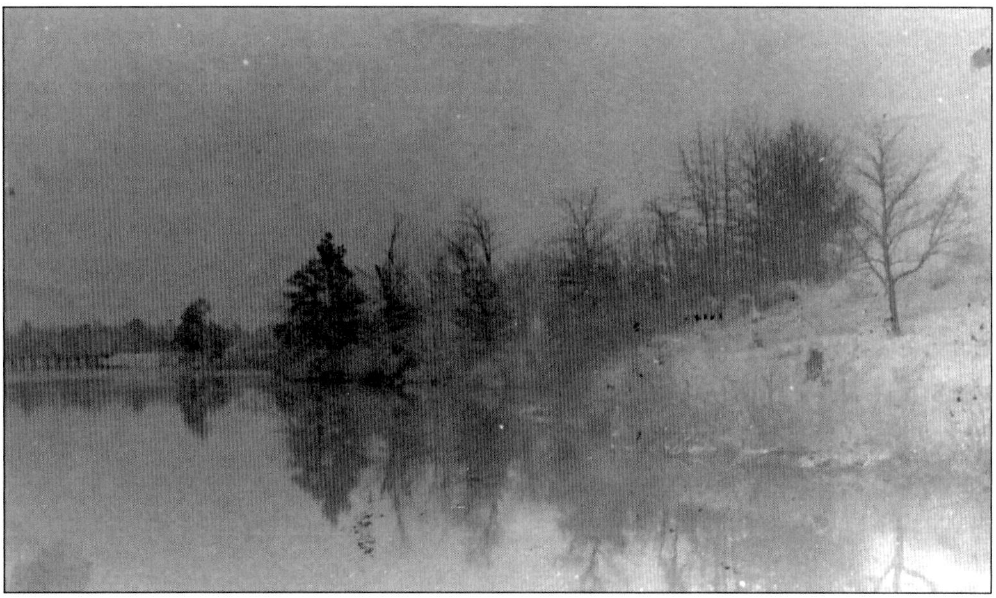

NEAR THE RAILROAD BRIDGE. The bare ground and the sharp rise of the bank from Barren Creek with the railroad bridge in the background indicate that this is the area of Mardela then known as Anderson town, which was the property of George Willey. This property is now developed.

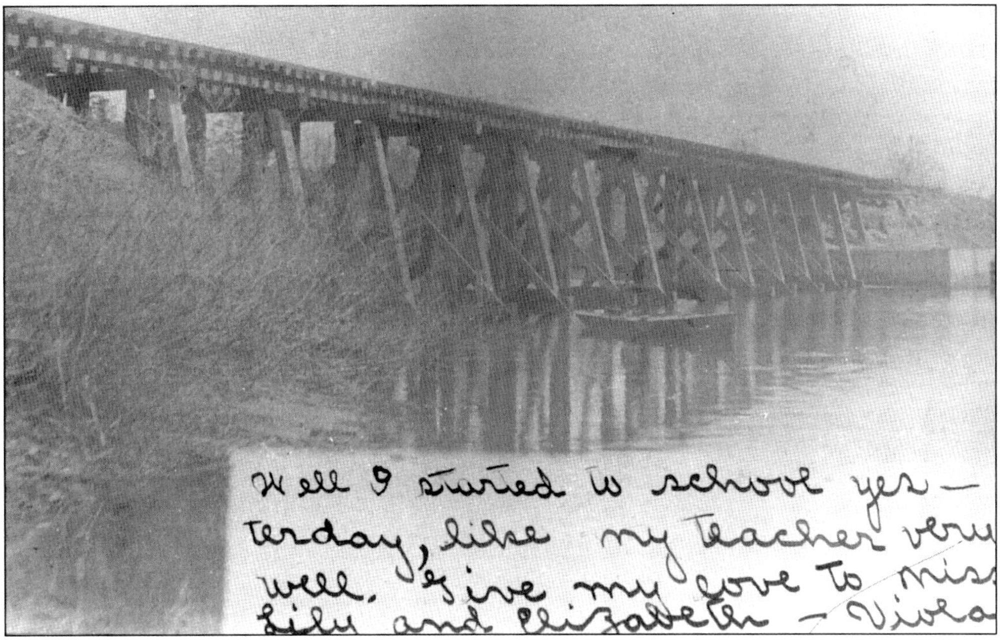

THE RAILROAD BRIDGE. The Baltimore and Eastern Railroad was completed in 1890 and was operated to Mardela for a time after the bridge over the Nanticoke River was abandoned. Service for freight continued to Mardela until about 1936 when the line past Hebron was abandoned. This meant the bridge was used for about 46 years. It was located a little west of present U.S. Route 50 where the abutment may still be seen. (Collection of the late Hilda Fowler.)

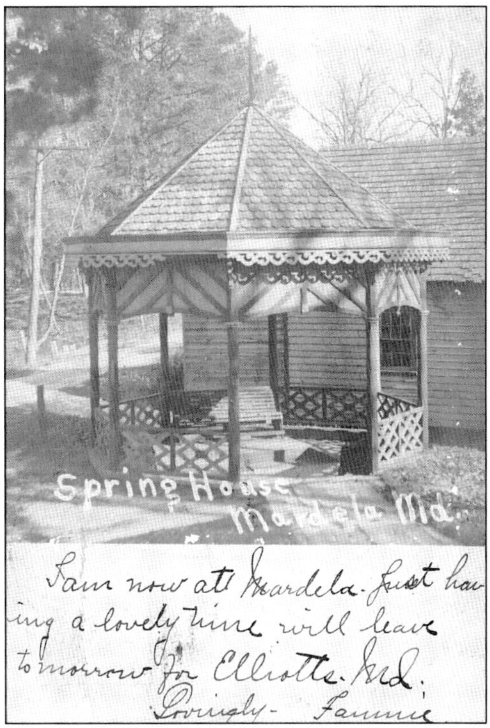

SPRING HOUSE, MARDELA. This shows the Springs when both the Bottling Company and the hotel were in operation. The plant is in the background and the Spring has been improved by a fancy spring house and a bench for those who wanted to sip the water.

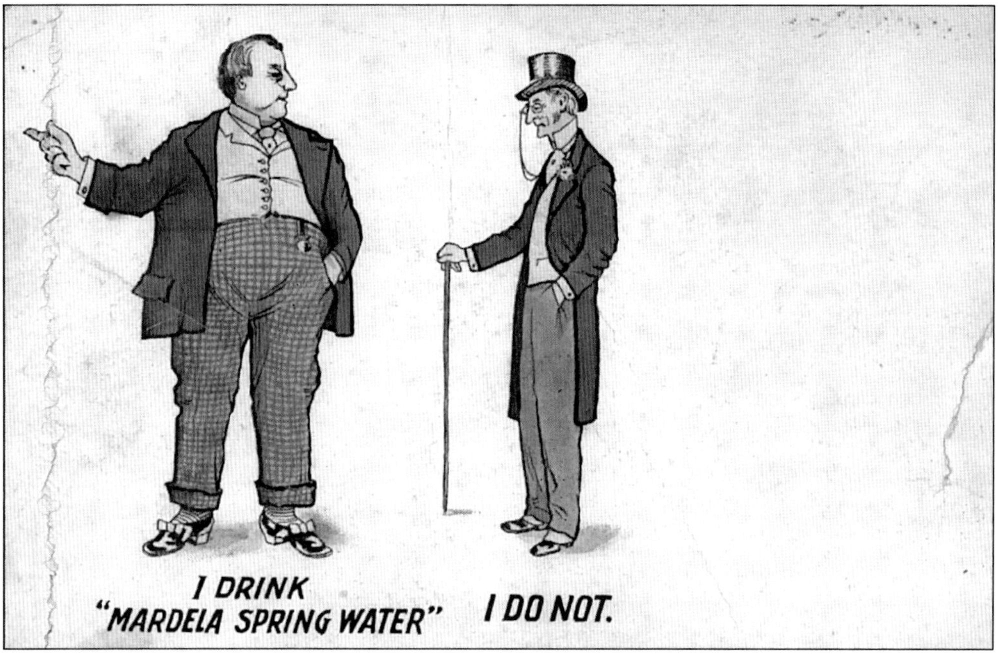

MARDELA SPRING WATER. This postcard was put out as part of the company's advertising campaign. How many people would be motivated to drink the Spring Water by this ad today? The bottles bring a premium price among collectors today.

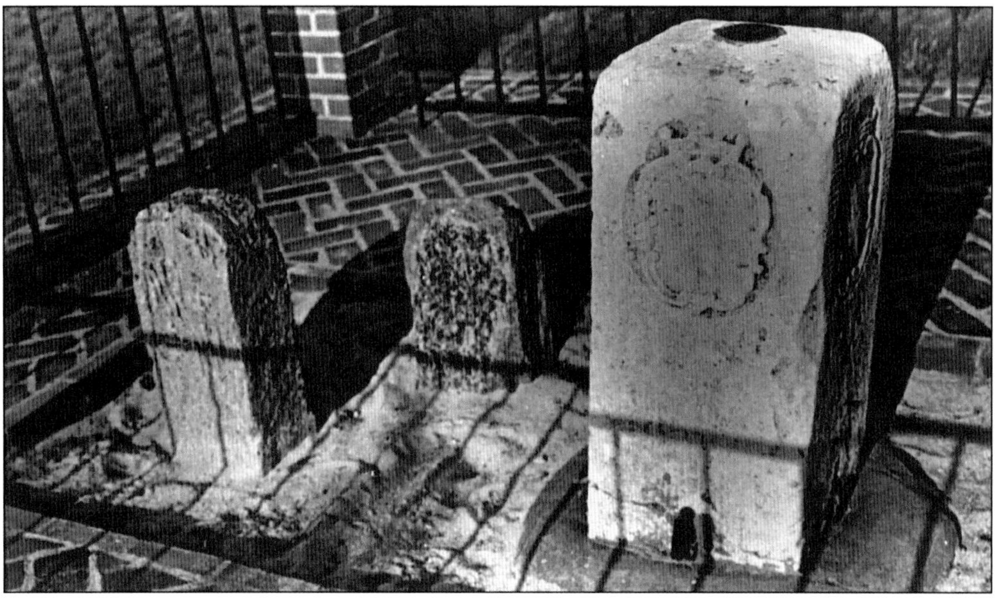

MASON-DIXON STONE. The Mason-Dixon stone, named for the surveyors, is located on the road between Mardela and Delmar. It marks the place that is the southwestern corner of Delaware. It is a crown stone and bears the arms of the Calverts on one side and Penn's arms on the other. A pavilion has been erected over the stones to protect them from the weather.

A plain stone was put in to mark each mile and a crown stone to mark each fifth mile. Local rumor has it that a boatload of stones was landed at Twiford's wharf below Sharptown and from there hauled to the proper spot and then put in place.

Four

Hebron

Hebron is a town that was created by a railroad, but is still healthy now that the railroad is gone. It was a stop on the Baltimore Chesapeake and Atlantic when that line was built in 1890, and the railroad authorities gave it its name.

Hebron's primary employer in the early days was the lumber mill, which produced baskets, boxes, and crates and was run by a man always referred to as "Boss" Bounds. The plant was sold to the Marvil Package Company at Bounds's death and was operated by Marvil until it was destroyed by fire.

The Hebron Savings Bank has now spread out with branches in Salisbury and Cambridge and is probably the town's largest employer. The town was for many years the home of a camp meeting, but when it ceased operations, the Hebron Volunteer Fire Company purchased the campgrounds as the site for its water tower and its Fireman's Carnival. The Fire Company for a number of years also owned the municipal water system, but sold it to the town.

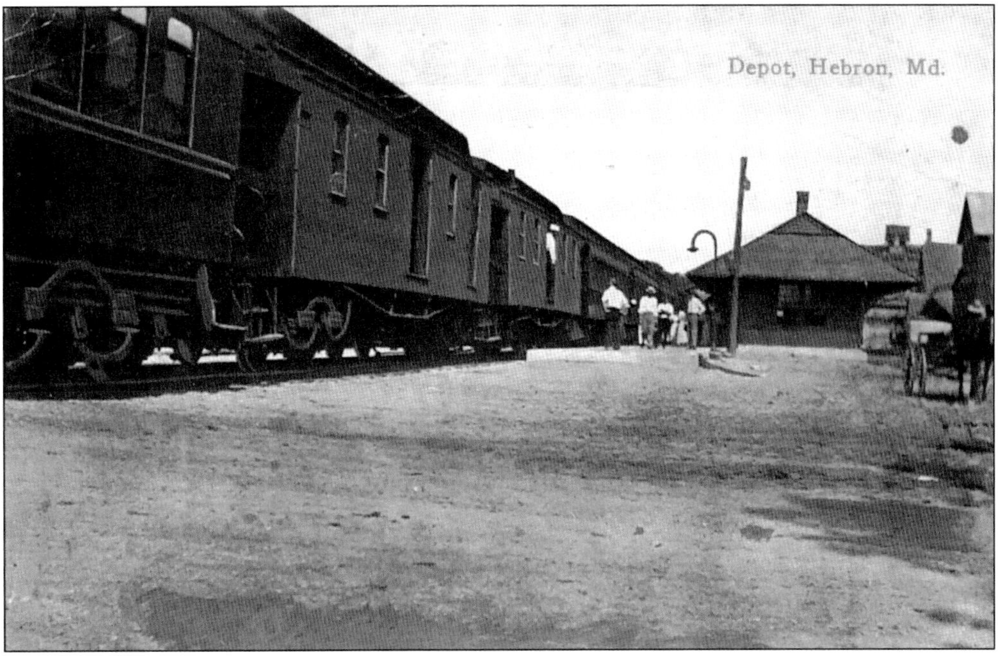

Depot-Hebron. This picture shows the B.C. & A train stopped at the Depot in Hebron, which is still there. It is now the headquarters of the West Side Historical Society. (Collection of James Jackson.)

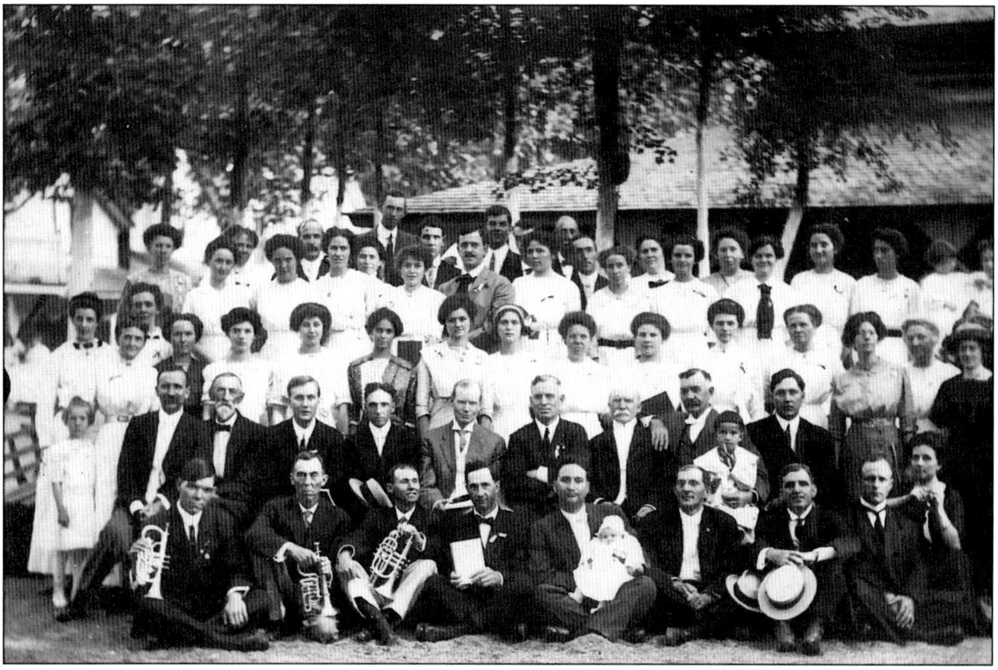

HEBRON CAMP MEETING. This shows the central building of the campground in the background and one of the tents on the left. This group is believed to be a church group from Salisbury who attended in a body bringing their own music with them. Notice the babe in the arms of his or her father in the front row.

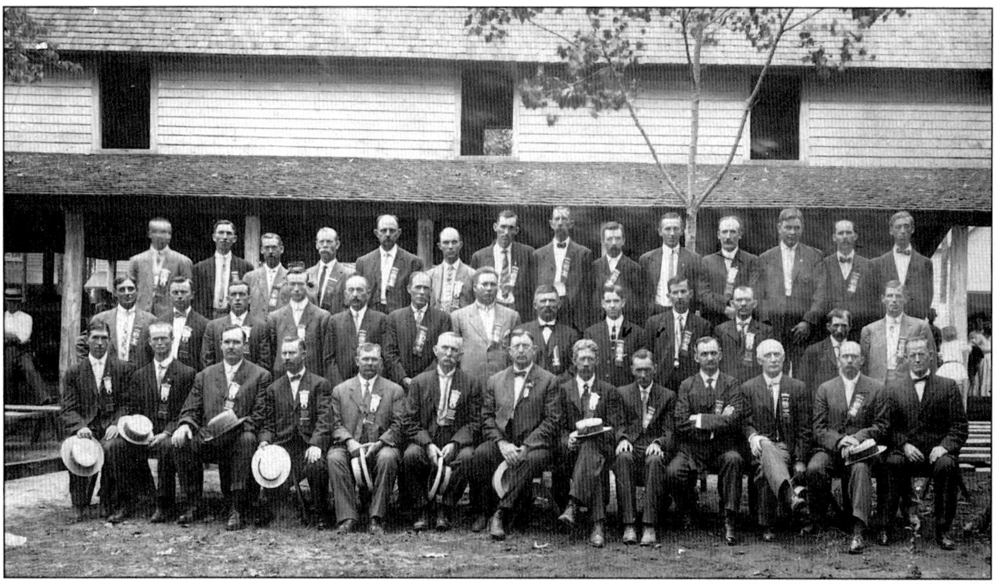

THE RED MEN OF HEBRON. This picture was taken at the Hebron Camp Ground. It is unknown what the occasion was. All of the Red Men are wearing badges and a few are also wearing medallions on ribbons around their necks. There are 40 men in the picture. (Collection of Oswald Wilkinson.)

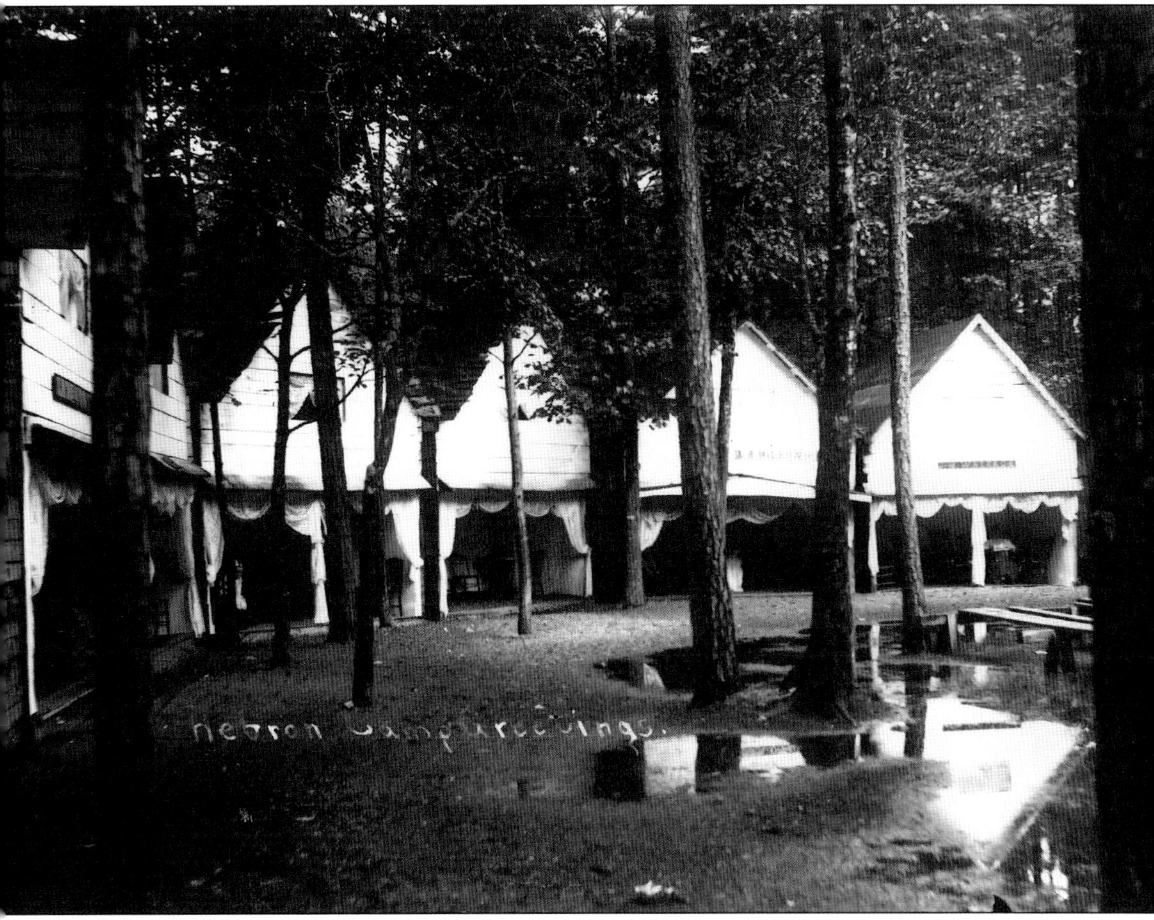

THE CAMPGROUND. This view shows the campground the morning after a rain. The trash has not been picked up and all the tents have their curtains pulled back, and the furniture has been moved back in each tent out of reach of the rain. It was as a teenager here that I started eyeing the girls as they strolled by. (Collection of the Edward Nabb Research Center at the University.)

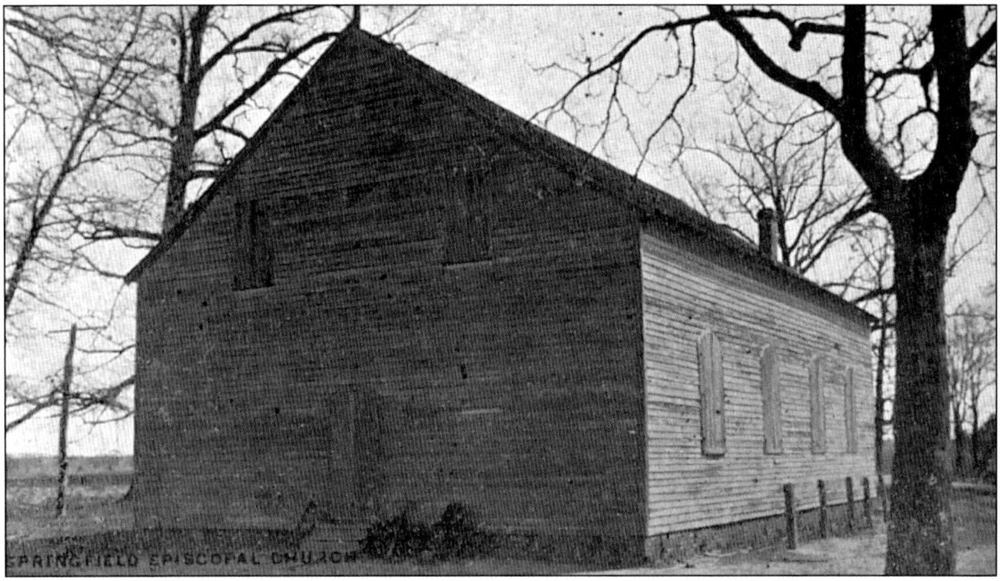

Spring Hill Episcopal Church. The card erroneously says Springfield. This was one of the Chapels of Ease of Stepney Parish. The church is built on 2 acres of a tract called Spring Hill that was donated by a Presbyterian, Mary Hampton.

The date of construction of the original church is unknown, but the present one was built in 1774 and has been in continuous use ever since. In 1880 the vestries of Spring Hill and St. Peters met and agreed to the terms of separation into separate parishes. The church's interior is the same today as it was when built.

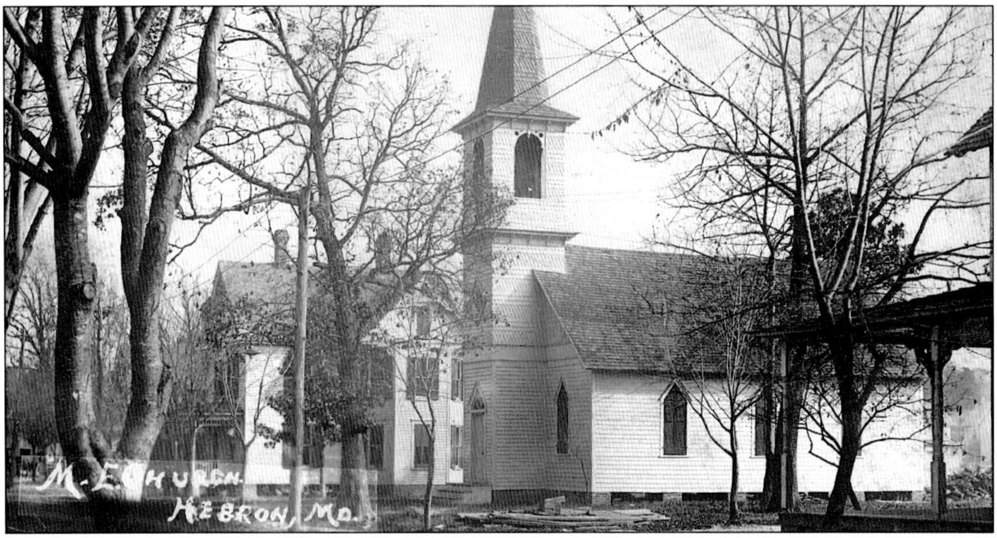

M.E. Church. This is the original Nelson Memorial Church, which was moved in 1916. The parsonage is shown next to the church. It is now the home of James Fox Jr., and it no longer has its two chimneys. The post office is now on the lot in the foreground. Mrs. Sally Nelson donated the church lot in 1892, and the church was named for her. It was replaced by the present brick building in 1916, and the Samuel Phillips building has been added since. (Collection of James Jackson.)

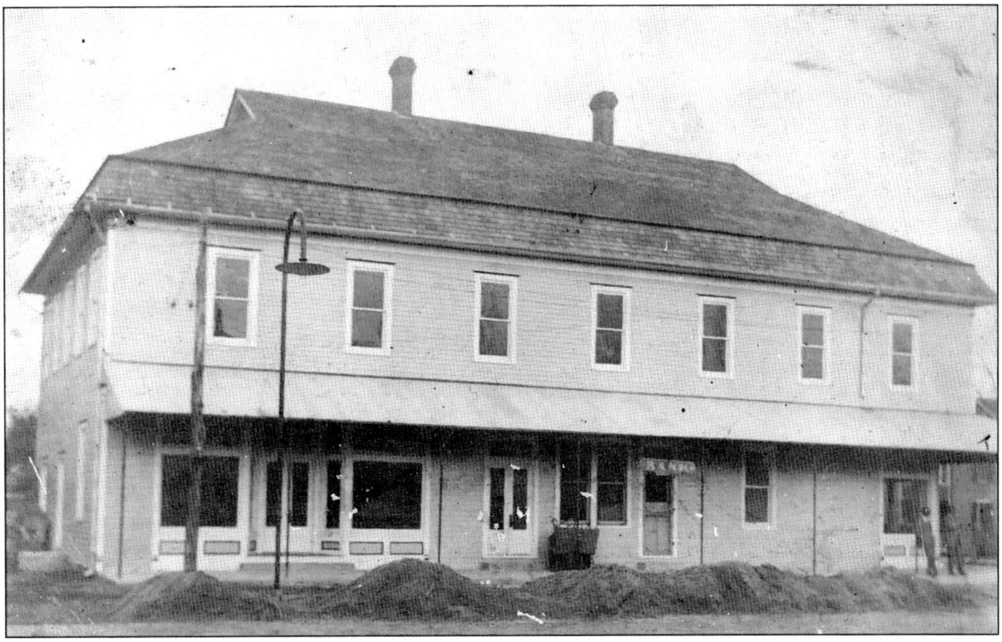

The Bounds Building. The post office is on the left, the bank in the center, and the drugstore on the right. This building faced Railroad Avenue, and the upstairs was the Lodge Room of the Red Men. The street was probably torn up to lay the original water supply system when the Fire Company owned it. The building has now been torn down.

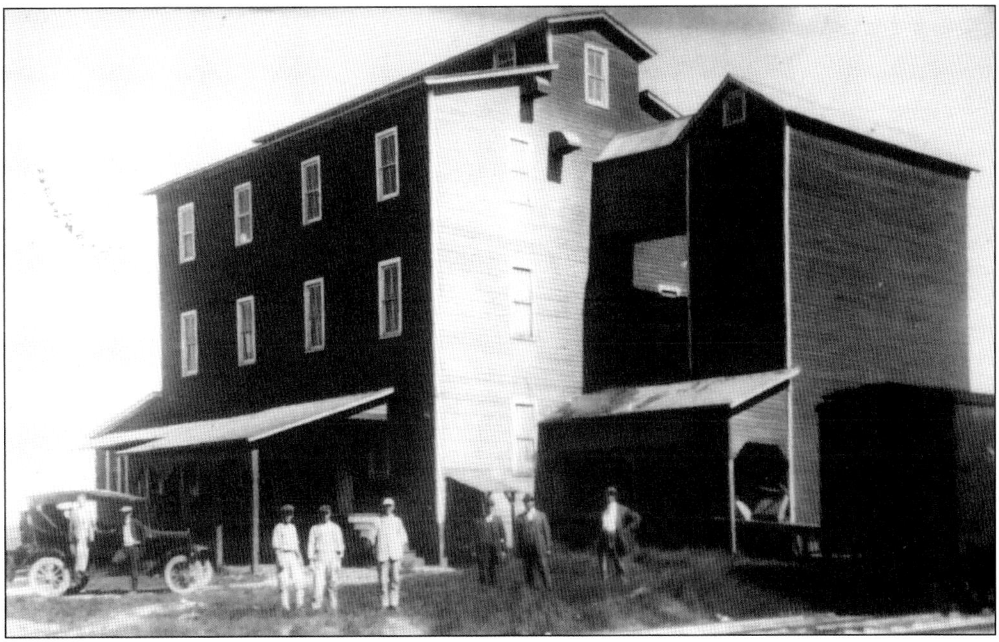

The Flour Mill. This photograph was taken about 1929. Two of the men shown are Grafton Mills and Howard Culver. (Collection of Oswald Wilkinson.)

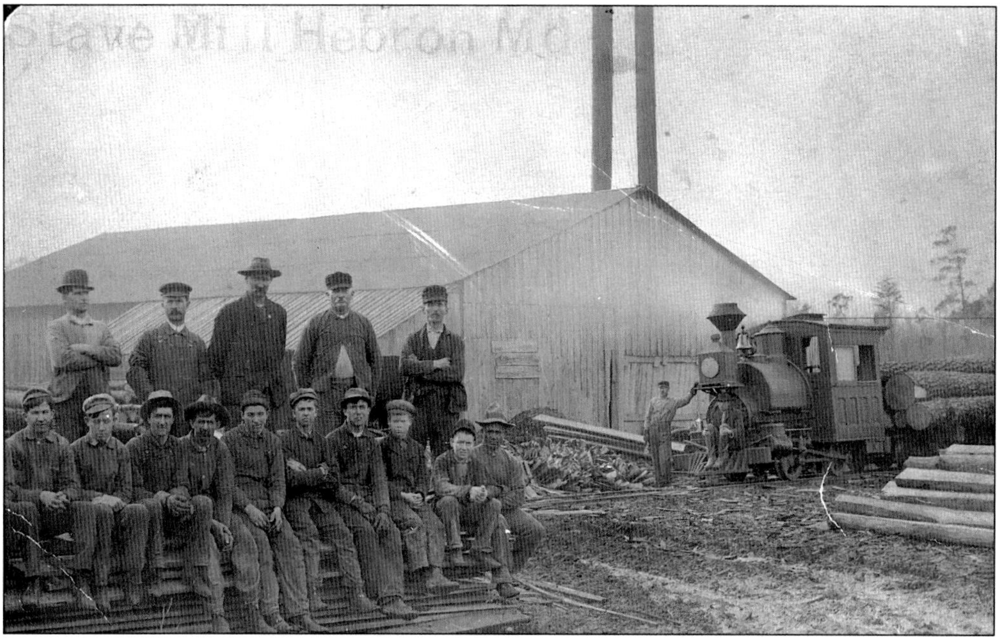

Basket and Crate Factory. This picture of the factory shows the grandfather of Oswald Wilkinson in the back row and his uncle in the front row, far left. The railroad train was a narrow gage line used to haul logs to the mill from the Devil's Woodyard between Rockawalkin and Quantico. You can see the logs still on a car attached to the engine.

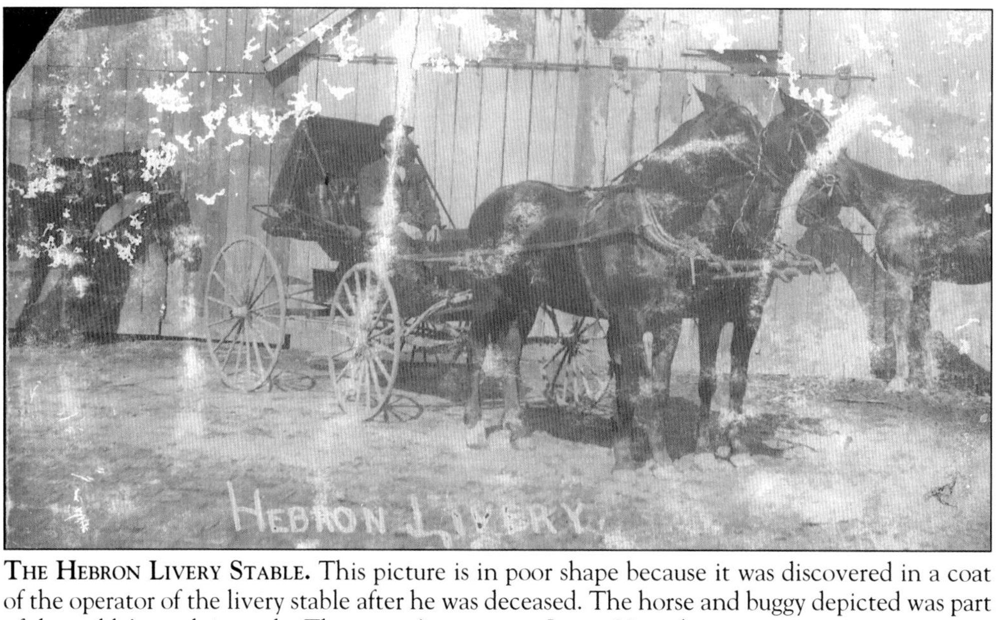

The Hebron Livery Stable. This picture is in poor shape because it was discovered in a coat of the operator of the livery stable after he was deceased. The horse and buggy depicted was part of the stable's stock in trade. The owner's name was James Humphreys.

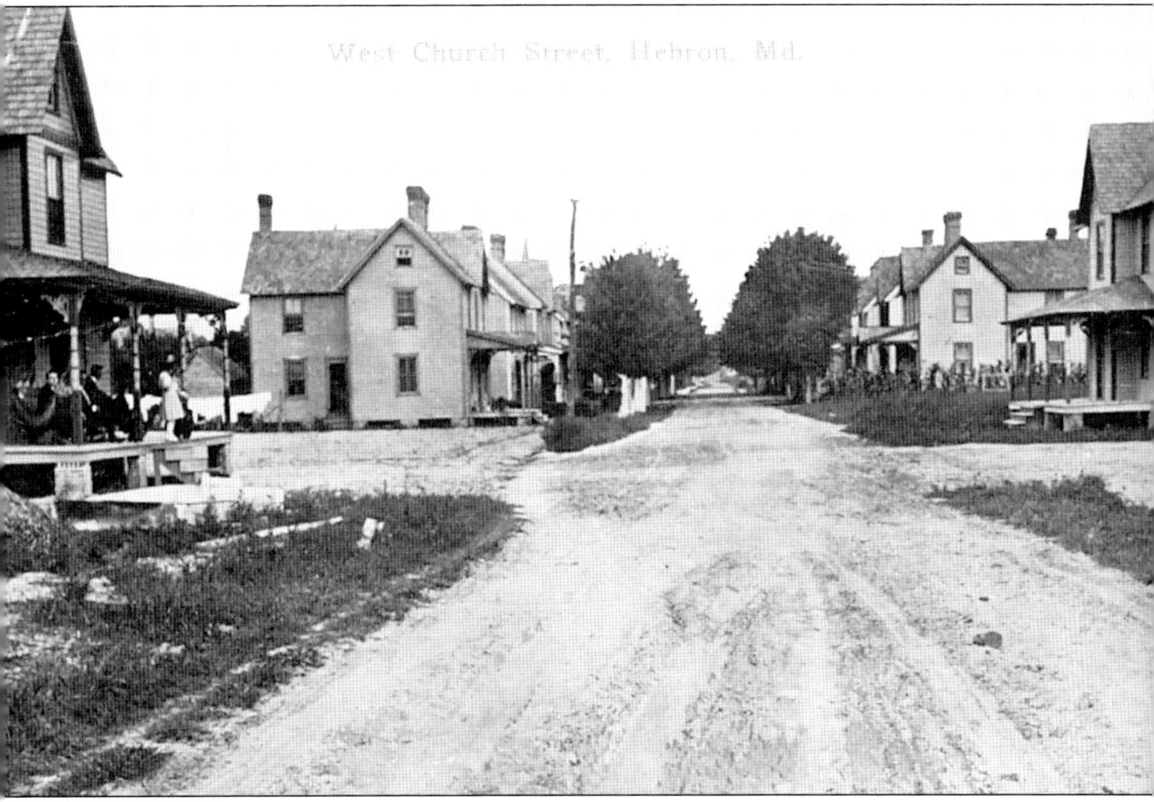

WEST CHURCH STREET. This scene was taken beyond Nelson Street. The homes of Oswald Wilkinson, Gordy Beach, and Margaret Webster and Eunice Wilson may all be seen.

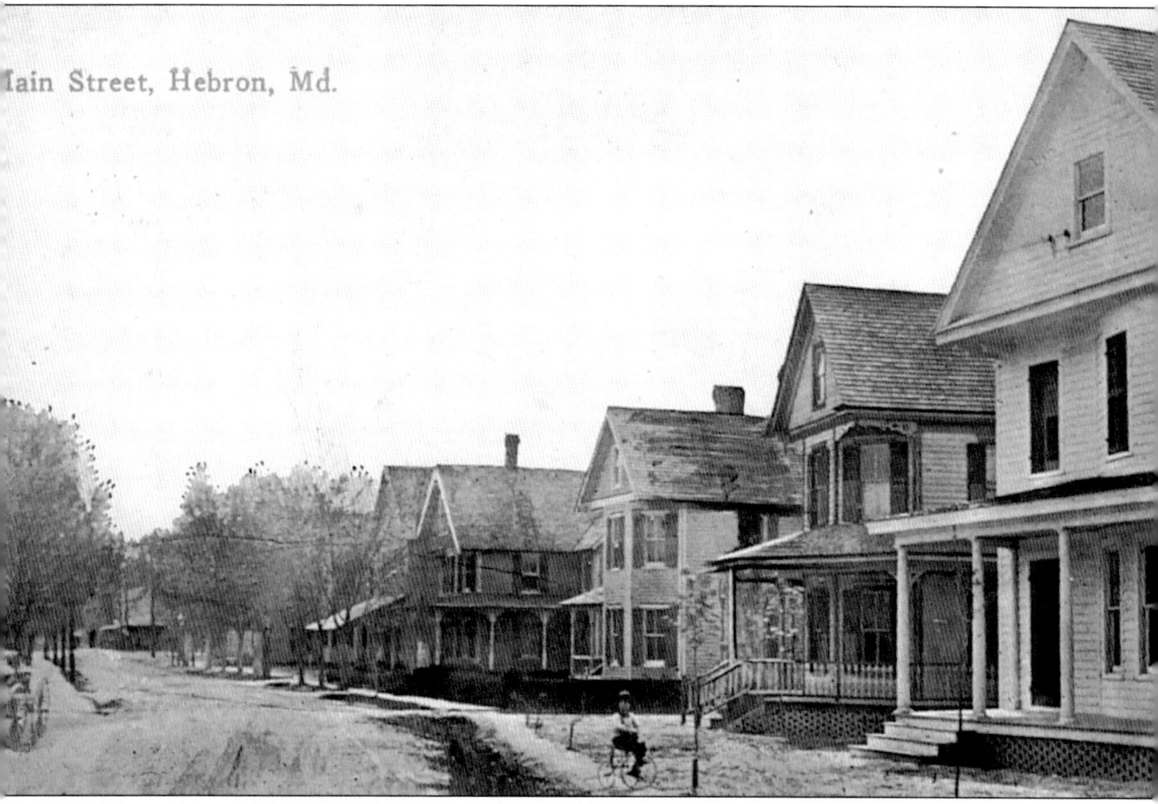

MAIN STREET HEBRON. This is now the 200 block North Main Street. The homes shown are those of Lee Holliday, Dr. Conoway, Lester Timmons, Carl Messick, and then Messick's store. The street is unpaved.

Five

ON THE RIVERS

The rivers, the Wicomico and the Nanticoke, are most important in the history of Wicomico County. They were the carriers of the first waves of its settlement, and until water transportation stopped, the steamer was the principal carrier of freight and passengers from Baltimore. Fish, oysters, and crabs were harvested by men in workboats until disease and over harvesting depleted the supply. Now pollution of the water has put bathing at risk, but a sunset over the water still has its old charm. Recreational use of the rivers has increased dramatically. Power and sailboats, skiffs and canoes dot the water; summer homes take up river frontage, and waterfront year-round homes pepper the landscape.

Whitehaven was founded by George Gale in 1704 on the south side of the Wicomico River. It was a small town containing only eight lots. Built in the center of a marsh, the rising water table caused it to move to the north side of the river, and today only archaeologists can determine where the town started. Perhaps a new day will be dawning with the restoration of the Hotel and Whitehaven's resurgence as a tourist attraction.

Green Hill was platted as a town and the plat was recorded among the Land Records, but then failed to attract citizens. The Lords Baltimore established a tobacco warehouse here, and during the Revolution the state sent troops to guard it. Now the empty church broods over the empty town though it is filled one day a year on the Sunday closest to St. Bartholomew Day.

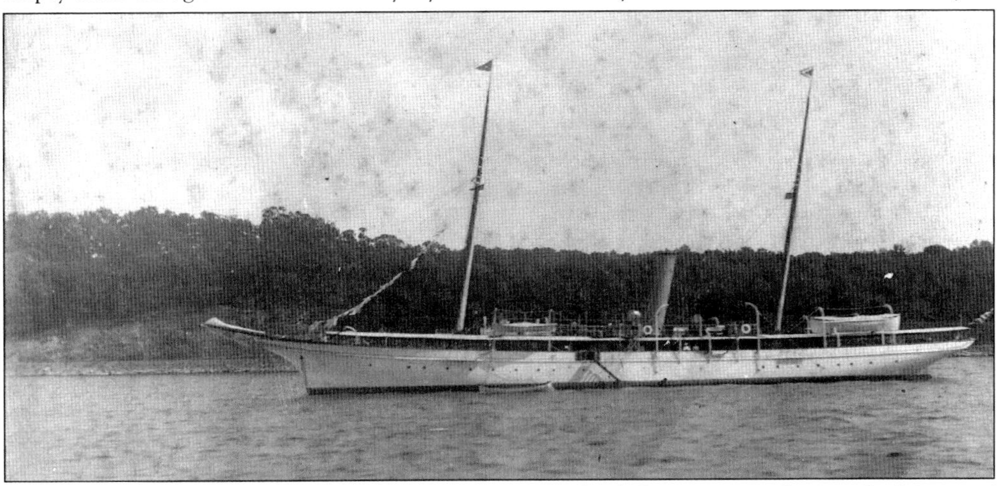

THE VIOLA. She was built by Smith & Williams Co. of Salisbury in 1914 for Marshall Jones of the Corinthian Yacht Club in Philadelphia. She was 66 feet long, had an 18-foot beam, a 7-foot draft, and the main cabin had a working fireplace. It required a crew of four seamen. This was the largest vessel ever built at the Smith & Williams's shipyard up to this time.

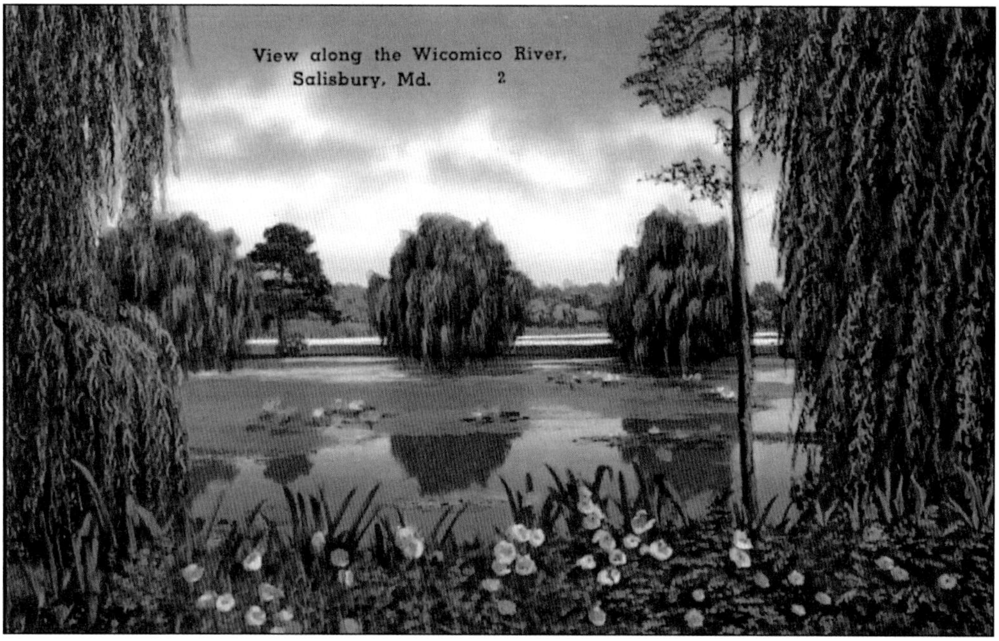

View Along the Wicomico River. This view is completely unrealistic. Only the pine tree is natural.

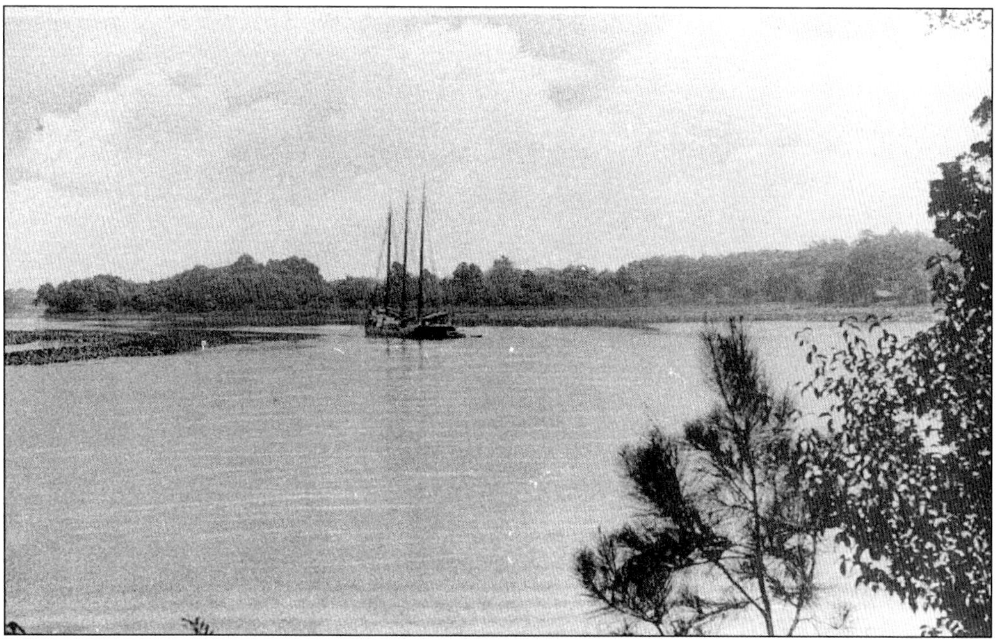

Wicomico River. This scene is real. The three master under bare poles is proceeding slowly up the river. The river is quite crooked and the tuckahoes growing in the mud are for real.

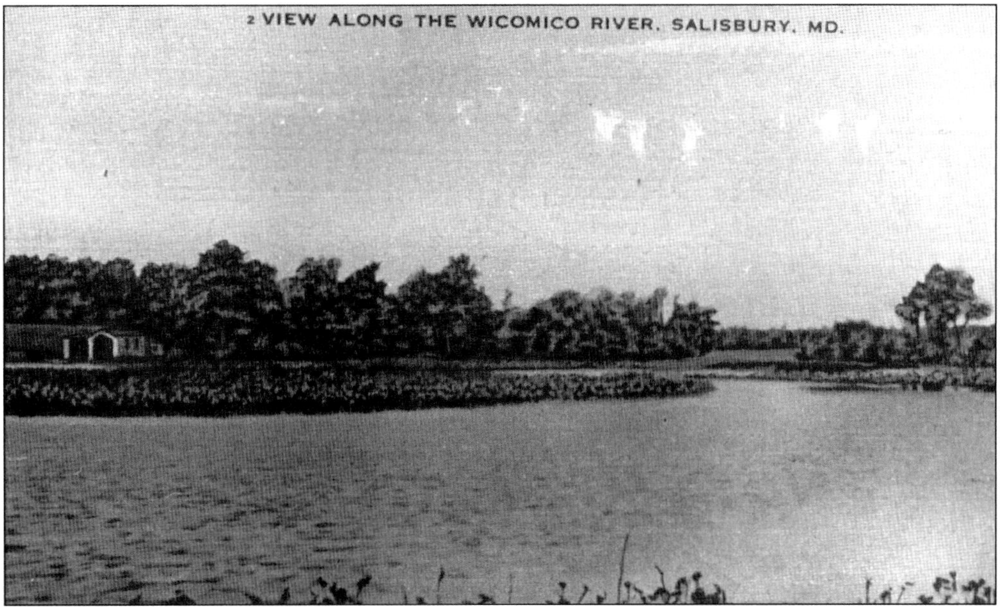

A View From Tony Tank Creek. This picture was taken at the mouth of Tony Tank Creek, which is at right in this photograph. The boathouse across the river is there.

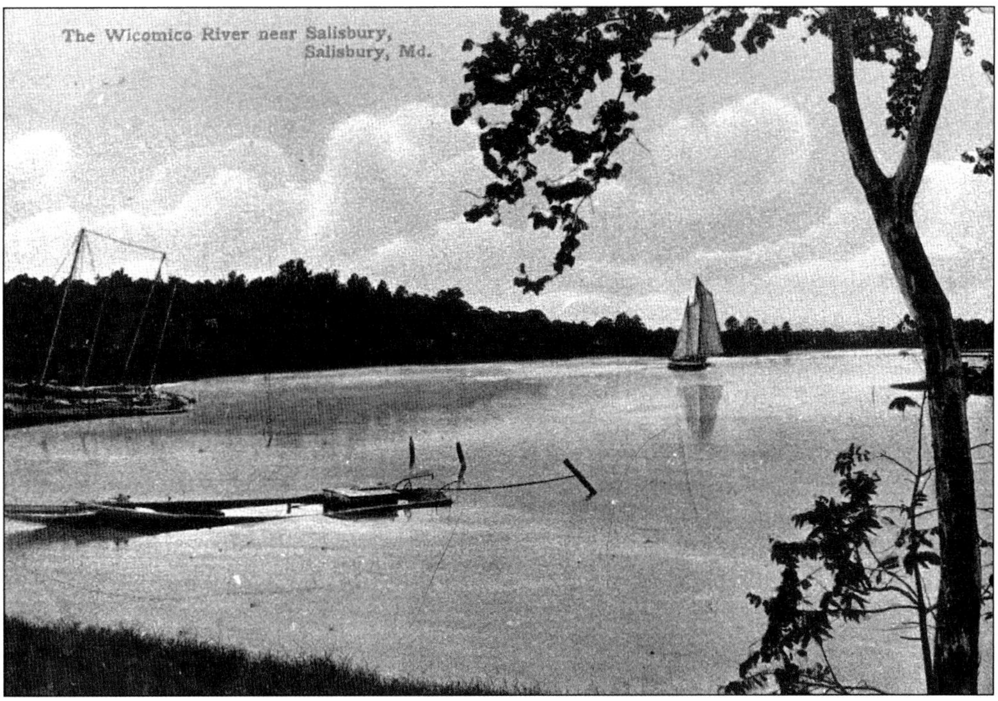

The Wicomico River near Salisbury. This scene was taken near Whitehaven, which was near the graveyard of abandoned ships and boats.

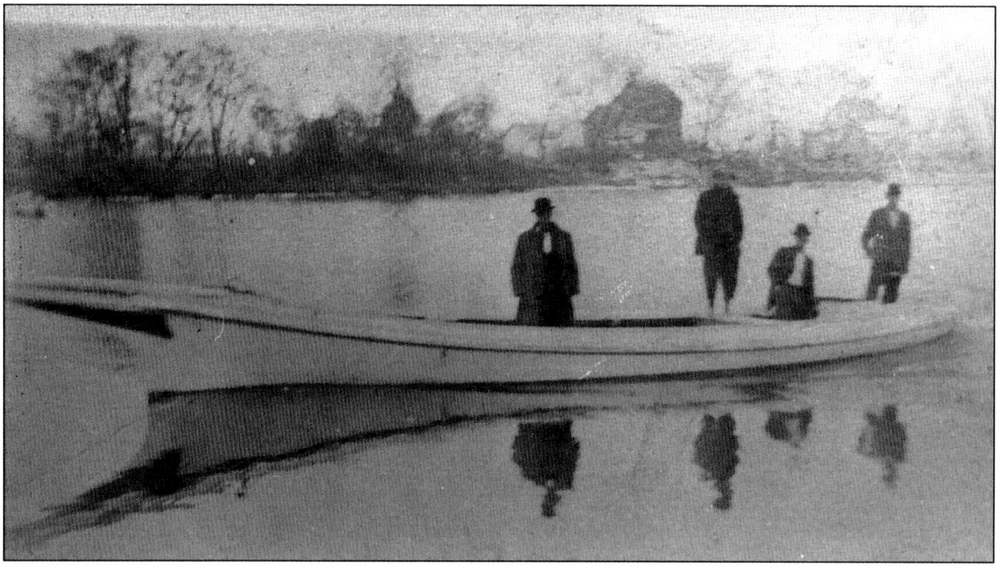

BOAT ON RIVER. This picture was probably taken on Sunday since the males shown are certainly not in work-a-day clothes. It is impossible to read the boat's name on the trailboard, but it is a typical log canoe. The people are unidentified but the provenance of the card points to the Wicomico side of the lower reaches of the river. The time is estimated to be the period of WW I. It would appear that the third man from the bow is steering from a small wheel, and the engine box is immediately in front of him. (Collection of Sylvia Taylor.)

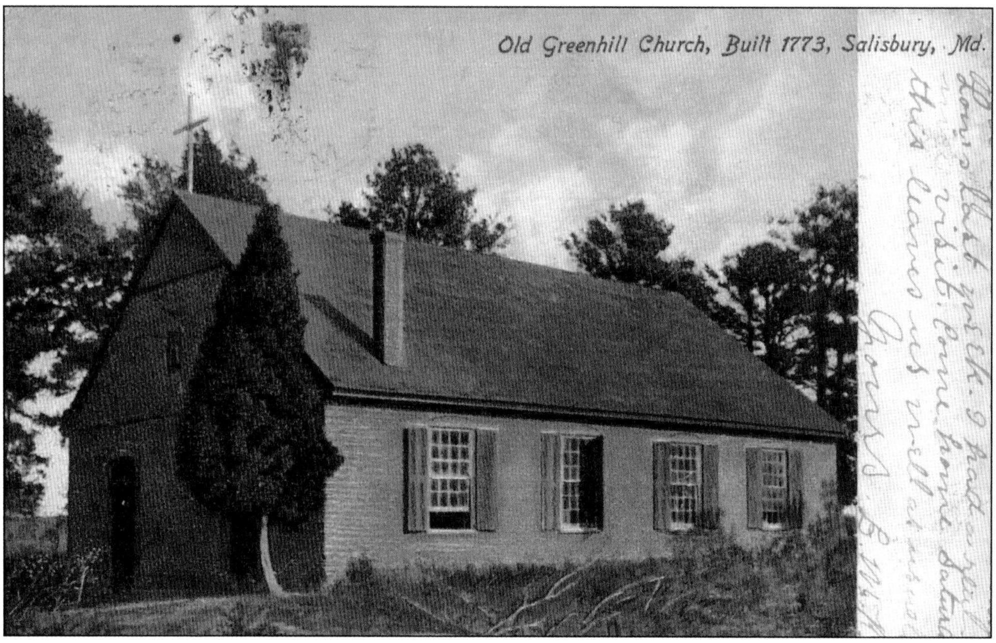

OLD GREEN HILL CHURCH. In this picture taken before 1907, the church had not been repaired and restored. Shutters were of the usual residential type with open louvers. The wildness of weeds and broken tree limbs is evidence of neglect. The church was subject to extensive repairs in 1927 and has been adequately maintained since then. An annual service is held at the Old Green Hill Church the last Sunday in August.

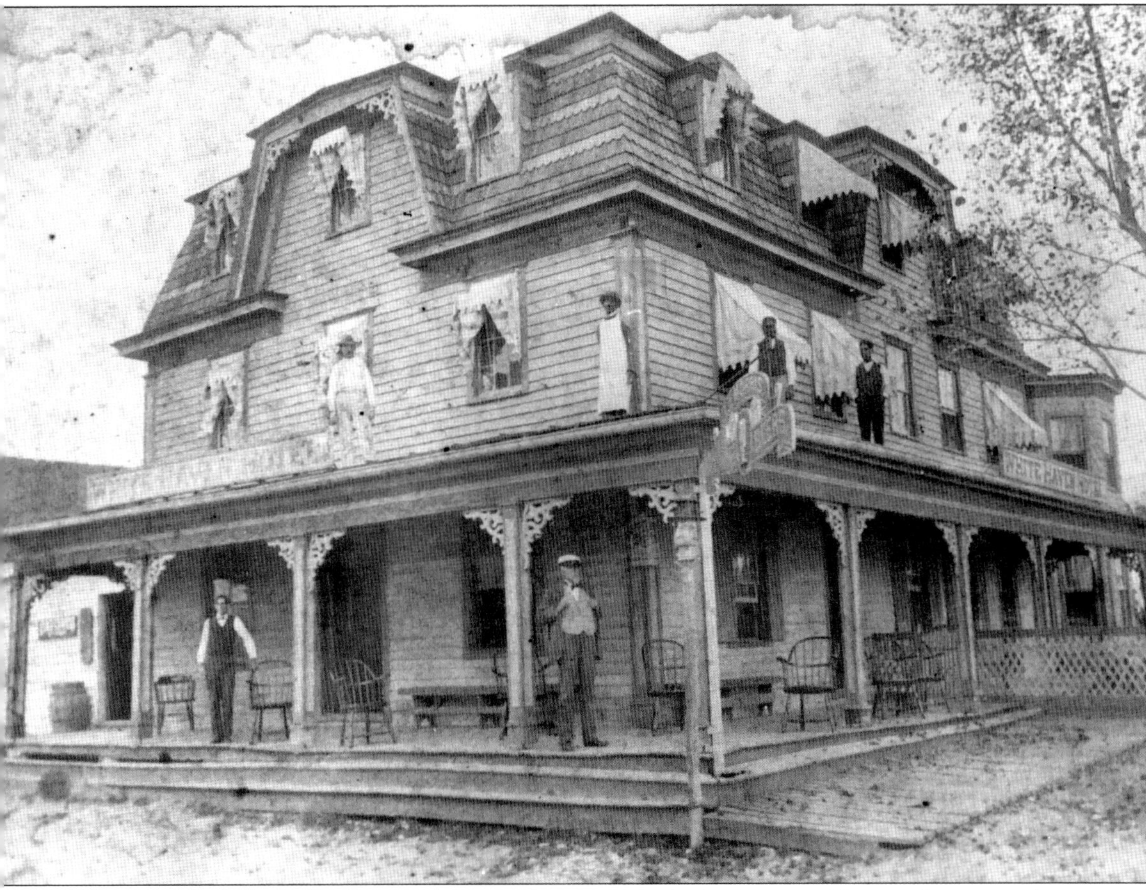

WHITEHAVEN HOTEL. The owner of the hotel was so proud of it, he posted his employees on the porch roof, and took station himself on the porch with his thumbs beneath his vest, to have a picture of the hotel. The ships that harbored here and the people who traveled them kept the hotel filled. The hotel has been jacked up and is presently undergoing extensive repairs and alterations. When finished it will be a Bed and Breakfast.

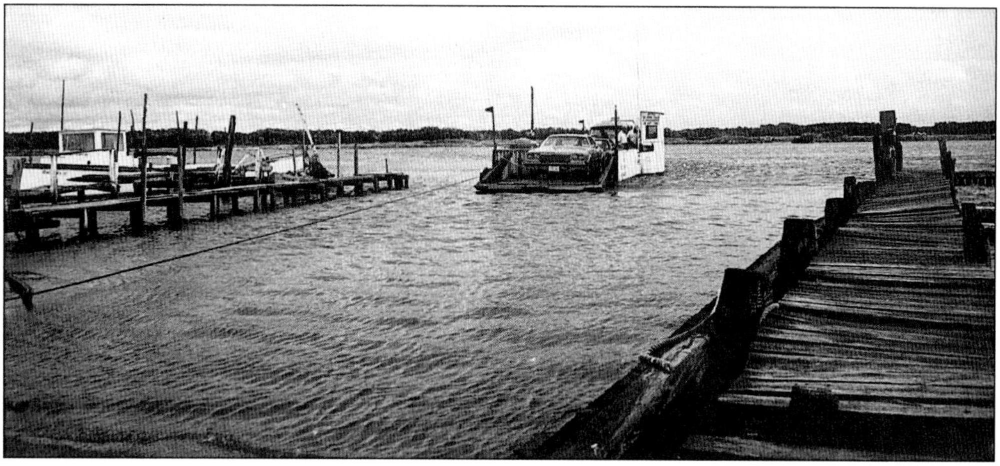

The Whitehaven Ferry. The Whitehaven ferry is one of the oldest in the United States in continuous use. Whitehaven switched from one side of the river to the other; its original site was on the south side of the river. In the late 18th century the balance began to shift and the town moved across the river. Only the ferry connecting the two sites remained constant. This is a cable ferry with the ferryman's house on one side to shield him from the weather. The reversible outboard motor is also in the house, which has a window on both sides. In the mid-19th century when the harbor in Salisbury silted up, the steamboats stopped here, and coaches from *Snow Hill*, *Princess Anne*, and *Salisbury* met the weekly vessel. In the days before steam, the narrowing of the river made sailing impractical beyond Whitehaven, and the packet boats stopped here and let off passengers for *Princess Anne*, *Salisbury*, and *Snow Hill*.

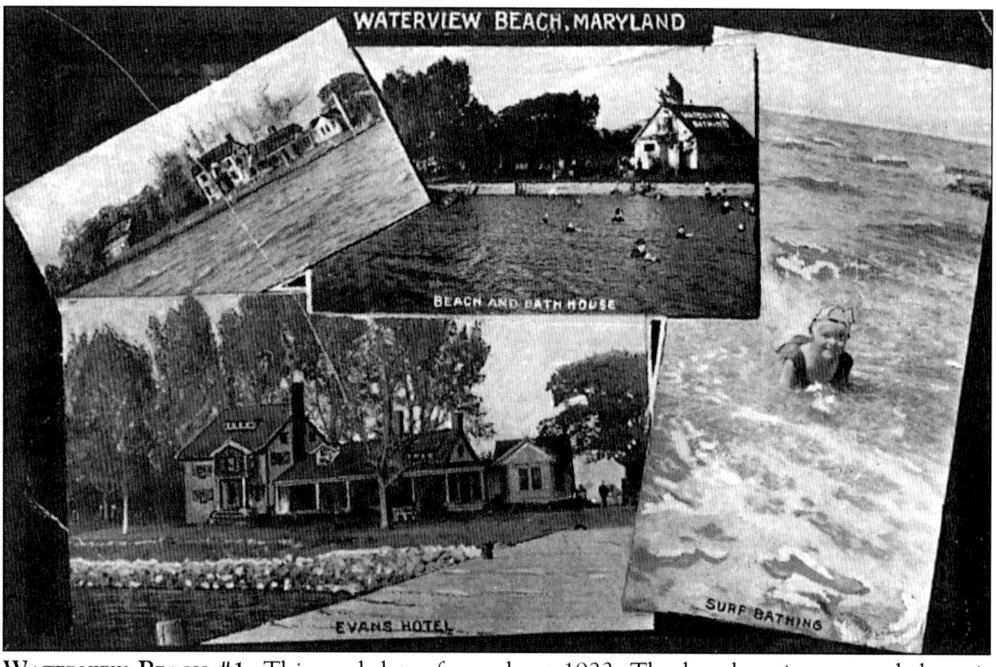

Waterview Beach #1. This card dates from about 1923. The hotel, as it appeared then, is shown in the lower left; Annabel Evans, the owner's daughter is at right; the barns are visible in the picture at upper left; and the bathhouse is at upper right. Not shown is the store and post office.

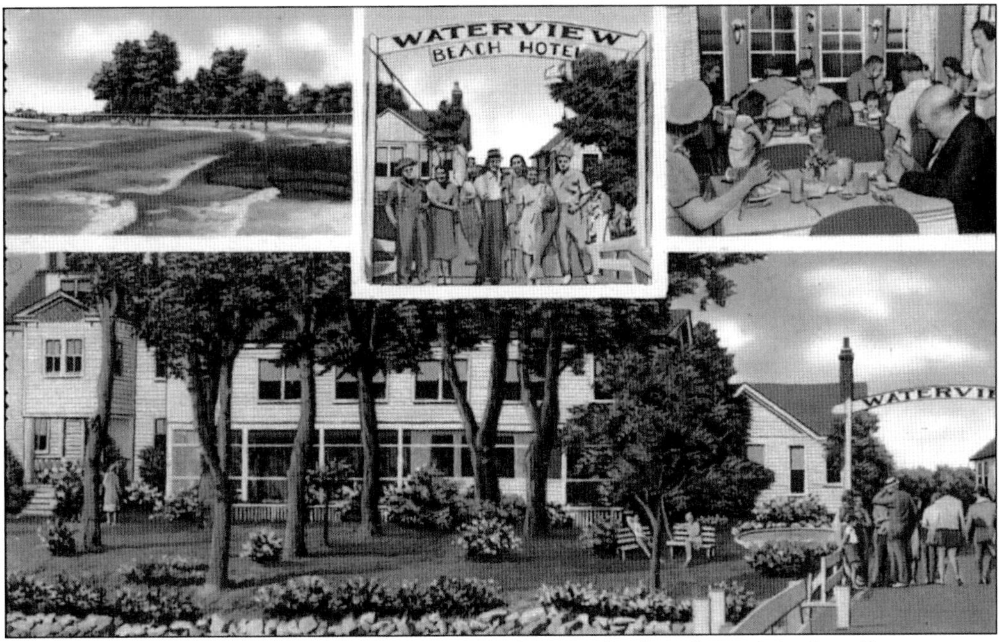

WATERVIEW BEACH HOTEL. This picture was taken in the last days of the hotel's operation, about 1933. William F. Evans opened it in 1919, and a major addition was made in 1929 that included the four rooms with double windows on the second floor. The rocks at left front had been hauled there from Port Deposit by Captain Robert Evans shortly after the Civil War when a storm had washed away an orchard in front of his home. Mr. William F. Evans, his son, lost the hotel during the Depression, and it closed after a brief period of operation by the late Parks Young. It was rented one summer by the Russian Embassy after which the hotel was allowed to deteriorate. The property has now become a waterfront subdivision.

The hotel site has been in residential use for several centuries, and the graveyard near the house has a tombstone dated November 5, 1792.

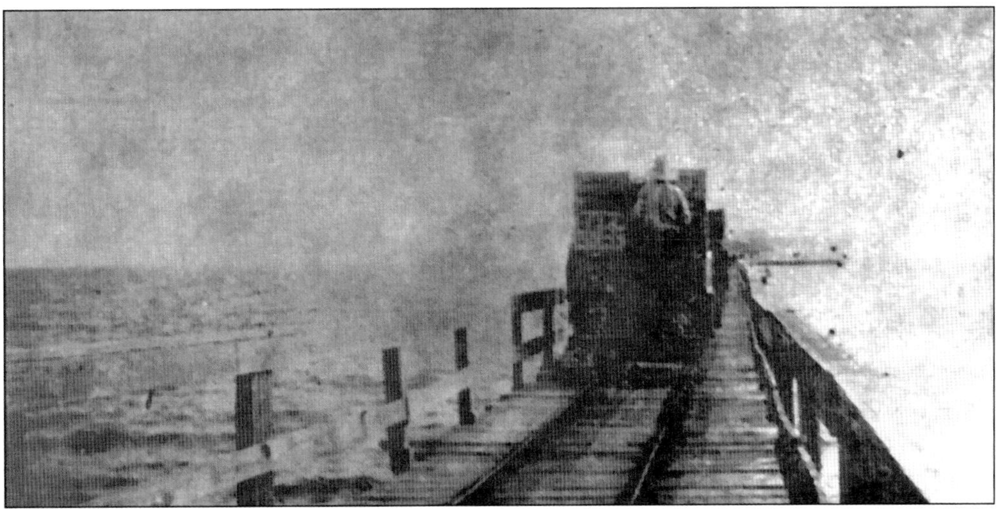

NANTICOKE WHARF. The wharf was built a long way from dry land and rails were laid down on the approach to relieve congestion and also to expedite loading. Shown here is a load of strawberries on its way out to the steamer.

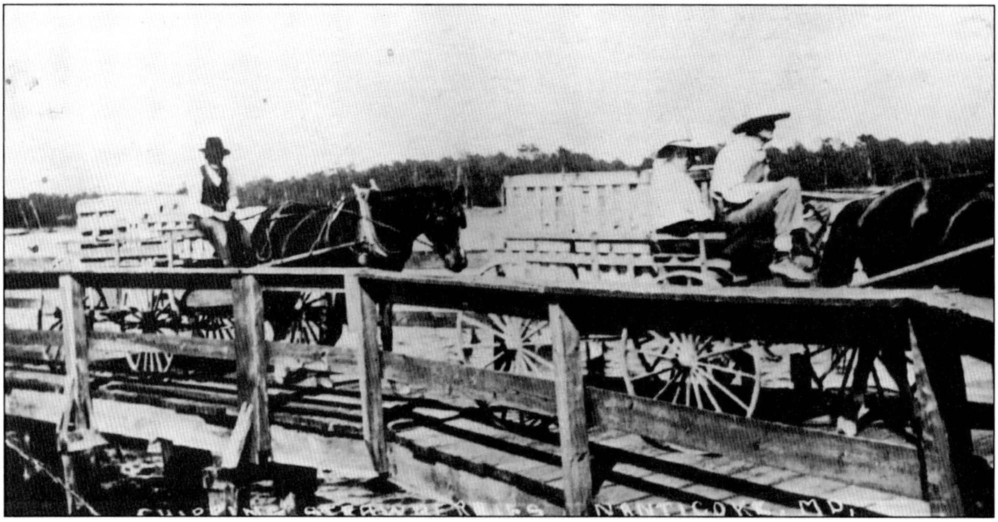

Shipping Strawberries at Nanticoke. These two men shown with their loads of strawberry crates were waiting in line to ship their berries to Baltimore on consignment. Local men acted as agents for produce brokers in Baltimore and had printed tags to attach to the crates. Farmers took their produce to the Nanticoke Wharf to be shipped on the *Virginia* beginning with asparagus in the spring. In addition people from Elliott's Island brought produce by boat to Nanticoke to be shipped. This picture probably dates from about the close of WW I because of the horse-drawn vehicles and because the quantity of produce shipped by boat dropped off markedly in the 1920s with the advent of the truck. (Collection of Betty Webster.)

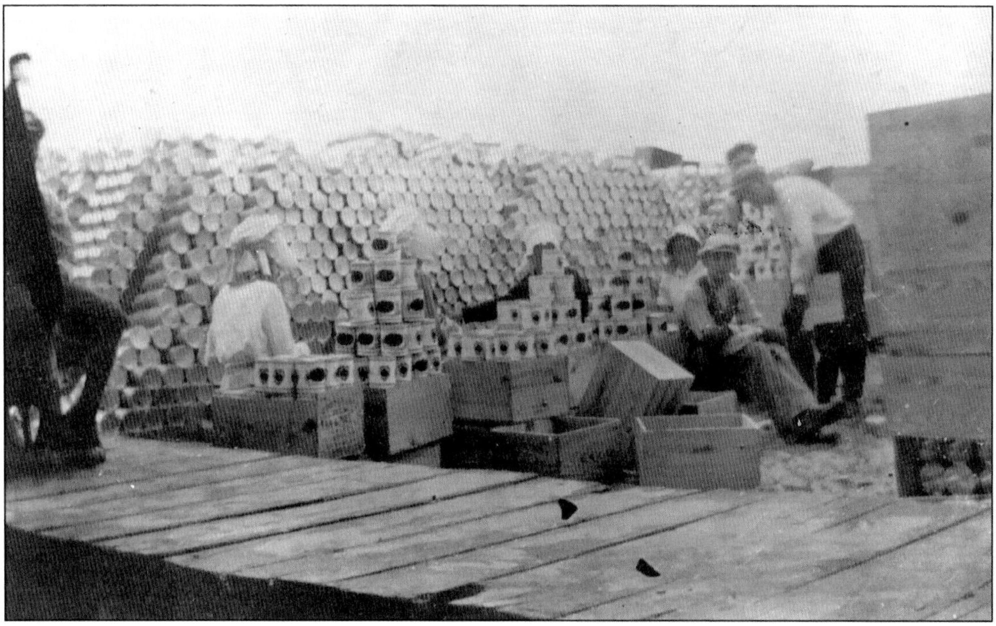

Canning Plant. There was a tomato canning plant located next to the steamboat wharf at Nanticoke, and here you can see the cans being labeled prior to shipping. The unlabeled cans are stacked on the left. Sometimes a buyer would want his own label used and he would send the labels down to be affixed to the cans. Notice the headgear on the women; it provided shade and protection against flies and mosquitoes.

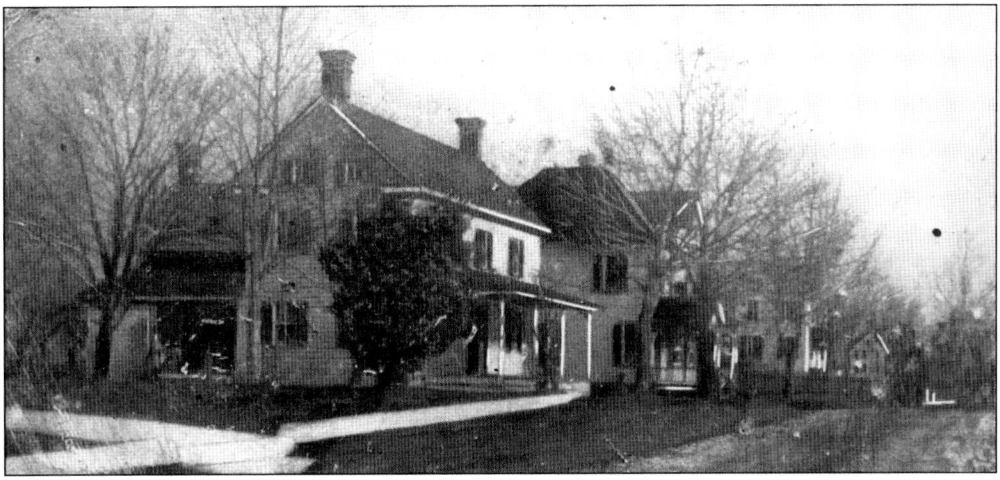

MAIN STREET, NANTICOKE. The state of the street reveals the age of this picture, which was taken shortly after the turn of the century. Electricity and telephones had not yet reached Nanticoke. The house closest to the camera was the Methodist Episcopal parsonage, now the home of the Albrights. The next house is the Ware Willing house, now owned by Wayne Spencer. The third house is the Rollie and Holton Douglass house, now owned by Franklin Willing. The house in the background was the Jessie R. Travers home. It is still owned by descendants of the Travers family. (Courtesy of A. Frank Holloway.)

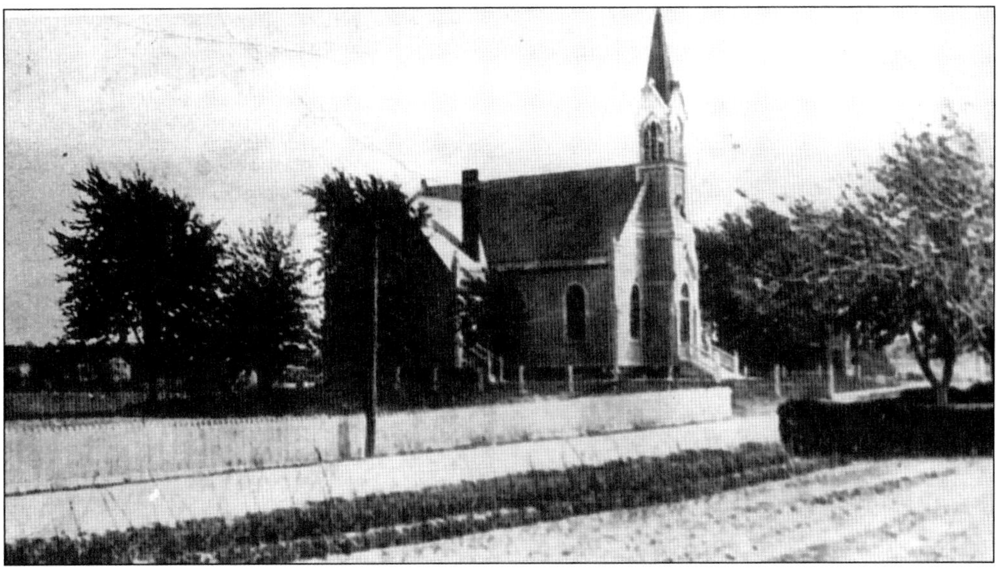

M.E. CHURCH, NANTICOKE. Work on the Nanticoke M.E. Church started in 1898, stopped during the winter, and resumed in the spring of 1899. The church was completed and dedicated on December 24, 1899. Except for the installation of plumbing, heating, and electricity, the church has been little changed since its completion. In a survey of structures of Wicomico County, made some years ago by Thomas N. George, a retired architect, the church was one of the finest examples of wooden Gothic architecture in the country.

According to local authorities this postcard picture was made about 1910. Judging from the single pole in the picture, which was a telephone pole, the only utility then available in Nanticoke, the date is about right. Commercial users of electricity, like the Waterview Beach Hotel, had their own Delco systems. (Courtesy of Sylvia Taylor.)

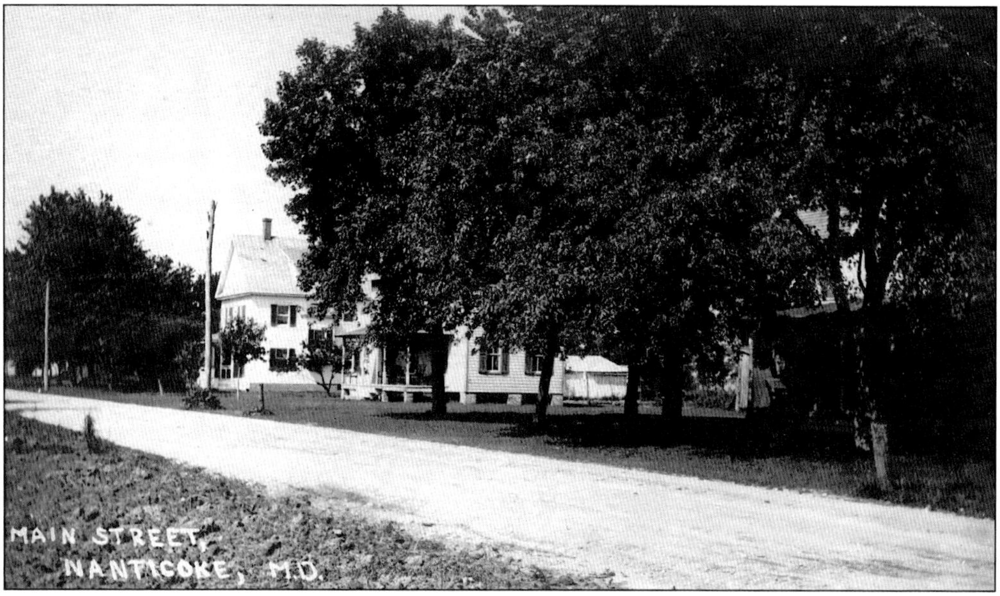

MAIN STREET NANTICOKE. This picture was taken before the street was paved. The house on the left was the house of David Messick; the Clint Walkers now occupy it. The chimney has since been removed. The next house is that of the Darbys; it is a vacation home and is not regularly occupied but is still in the Darby family.

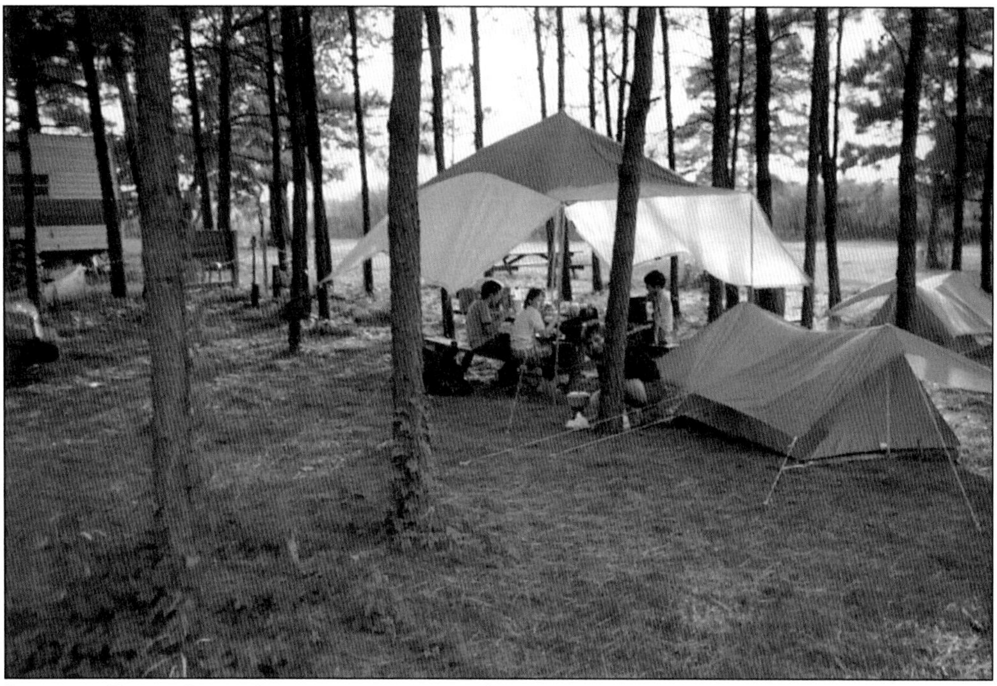

ROARING POINT CAMP GROUND. Hance J. and Patti W. Pepper bought Roaring Point Farm at Nanticoke and opened part of it as a recreational campground in 1974. The camp is located at the site of the Nanticoke Steamboat Wharf and the Willing home, which was built in 1798. After the death of founder Hance Pepper in 1987, the camping operation was sold to Mr. and Mrs. Alvah Constantine.

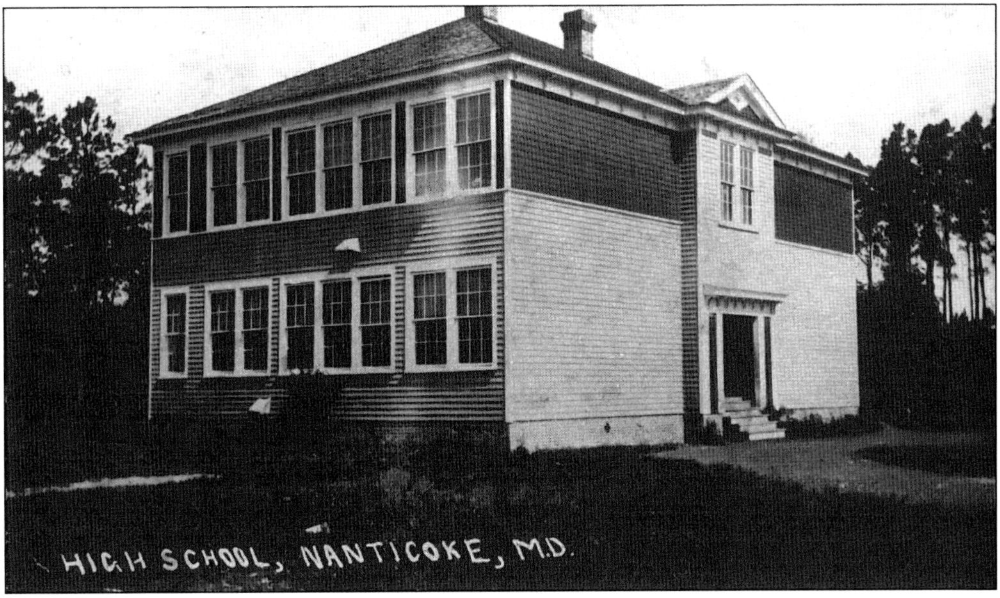

NANTICOKE HIGH SCHOOL. The Nanticoke High School building was built in 1914 and continued in use as a high school for more than 30 years, graduating its last class in 1948. After this it was used only as an elementary school, until 1967, when it was closed and its students bussed to Quantico and Hebron. The last three teachers, Mildred I. Turner, Camilla Leech, and Jeannette Insley were also transferred to Quantico. This postcard picture was obviously made before 1948. (Collection of Sylvia Taylor.)

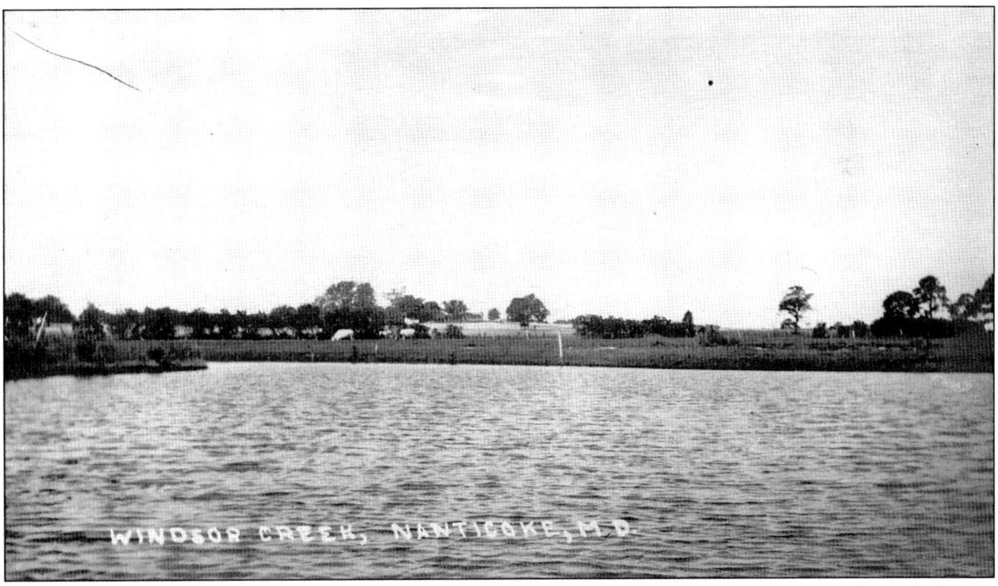

WINDSOR CREEK. This creek is between Nanticoke and Bivalve. The long cigar-shaped object, shown on the card resting parallel to the shoreline, is the fuselage of a DC3 airplane. It did not crash. It was purchased at Dover Air Force Base by the late Parks Young and hauled to Nanticoke where it rested for a while on property of the late Paul Evans. Later it was moved to the property belonging to Young where it remained until his death several years ago. Since than it has been removed and a house built on the premises.

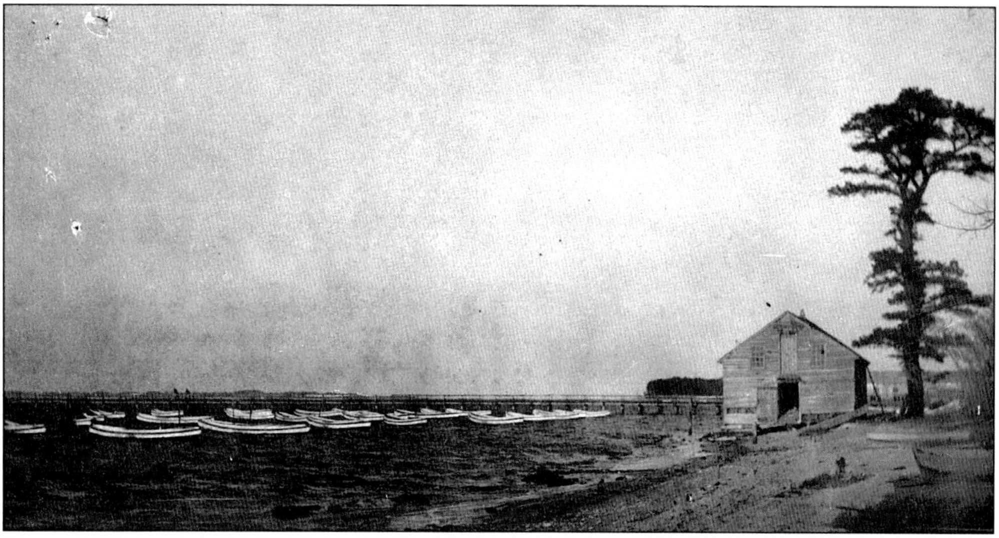

RIVER AT BIVALVE. This card shows the end of the road at Bivalve, formerly Waltersville. The boat anchorage is shown, as well as the oyster house by the water's edge. The card says, "on the Nanticoke looking north. The Pride of the oysterman's life. Does it look natural." Bivalve was a regular stop on the Nanticoke River Line and was served by the *Tangier* until 1923.

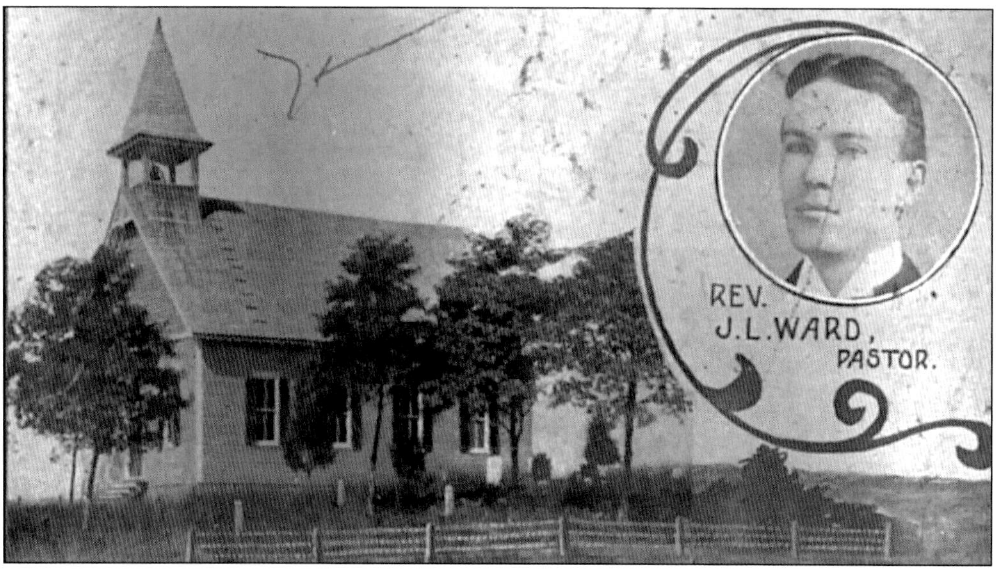

THE METHODIST PROTESTANT CHURCH, BIVALVE, MARYLAND. This picture of the Methodist Protestant Church in Bivalve was made between 1903 and 1907, the period during which Rev. J.L. Ward was the pastor. The church was built in 1886 in what was then known as Waltersville. (Bivalve was named for the post office founded in 1887.) The original meeting place for the Methodist Protestant Society had only one room.

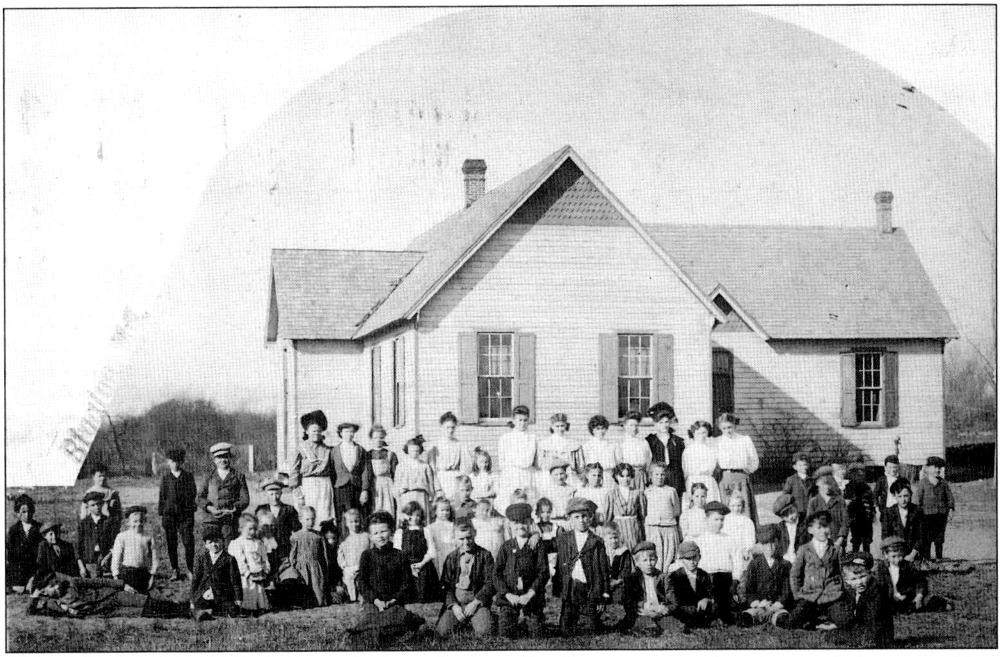

The Bivalve School. Mrs. Nettie Leatherbury had been married and retired from teaching here when she received this card showing her former students in 1907. This was a three-room school, and in rural areas the school board depended on the birth rate to determine the size of the classes.

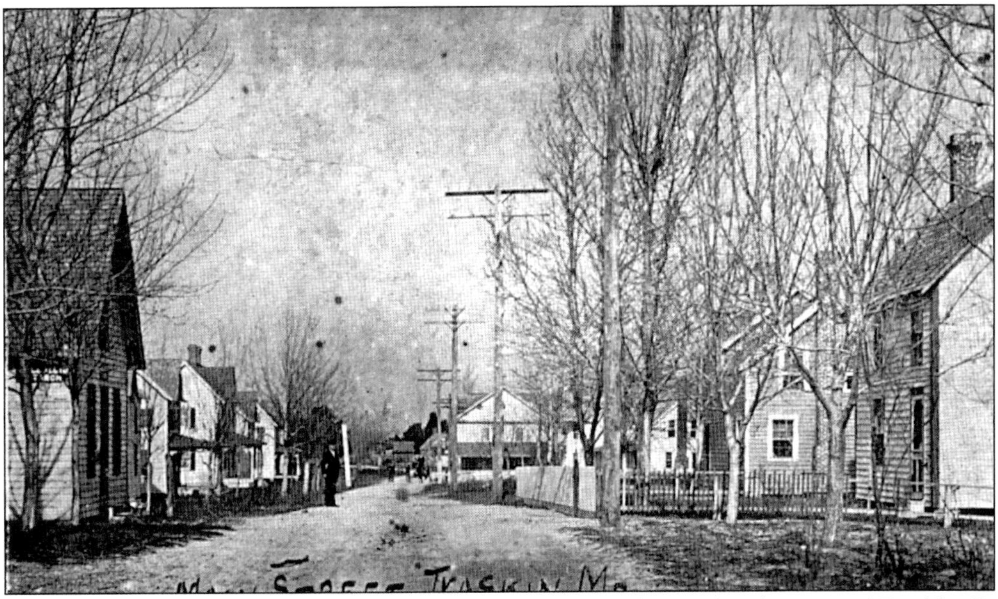

Main Street, Tyaskin. The most prominent building on this card is the store of Franklin B. Culver in the middle of the picture. His home is behind the picket fence, this side of it. The store was later taken over by Ernest Larmore, who married Culver's daughter. The store has been abandoned and is now covered by Virginia creeper. The road shown in this photograph led down to the steamboat wharf and canning factory. Among the houses on the left were those of the Rothwells, Mrs. Messick, and Jim Buck Culver, the son of Franklin.

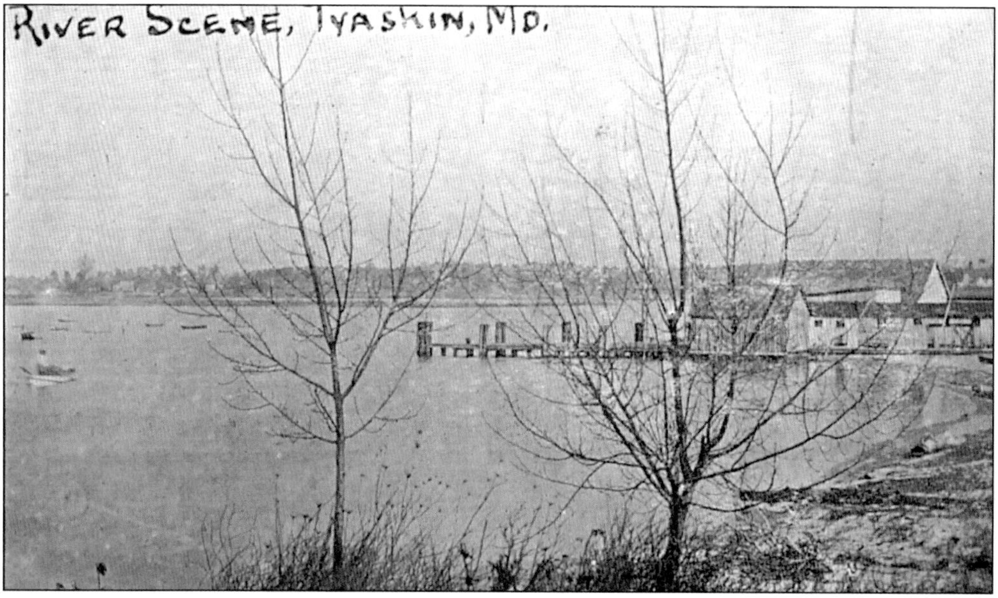

River Scene, Tyaskin. The scene shown is on Wetipquin Creek, which is off the Nanticoke River. It is Dashiell's Island that you see in the background. The building to the right of the wharf was the canning house, and the building behind the wharf was the fish house. The schedule of the Nanticoke River Line was marked "tide permitting" for stops at Tyaskin, indicating that the steamer could not get into the creek at low tide.

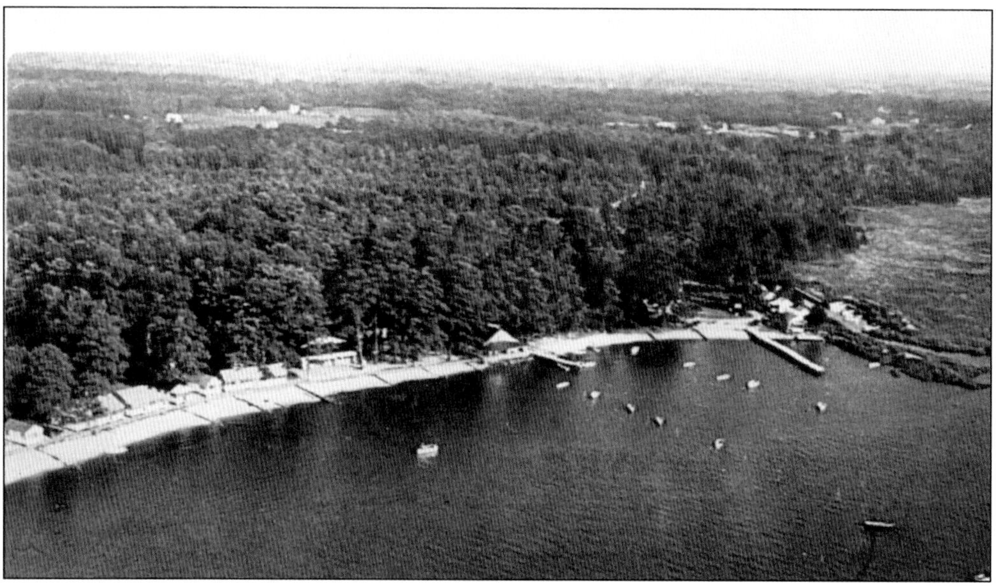

Sandy Hill From the Air. This card was made about 1963. The building in the center near the short wharf was the bar, and the larger building to the left was the Recreation Hall. To the immediate right of the Recreation Hall is the big tree shown on the next postcard. Note the jetties running through the sand into the water to hold the beach in place.

The clusters of buildings at far right are the summer residences of private owners and are not a part of Sandy Hill.

THE BIG TREE. This monster pine tree once stood outside the Recreation Hall at Sandy Hill (it can be seen in the background) as one of the attractions. When I was a boy, Sandy Hill also boasted a merry-go-round. Both the tree and the merry-go-round are long gone.

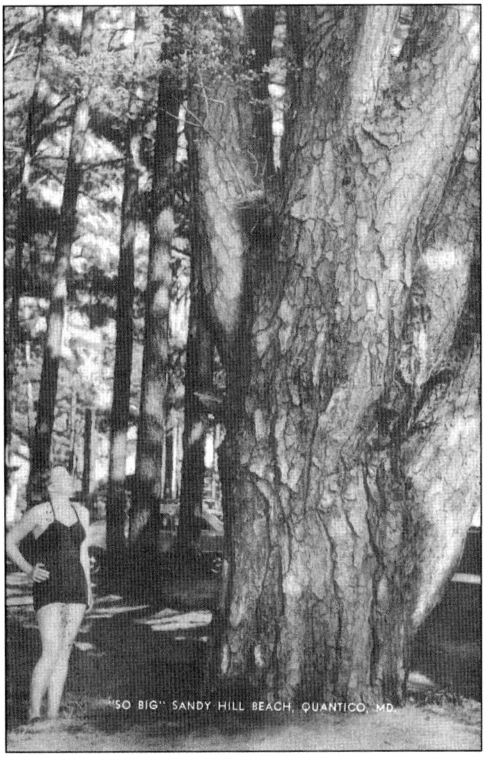

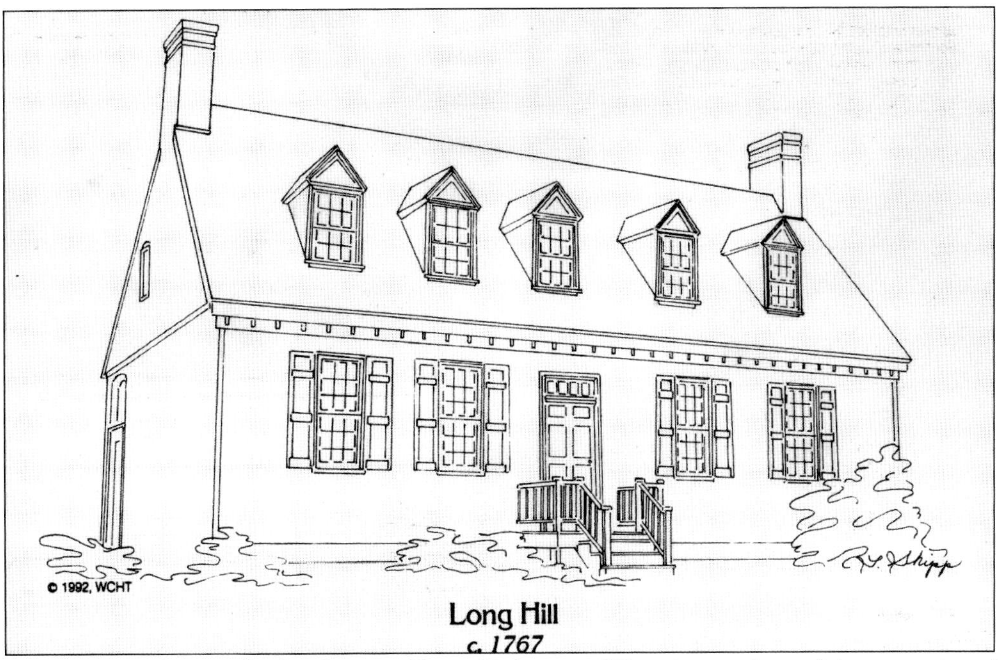

LONG HILLS. This was the family seat of James Disharoon. When it passed out of the possession of Cadmus Dashiell, it went to the Hamberry family, who owned it until recent years. The Hamberrys, in a fit of extravagance, had murals painted directly on the paneling, which is all intact. The brick is all Flemish Bond. The house has been sold and restored in the last few years.

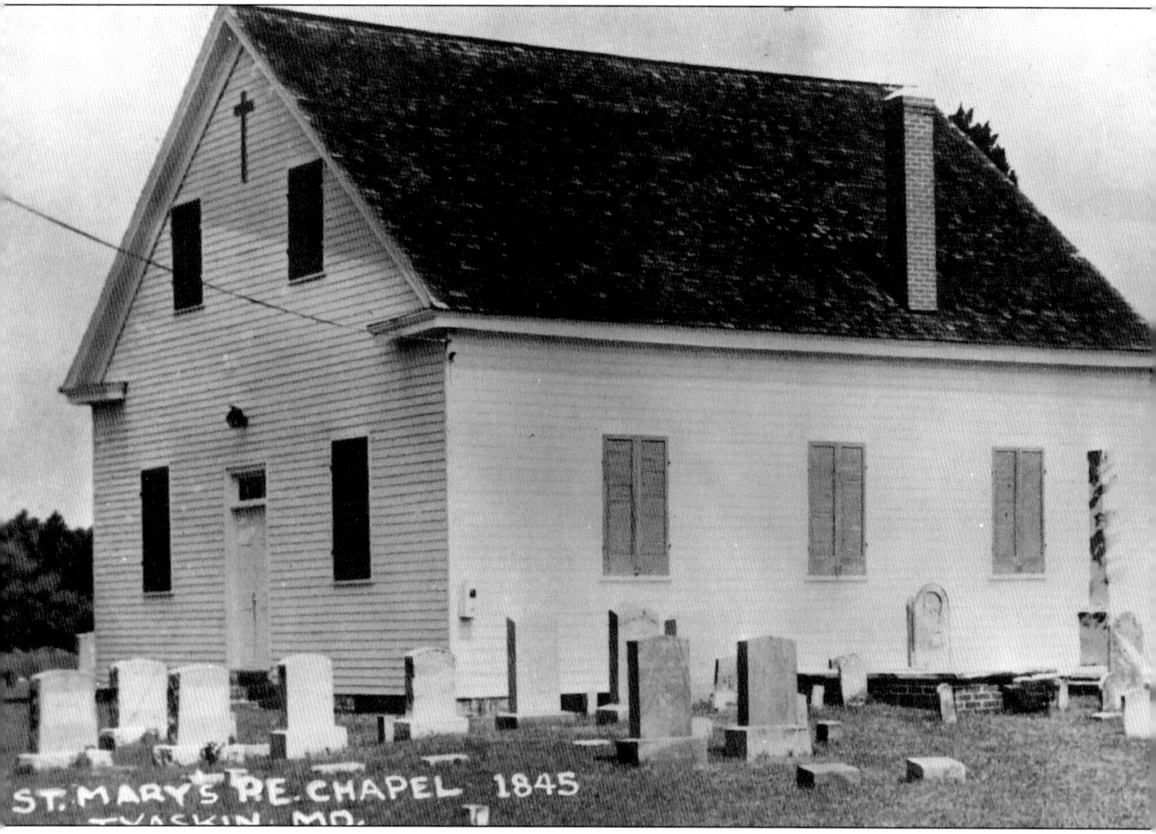

ST. MARY'S CHAPEL. St. Mary's Chapel was built in 1845 to replace one that had been built in 1834. In 1913–16 extensive repairs were made, and the plaster walls were replaced as well as the present pine ceiling. Several years later, the chimney, which is shown here, was built to serve the church, along with a chimney on the other side to serve a stove on each side.

The churchyard shown here is the oldest in continuous use in the county. It has been used since the original church was built. This is not one of the original chapels of ease in Stepney Parish, but was built when the church had to move closer to the roads rather than the river. (Collection of Betty Webster.)

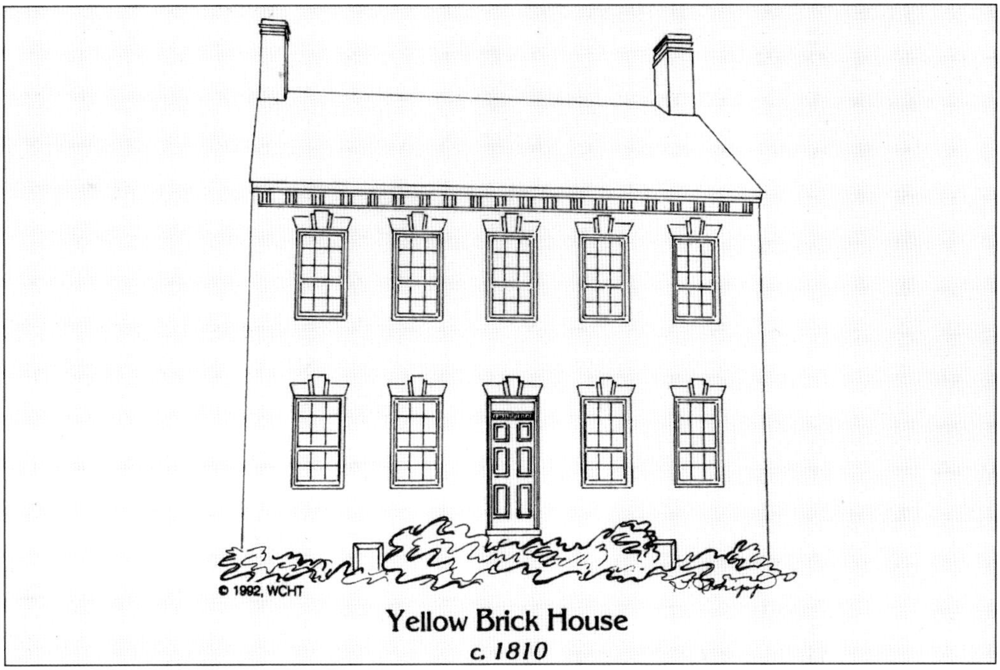

The Yellow Brick House. This house is located on the north side of the road from Cox's Corner to Whitehaven. The brick is English Bond. In its unrestored state, the house was suffering from a fire in what had been used as a kitchen. The house originally had a detached kitchen that had been removed.

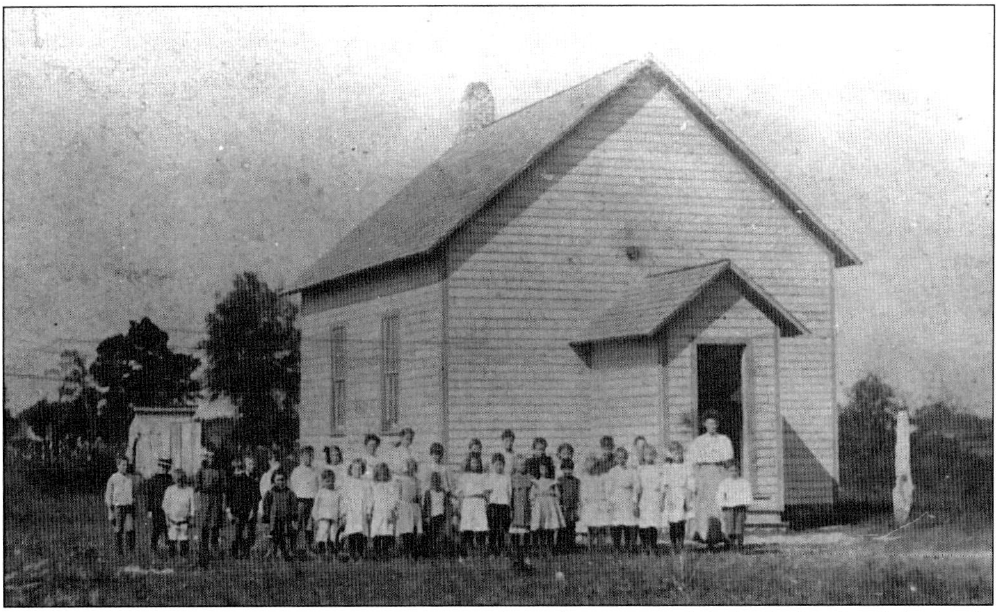

One-Room School. This picture may be at either Clara or Royal Oak. Both schools had only two windows on the side but neither had the protected entrance. There are 33 students and a teacher in this photo. The provenance of the picture is from the west side. The Chick Sales (an outhouse) looks too small for a divided HIS and HERS partition behind the boards in front, but it is possible. The style of clothing suggests a pre-1910 date. (Courtesy of Sylvia Taylor.)

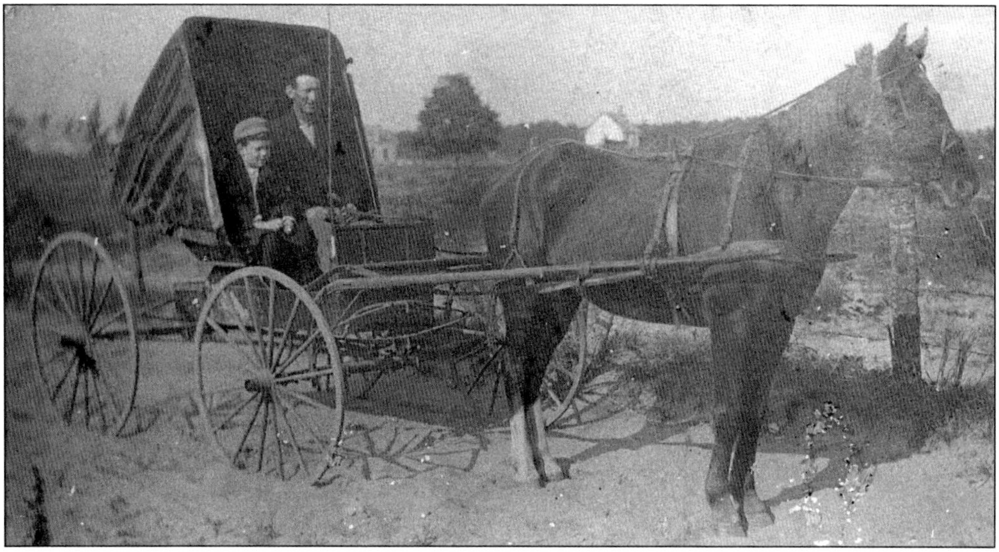

Horse and Buggy. This picture illustrates more than the father and son in the picture. It illustrates a way of life that is long gone, including the carriage with the folding top, the horse with its harness, the buggy whip upright in its holder, and the sandy roads of the Lower Shore. This picture dates from about 1910 but is unidentified except that it was collected on the west side of the county. (Courtesy of Sylvia Taylor.)

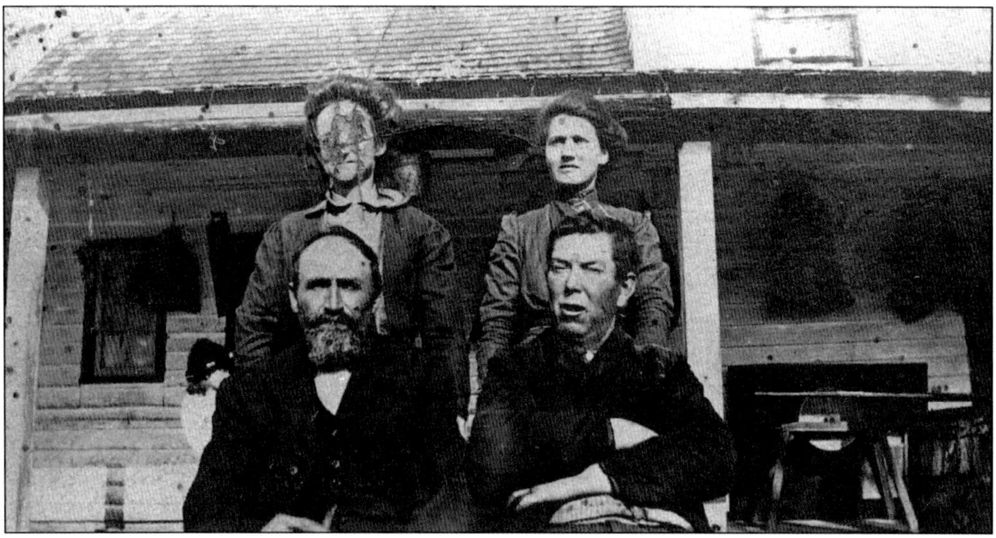

The Bounds-Hayward Family. The Bounds couple (left) is shown in the marriage license records to have gotten married on November 26, 1861. The Haywards (right) were more famous for something else, though. Uncle Zeb was a bootlegger of note during the Prohibition era. A story is told about him that a man came to the Waterview Hotel to spend a week and wanted some whiskey. He found it at Uncle Zeb's and brought it to the hotel where he placed it in a leather satchel. The man's hands were a little unsteady by the time he finished his use of the bottle and some of the whiskey got on the outside of the satchel. When he looked for an eye opener the next morning, he got more than he was looking for, what he had spilled had eaten a hole through the satchel. This is no lye. (Collection of Sylvia Taylor.)

Six

Rockawalkin and Quantico

Rockawalkin was the first railroad stop on the way to Claiborne. It was the center of a rural area between the road to Cambridge and the Wicomico River, extending west to Upper Ferry. Beyond that was Quantico.

Quantico is an ancient town, and also an Election District of which the country club pictures are a part. We have never seen a view card from the town of Quantico.

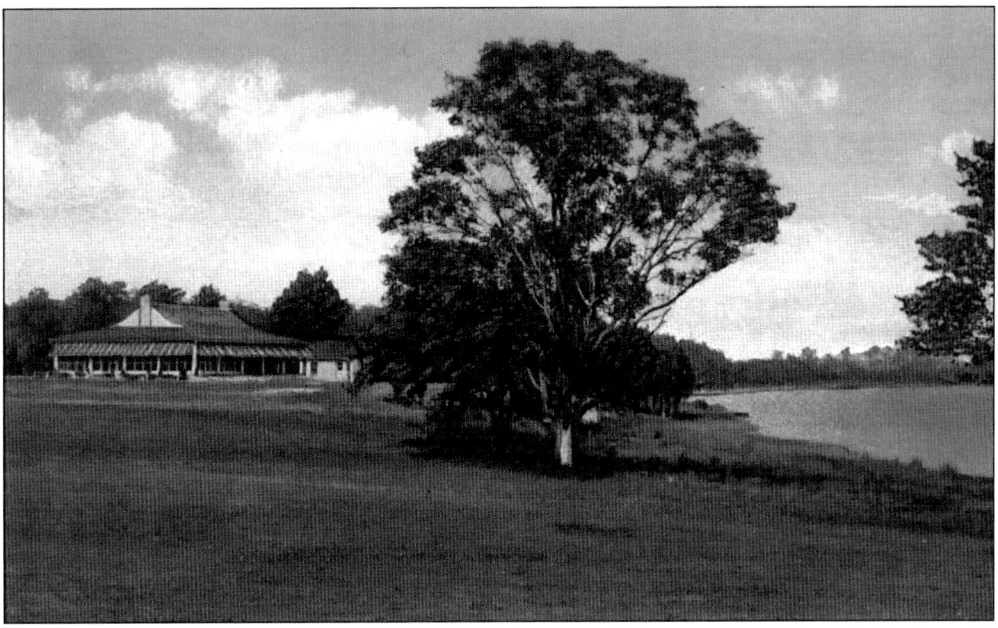

Green Hill Country Club. The Green Hill Country Club was organized in 1925 when 23 men pledged $250 each to buy the property, which was on the road to Whitehaven. John K. Gunby was the organizer. They built a nine-hole golf course and the clubhouse shown on the picture. The club operated under an unwieldy group of 23 directors until 1932 when it was re-organized and the name was changed to the Green Hill Golf and Country Club. In 1934 the mortgage on the club was foreclosed and the property was sold for $8,000. The property was resold to Pratt Phillips in 1936. The Green Hill Yacht and Country Club was organized in April 1949 and has been operating successfully ever since.

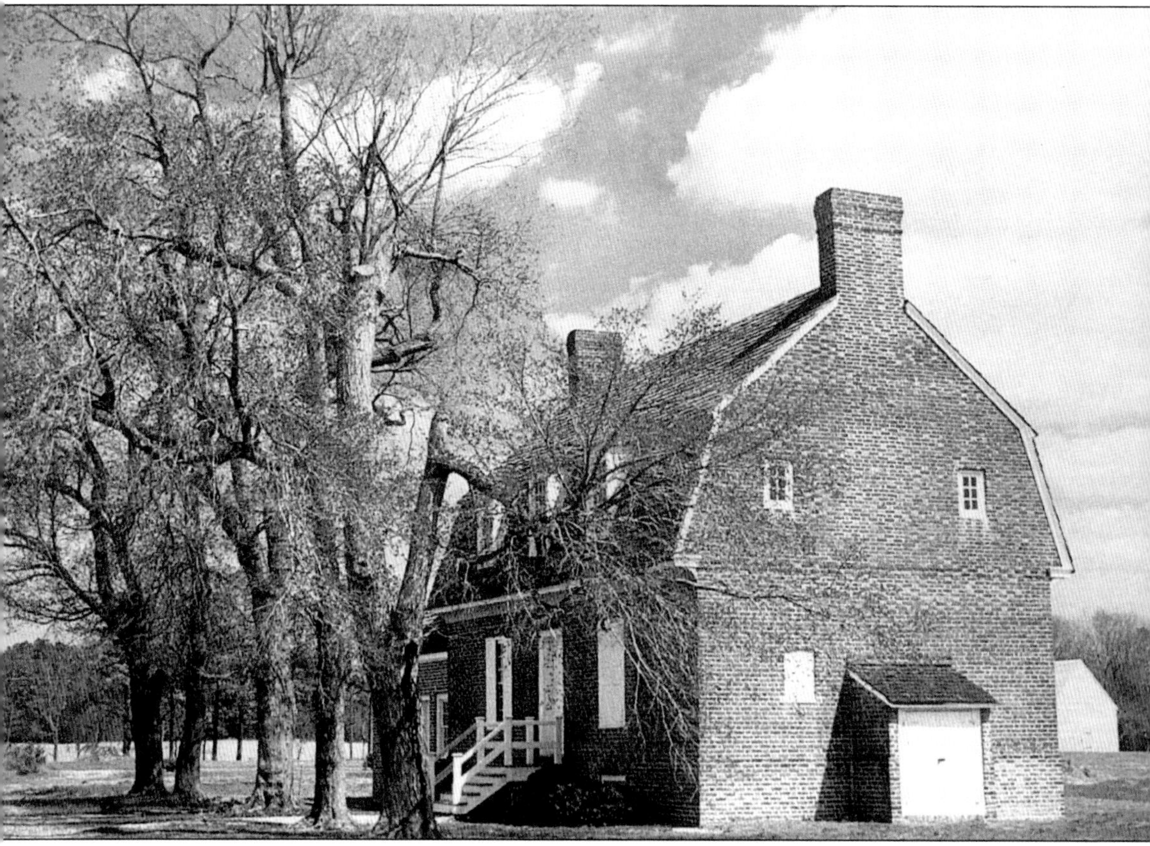

PEMBERTON HALL. Pemberton Hall was built in 1742. The property was sold by the Handy family in 1844 for $10 an acre, including the buildings, to Jehu Parsons, who was then "Mr. Salisbury." In his Will, he left it to one of his sons, who sold it to the Taylors. The house fell on evil days when it passed to the Taylor family, who turned Pemberton Hall into a tenant house. The Taylor heirs finally sold the property to a group of Salisbury buyers who, at the urging of Polly White Burnett, agreed to give the acre the house sat on to the State. The restoration of the house is now complete. Although Wicomico County does not own Pemberton Hall, the house is the center and major attraction of Wicomico County's Pemberton Historical Park. The Wicomico Historical Society's headquarters is also in the Park.

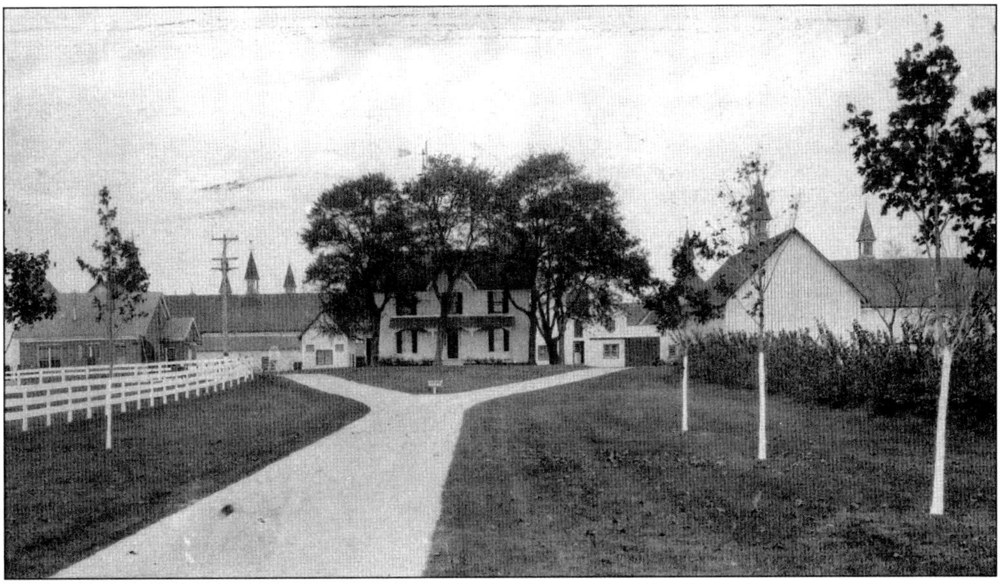

The Homestead Dairy Farm. In the early 1920s nearly all of Salisbury got milk from this dairy. It was the play toy of Congressman William H. Jackson. He built the barns, the silos, and the superintendent's house, which had a paved driveway leading up to it. Jackson reportedly lost money on it every year, but it was his hobby and he didn't care. After his death it was sold to John Holt, and the dairy operation ceased. It now belongs to the E.S. Adkins Co.

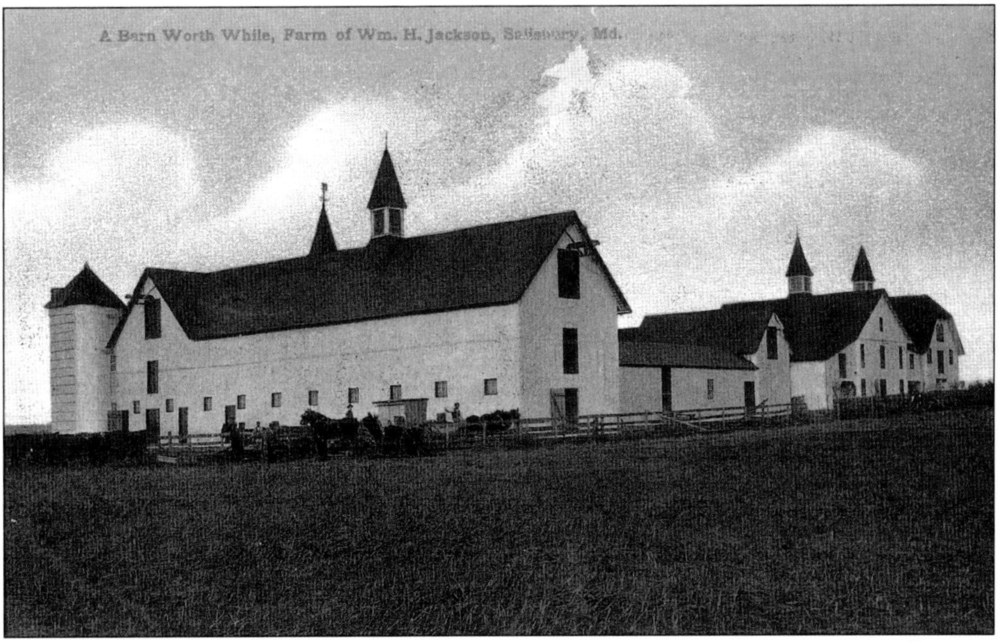

Large Barns. The big barns on the Rockawalkin property of Ex-Congressman William H. Jackson were built in 1914. The son of a nephew of Mr. Jackson's wife asked me for a photocopy of this card because his father had worked on building them. Mr. Jackson built them because of his need for them to house the cows for the Homestead Dairy Farm, which he had started a short time earlier.

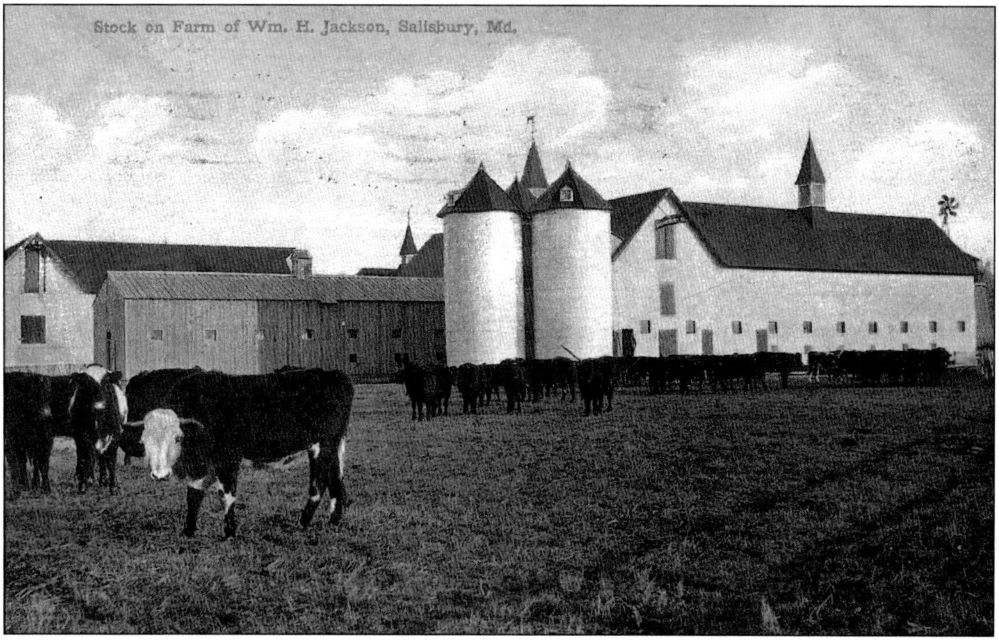

This picture provides a closer look at the residents of the dairy farm.

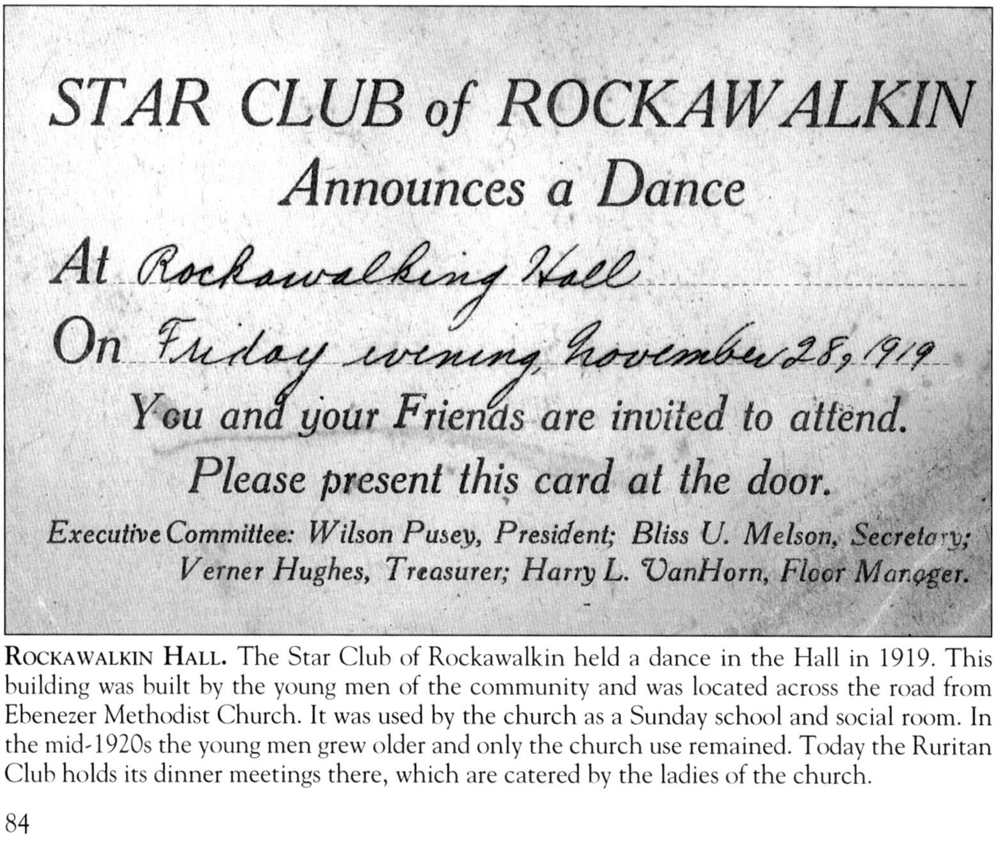

STAR CLUB of ROCKAWALKIN

Announces a Dance

At Rockawalking Hall

On Friday evening, November 28, 1919

You and your Friends are invited to attend.

Please present this card at the door.

Executive Committee: Wilson Pusey, President; Bliss U. Melson, Secretary; Verner Hughes, Treasurer; Harry L. VanHorn, Floor Manager.

Rockawalkin Hall. The Star Club of Rockawalkin held a dance in the Hall in 1919. This building was built by the young men of the community and was located across the road from Ebenezer Methodist Church. It was used by the church as a Sunday school and social room. In the mid-1920s the young men grew older and only the church use remained. Today the Ruritan Club holds its dinner meetings there, which are catered by the ladies of the church.

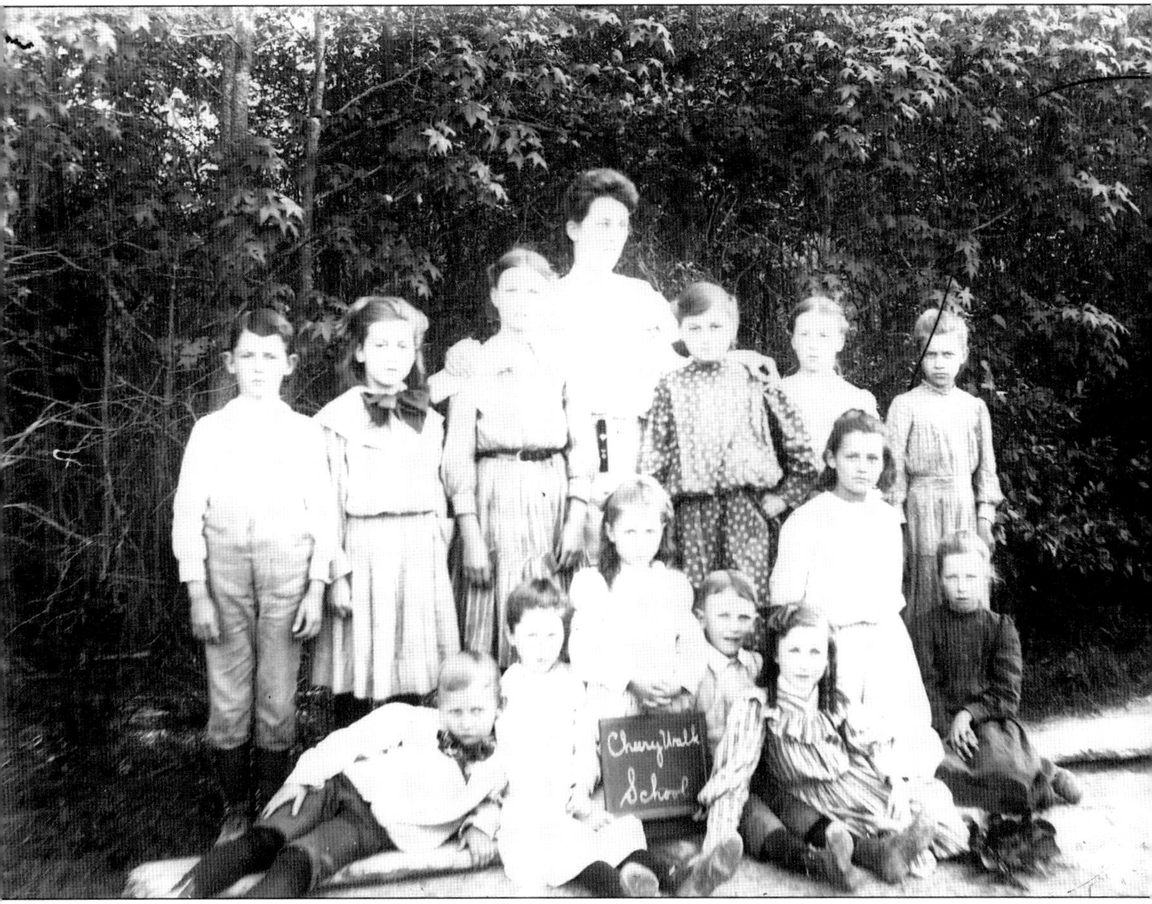

CHERRY WALK SCHOOL. This picture is of School No. 5 located on the southerly side of Cherry Walk Road. This is another of the partially identified pictures. Cherry Walk is a rural neighborhood west of Quantico. (Courtesy of Nabb Research Center at Salisbury University.)

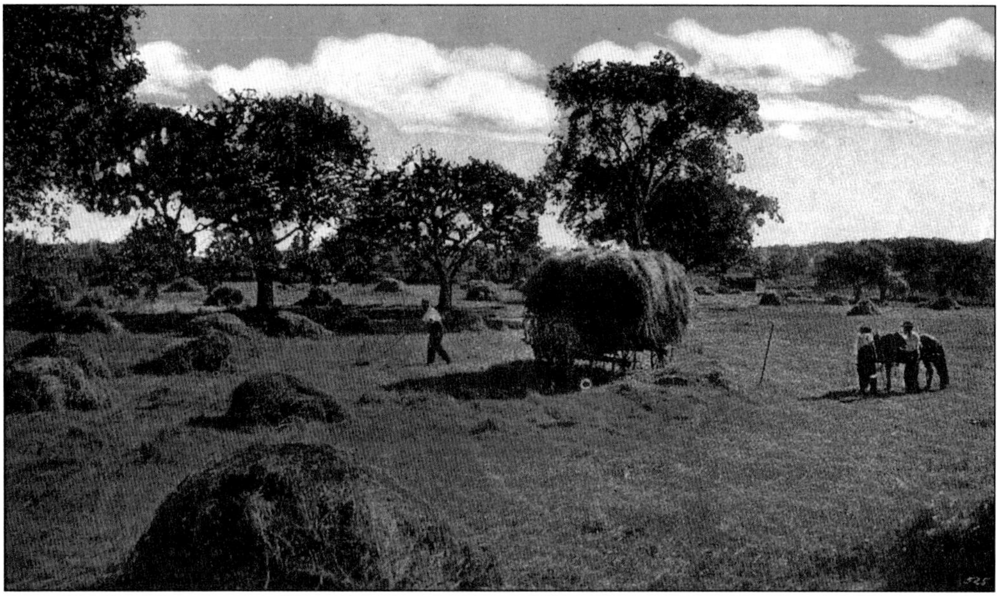

Quantico Greetings. This is a greeting, not a picture of a scene near Quantico. While I have never seen a view card of Quantico, it is a thriving village with a long history and was once known as the goose capital of the world.

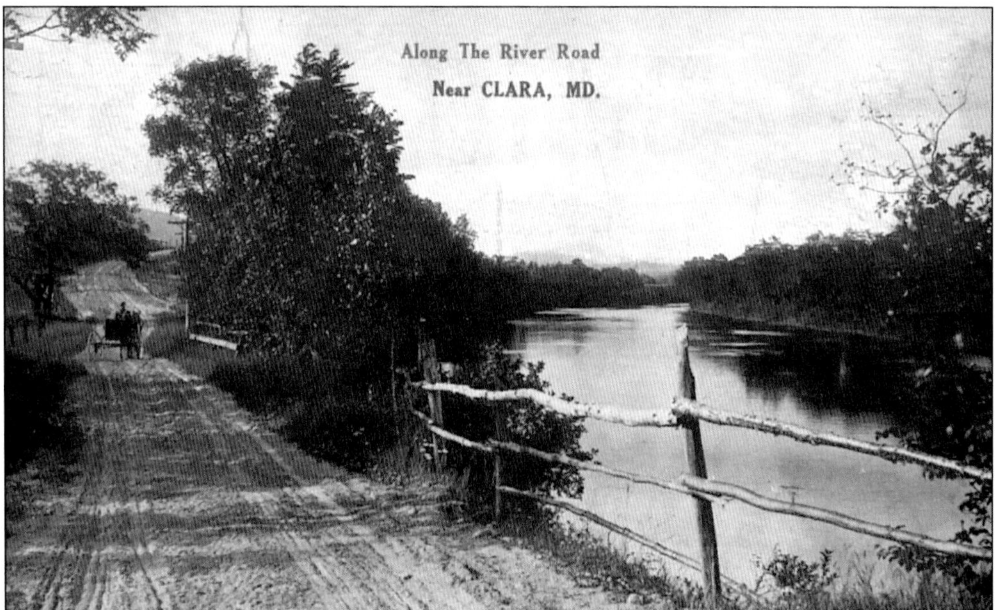

Clara. Clara's first post office opened on February 6, 1901, and stayed in use until 1943. Clara was essentially a rural neighborhood. It had a post office in a general store, a one-room school, and a canning factory.

Seven

The East Side

The East Side of Wicomico includes the towns of Parsonsburg, Pittsville, Willards, Powellville, and the areas around them. Except for Pittsville, the area was poorly represented photographically. Even the stores of Willards and Powellville, housing the post offices, had only a few of the "Greetings From" types of cards. The broiler industry changed the East Side. The hatcheries in the county were located here and farmers took to broiler raising as a second source of income. Soon almost every farm had a chicken house, raising chickens for eggs or flesh. Agricultural science cut the growing cycle from 13 weeks to eight and increased the task of disposal waste and the risk of pollution from the run off into streams and rivers.

Parsonsburg is an unincorporated village begun in 1854 with its own active fire company and a strong Methodist church. It was named after the storekeeper who operated the first post office, Isaac H. Parsons, on the East Side.

Originally called Derrickson's Crossroads after the store located there, Pittsville became Pittsville after the building of the Wicomico and Pocomoke Railroad. It was named for Hillary R. Pitts, president of the Wicomico and Pocomoke Railroad. It is now a bustling community with water and sewer systems, a strong volunteer fire company, and a very active town government.

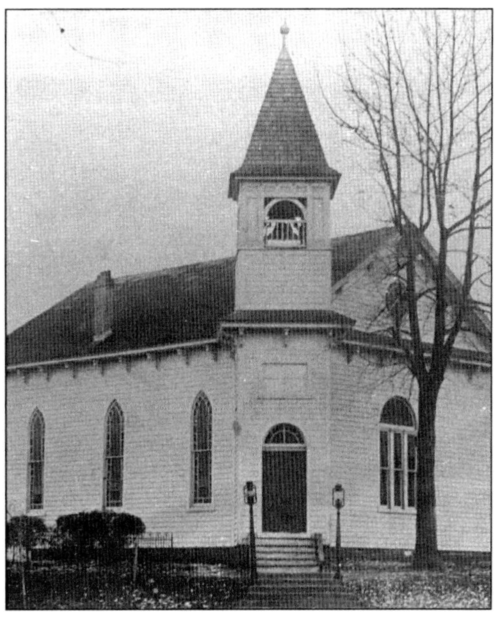

Jerusalem Methodist Church. The Jerusalem Church was started by George Kendall Perdue in 1839. He had prayed that a pine tree under which he had prayed might be cut down and a church built on the spot. He rose early on Christmas morning, cut down the tree, and began to hew it into lumber. Mr. Gillis Figgs soon came along and then other neighbors joined in. The original church was finished in March. The church had been built so that the water from the western eaves drained to the Wicomico River and the water from the eastern eaves drained to the Pocomoke River. Twenty-five years later the pulpit was remodeled and new pews were built by George W. Parsons and the tallow candles replaced by oil lamps. The original church was vacated in September 1875 and the present church built. (Collection of the late Hilda Fowler.)

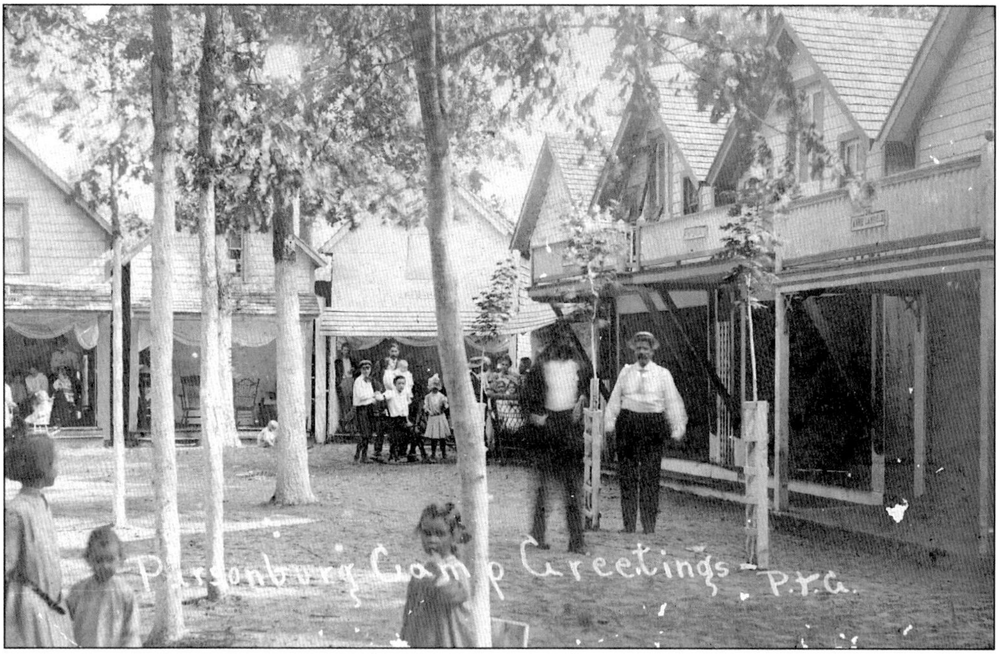

Parsonsburg Camp Greetings. This card was mailed on August 23, 1909. It shows a tent on the right with a roof-type overhang, which is unusual. All of the trees in the campground are white washed. The woman in the background has two children in a wicker stroller.

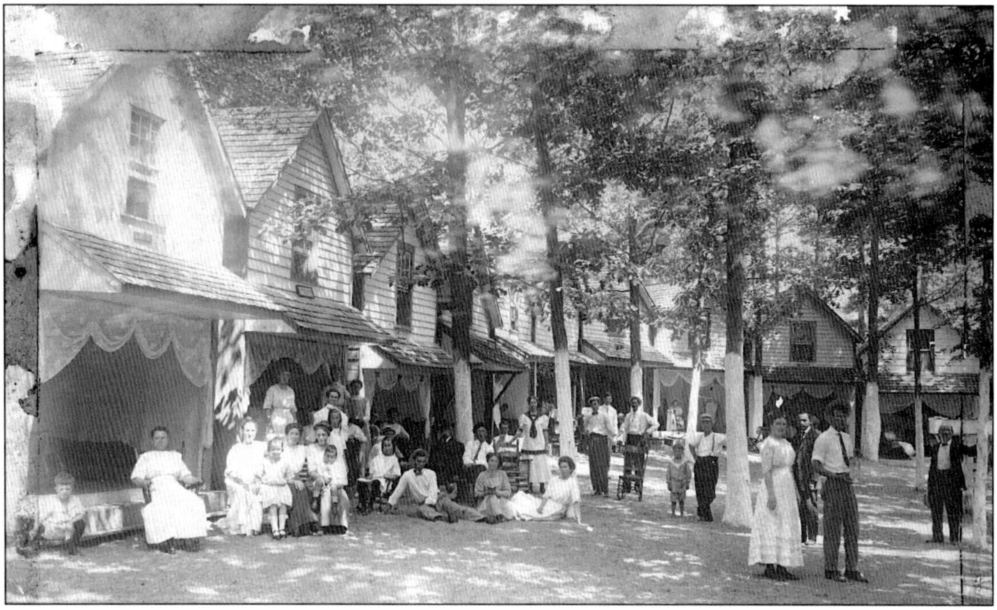

Parsonsburg Camp. The Parsonsburg Camp was run by the Jerusalem Methodist Church and adjoined the church property south of the railroad tracks. This shows that a good many of the cottages were built close to each other around the promenade in the camp. The preaching took place in an open pavilion in the center. There were no loud speakers to amplify the minister's voice, and possibly this was where the term "shouting Methodist" originated. As I remember it, the young kept promenading despite what was going on in the center.

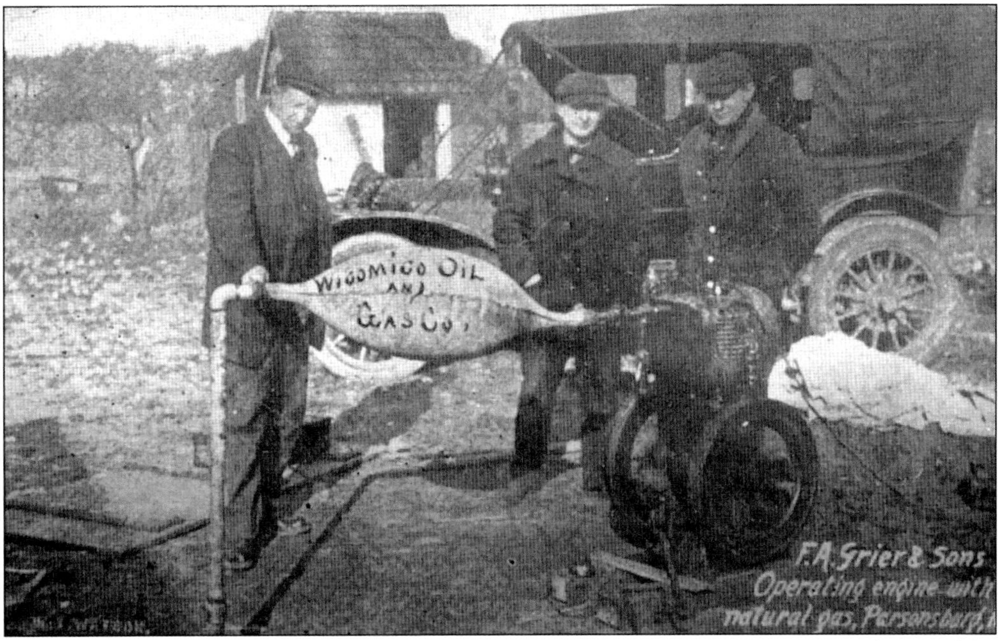

WICOMICO OIL AND GAS COMPANY. The Wicomico Oil and Gas Company was chartered for $300,000 in Delaware and plans were to sink ten wells. It announced it had 1 square mile of land under lease between Pittsville and Parsonsburg. The first well was to be driven on the land of George Meade Maddox. The next one was to be built one quarter of a mile from Parsonsburg on the land of S.P. Parsons. Drilling was in the hands of Flint and Strother of Clarksburg, West Virginia. The oil proved to be elusive but natural gas was found and piped into the houses at Parsonsburg. The story is that one Sunday the people returned from church to find their kitchens flooded. Water was coming through the gas pipes. Many people will remember the second time that oil was projected on the shore, and oil leases were sold on much of the land in the county. (Courtesy of the late Hilda Fowler.)

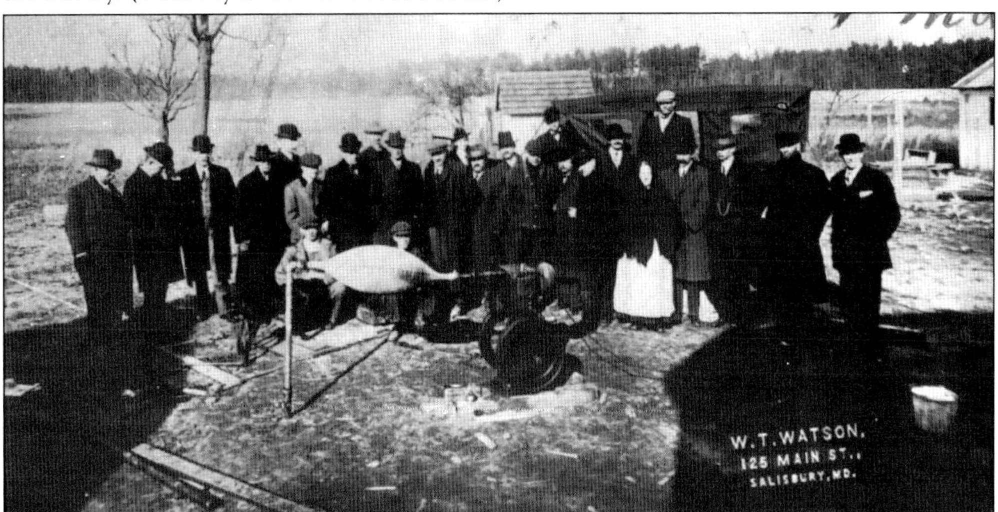

OIL FIELD, PARSONSBURG. This picture was made near Parsonsburg. It was the natural gas well that was hooked to the houses in Parsonsburg. All of the hierarchy of the Wicomico Oil & Gas Company were present. The stockholders only had this picture to show for their money.

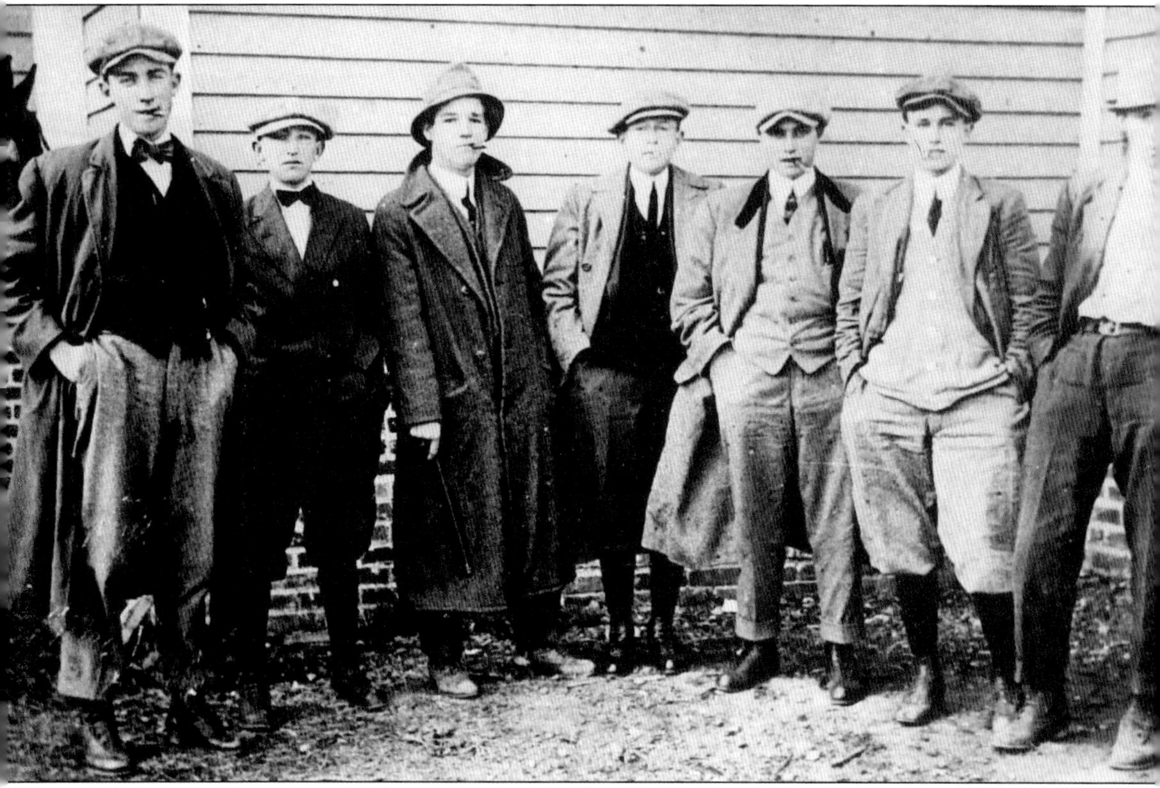

PITTSVILLE BOYS, 1906. This postcard of unidentified boys in Pittsville in 1906 is remarkable for what it shows. All of the boys, except one, are smoking cigarettes or cigars, obviously the thing to do in 1906. Today the numbers would be reversed. (Collection of James Jackson.)

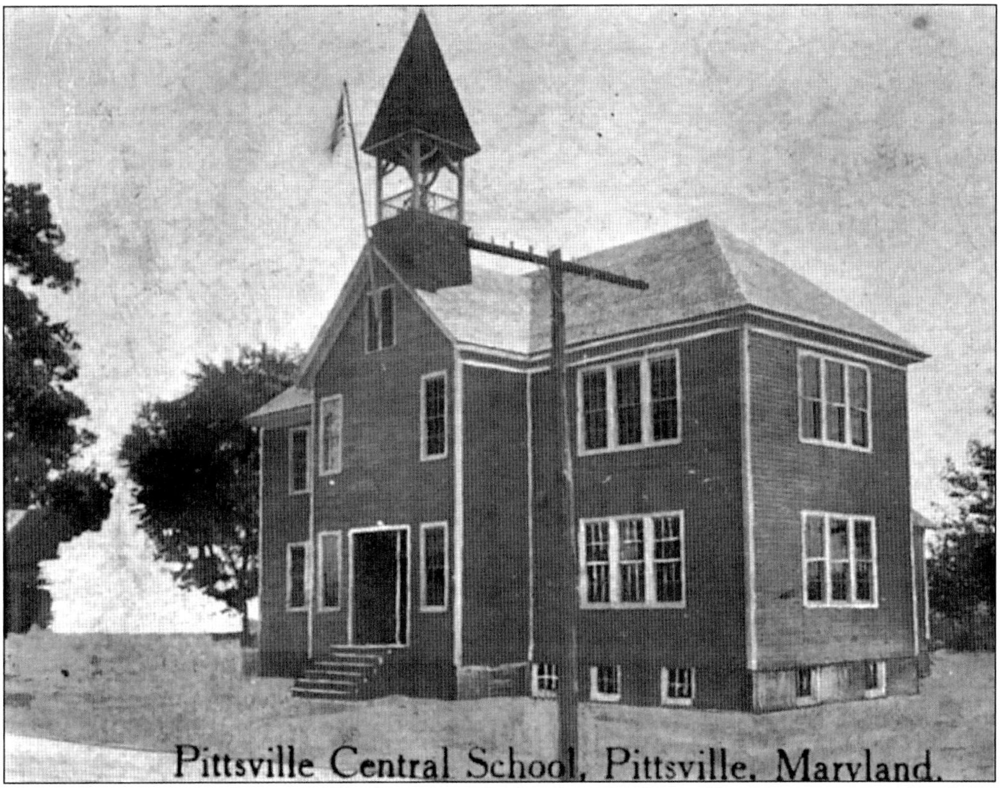

PITTSVILLE CENTRAL SCHOOL. The first central school in the Pittsville area, it was a high school as well as an elementary school. (Collection of Casey Parsons.)

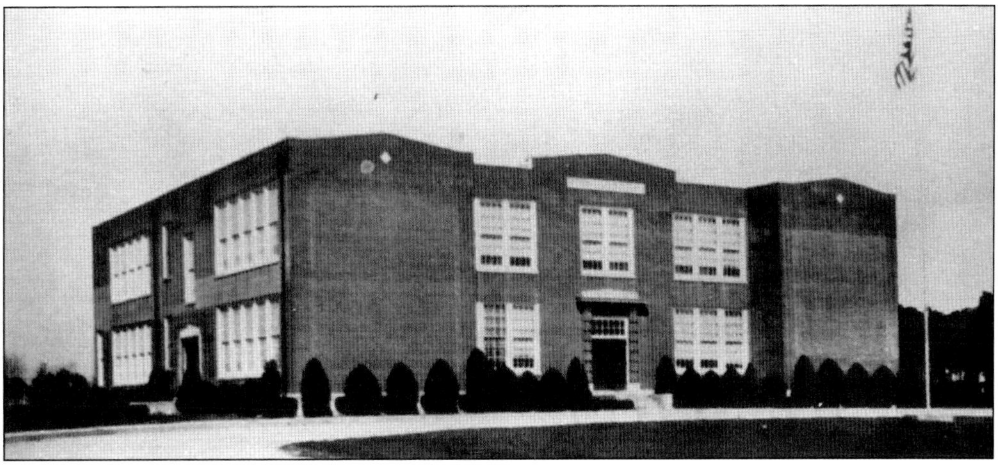

PITTSVILLE SCHOOL. On November 20, 1930, the student body moved into the new school at Pittsville. There were 287 students, and the campus contained more than 10 acres. The structure is red brick and contains nine classrooms, including the chemistry laboratory and the library, principal's office, teachers' room, and an auditorium that seats 500 students. One hundred eighty-six students moved over from the old building. It was dedicated on January 22, 1931, and cost $65,000. Originally it contained a high school, but it has been discontinued and the students moved to Salisbury. It is now only a primary and middle school. (Collection of James Jackson.)

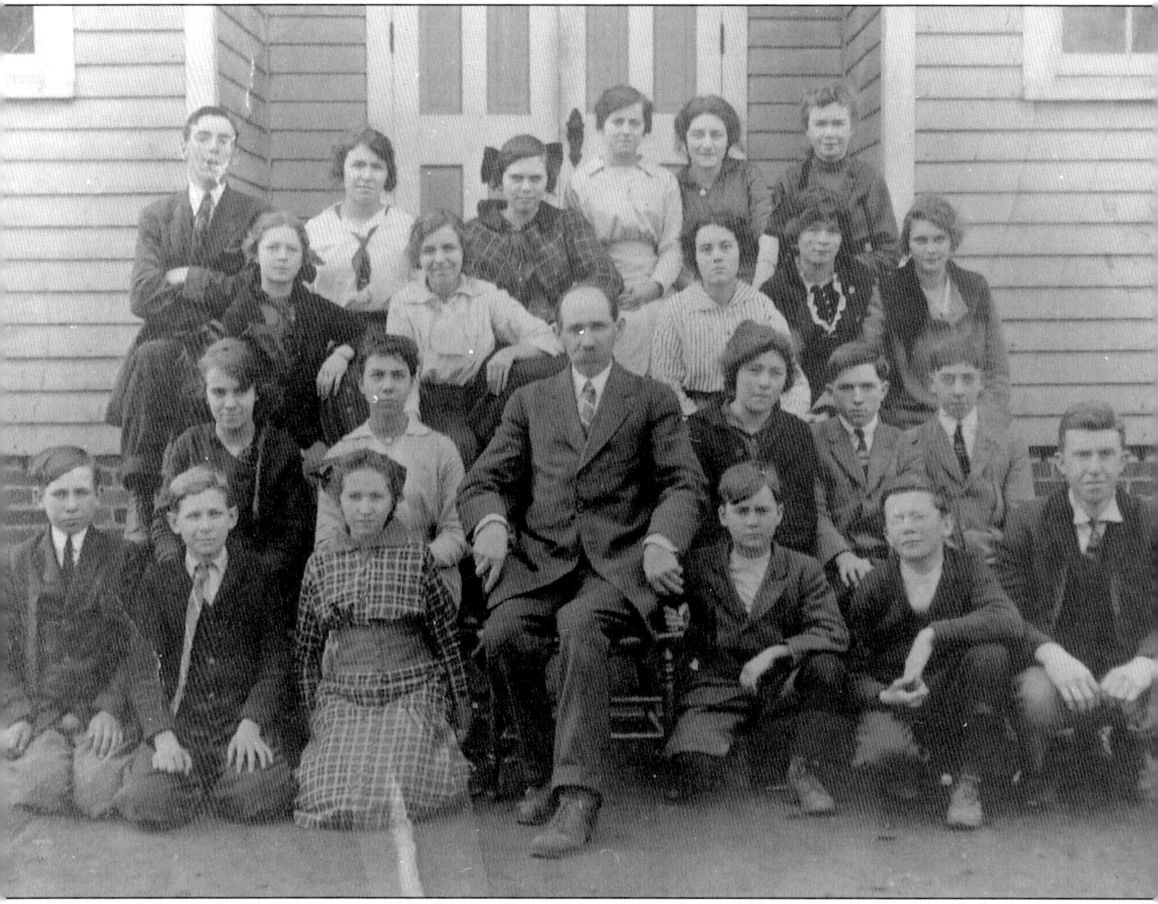

PITTSVILLE HIGH SCHOOL. This postcard was made in 1915 after the opening of the "new" school building. Pictured from left to right are the following: (front row) Guy Carey, Charles Truitt, Nellie Truitt, William Farlow, Lester Timmons, and Ralph Davis; (second row) Grace Campbell, Margurete Jarman, Hattie Campbell Wells, Allie Hamblin, Roy Farlow, and Mr. Tommy Truitt, the principal (seated); (third row) Lillian Dennis, Mary Brittingham, Lottie Parsons, Grace Windrow, and Bessie Collins; (back row) Owen McNeal, Annie Massey, Margaret Bratten, Elva Hudson, Grace Parsons, and Elsie Timmons. (Collection of Grace Parsons.)

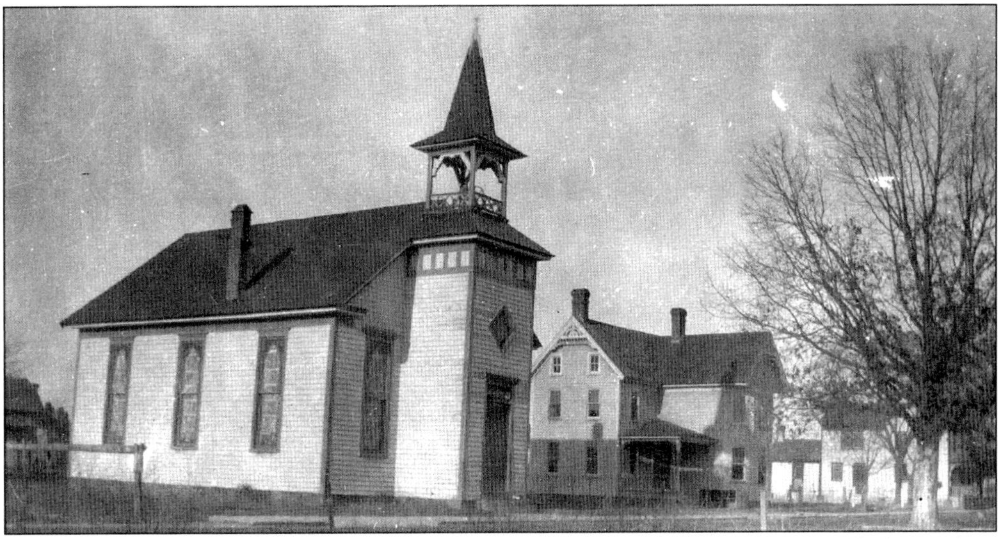

Grace M.P. Church, Pittsville. The church was founded in 1825. Originally located on Friendship Road, it was moved into Pittsville proper in 1875. The church maintained its separate identity through the unification of the Methodist Protestants with the Methodist Episcopalians in 1939. Ayers and Grace were assigned to separate circuits so they would have separate preachers. In 1966 the situation ended, and Grace and Ayers and Eden, at Willards, were assigned the same pastor. Grace limped along until 1989 when it finally gave up the ghost. When the church building was sold for $5,000 the money was used for the joint parsonage. The building, organ, and furnishings were sold to the Full Gospel Church. (Collection of Casey Parsons.)

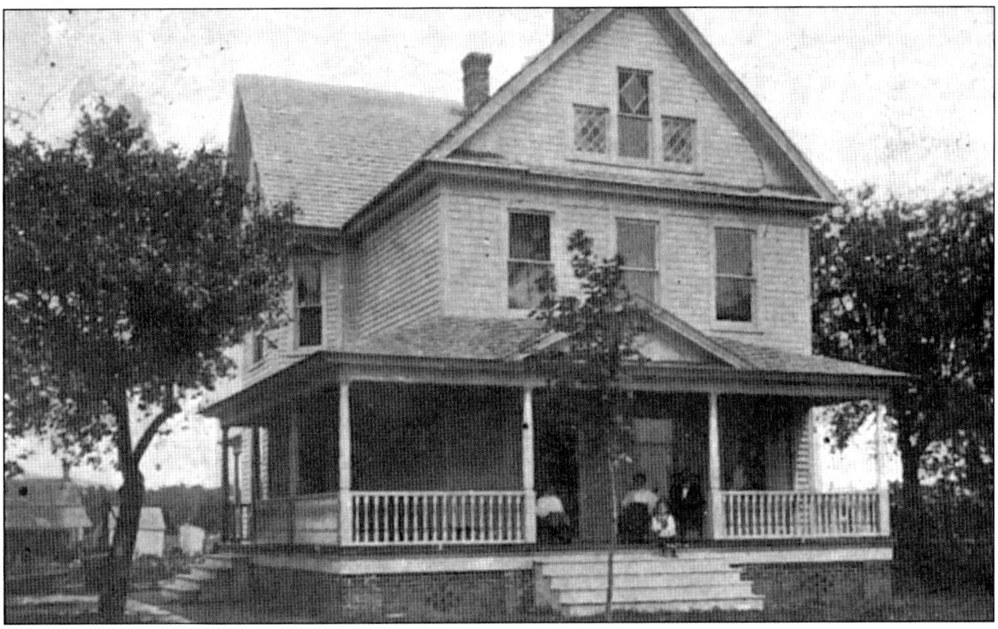

Methodist Protestant Parsonage. The preacher and his wife and children are all on the front porch. The parsonage was alongside the church, which was on Main Street in Pittsville on a lot that backed up to the Baltimore, Chesapeake and Atlantic Railroad. The card is about 1920. (Collection of James Jackson.)

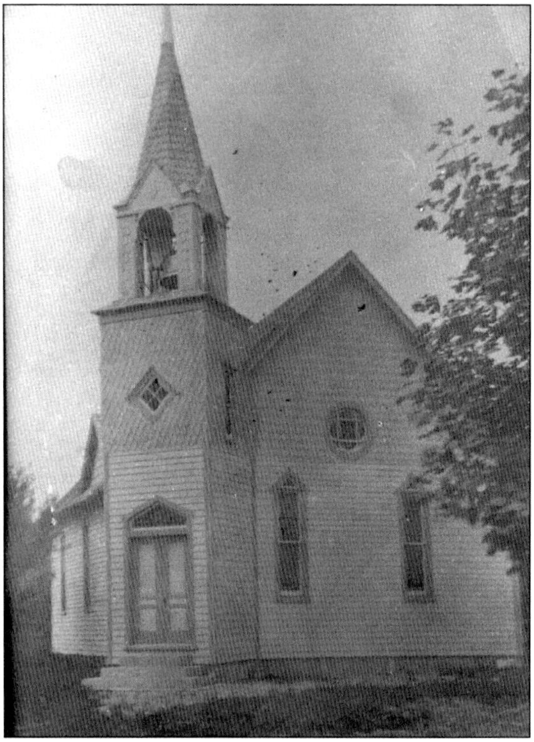

Ayers M.E. Church, Pittsville. The dedication of Ayers Church was to take place on October 6, 1889, but the dedication did not take place as planned because of inclement weather. The Reverend George E. Ross, president of Dickinson College, preached the dedicatory sermon. The church cost $1,300 to build, and the congregation still owed $800 on it but nearly $300 was raised at the dedication. (Collection of James Jackson.)

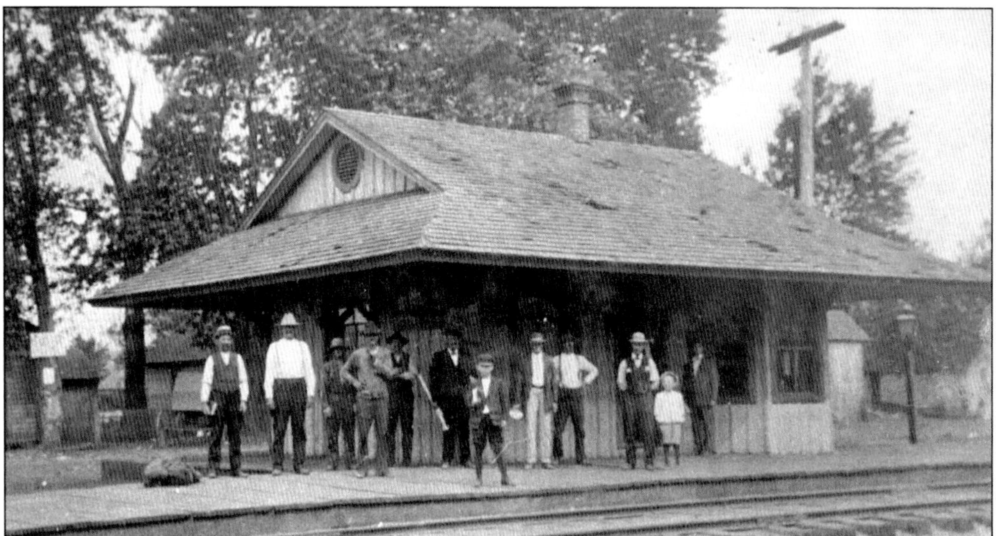

Pittsville Railroad Station. This postcard shows the railroad station as it existed in 1906. The earlier station of the Wicomico and Pocomoke was too small and was sold and moved away. The lower floor of the Red Men's Hall was used as a station until this one was finished. The Wicomico and Pocomoke was all single track. The size of this station was determined by its importance as a shipping point for strawberries. This station was disposed of after the railroad went into receivership and it was moved north of Pittsville to a farm. It has now been rescued, restored, and moved to Maple Avenue where it is an accountant's office. (Collection of James Jackson.)

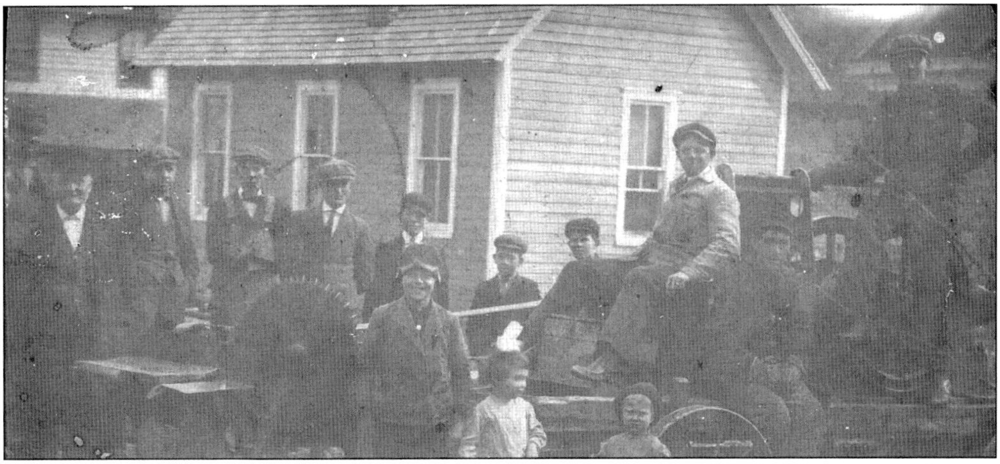

Post Office, Pittsville. This one-room building was supposedly the first post office in Pittsville; Mrs. May Farlow was the postmistress. On the right side of the picture is a man and boy with a piece of equipment that has a large wire buffing wheel on the end of it.

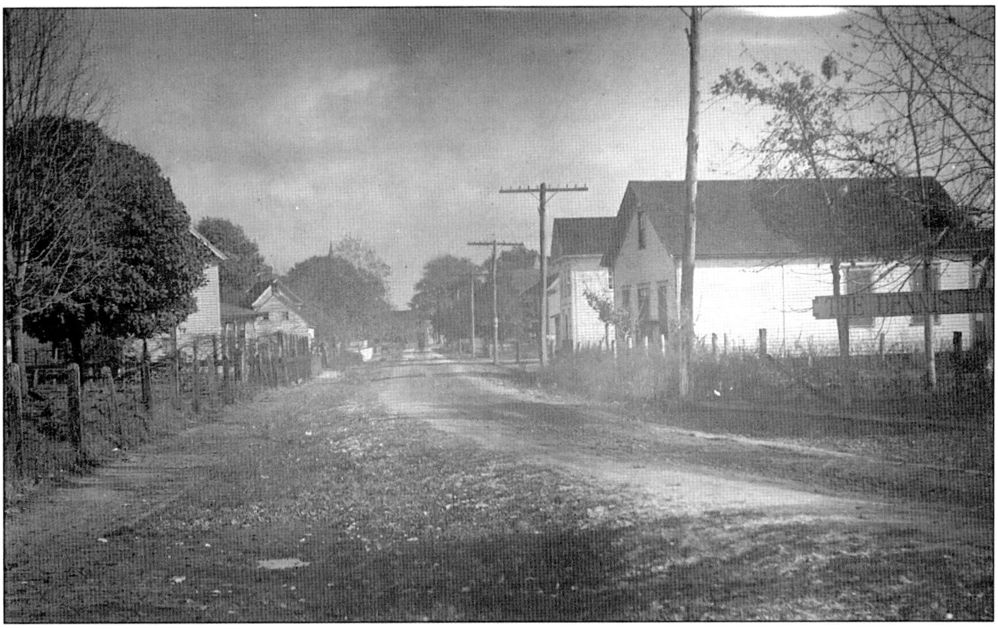

Main Street Pittsville. The sign of the Dennis Hotel is visible on the right with the stores behind it, and on the left is a single store. At the height of its prosperity there were six stores in Pittsville. The closest store on the right has been moved and is now Jackson's Floral Designs. This building contained a lodge room on the second floor. The time is about 1910. (Collection of James Jackson.)

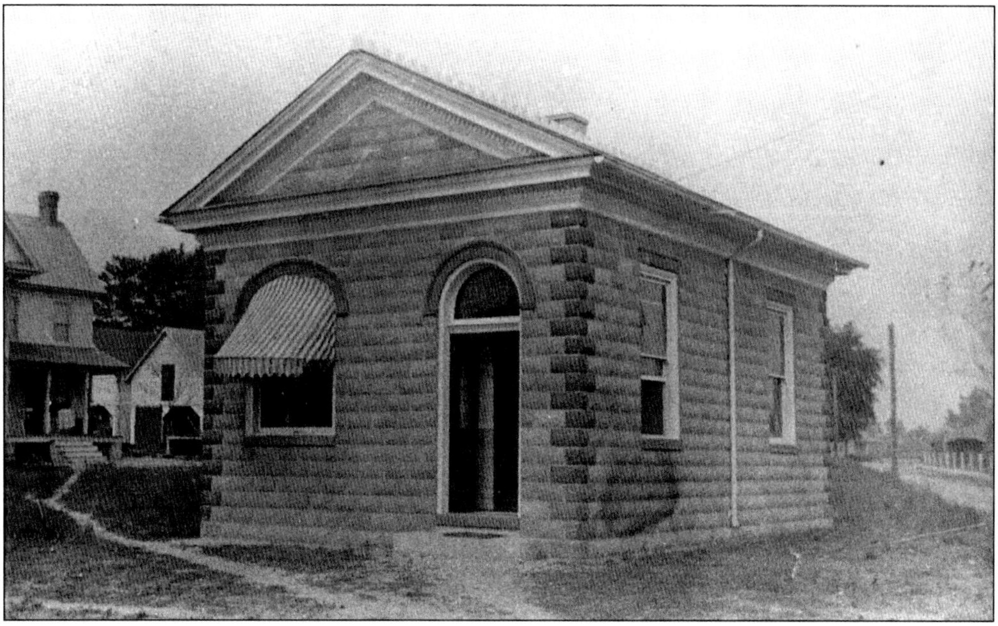

TRUCKERS AND SAVINGS BANK. This new bank was opened for business about May 11, 1906. Ebenezer A. Davis was the first president and held that position from 1906 until his death on January 2, 1944. The bank sold additional stock and moved its headquarters to Salisbury. It was later merged into Equitable Trust Company, and has now become a part of Bank America. (Collection of James Jackson.)

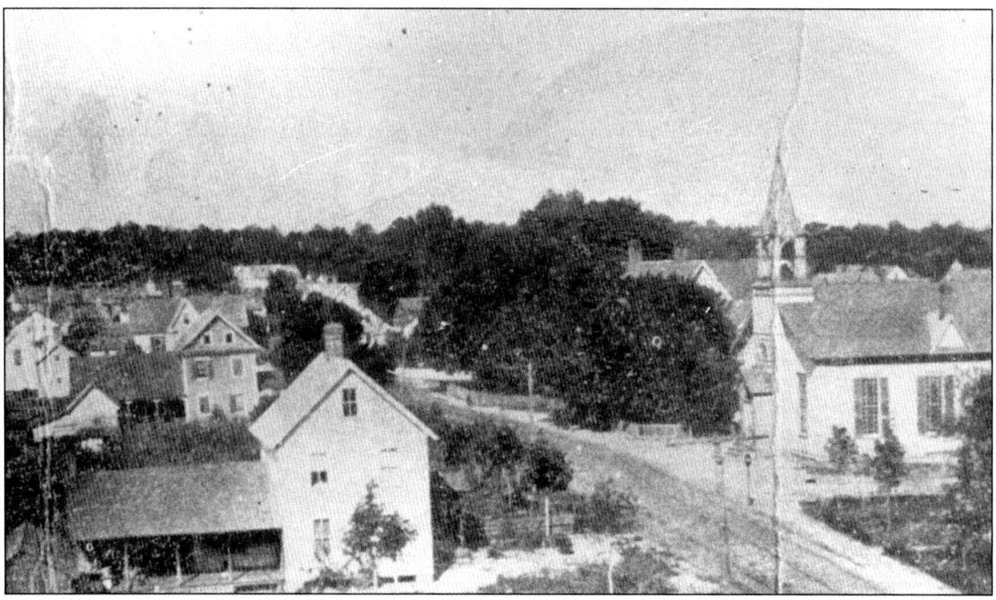

MAIN STREET, PITTSVILLE. This is a picture of Main Street in Pittsville. The Ayers Church is shown on the right, and on the left are a number of the houses in Pittsville.

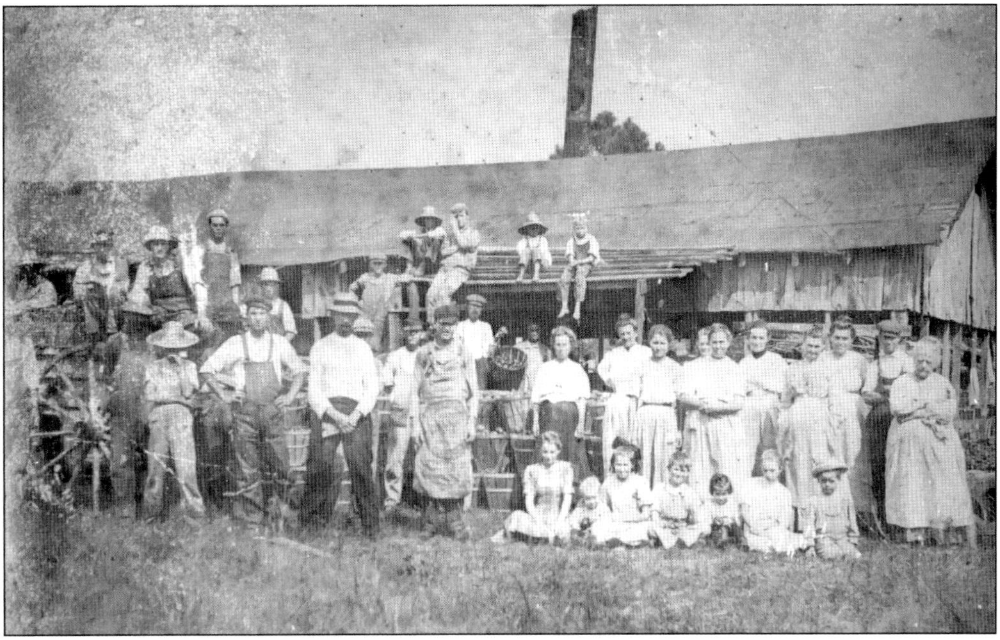

The Canning Factory at Pittsville. You can see the baskets of tomatoes in the middle of the picture. It was probably taken at the noon break since so many children are in evidence. Small canning factories like this were located all over the Shore, ran for only a few weeks in the summer time, and were not too sanitary.

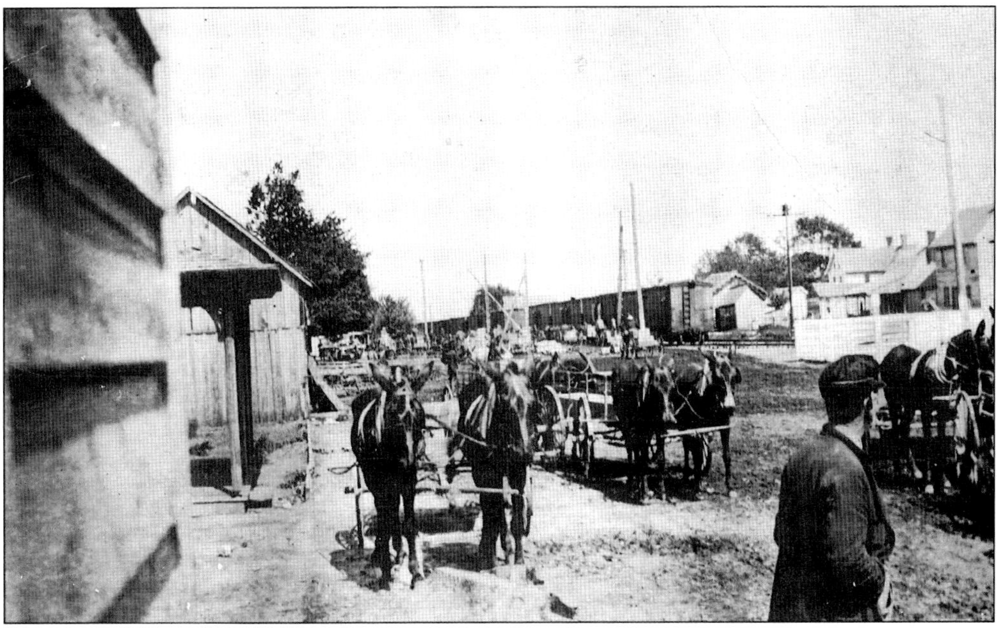

Strawberry Time. This picture dates from 1915. The railroad cars are lined up in Pittsville as the loaded wagons carrying strawberries are lined up along the cars waiting to unload when the berries were sold. The empty wagons in the foreground belong to farmers passing the time of day after selling their strawberries.

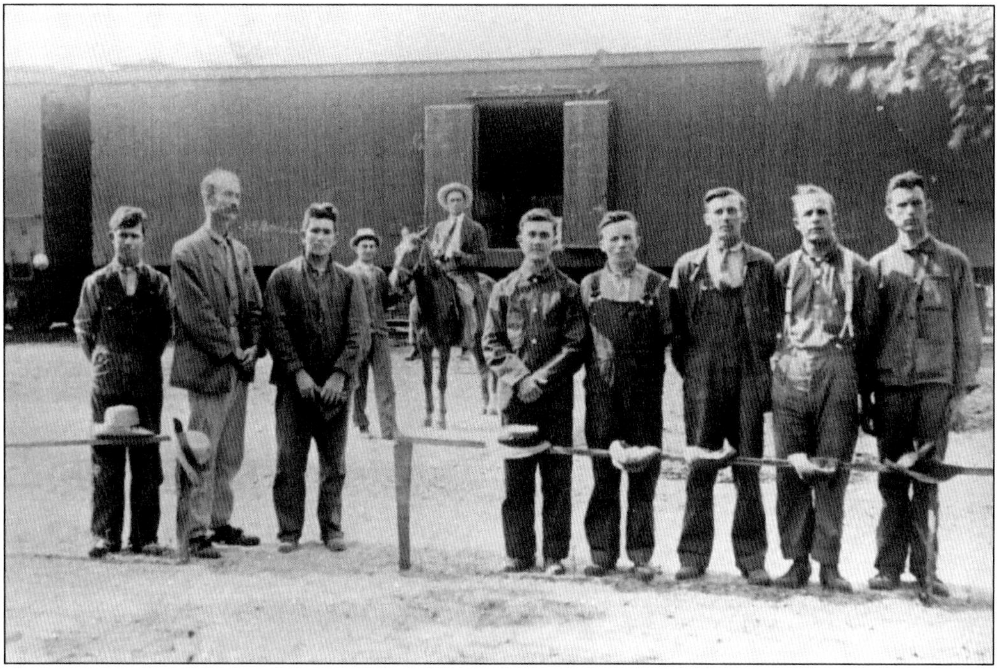

WORKERS AT PITTSVILLE. The strawberry workers at Pittsville have been identified in part, but the occasion is dim as well as the year. The season of the year was strawberry time when the crates were loaded on the train in the cars and piled two crates high as per the picture. The train stopped at Salisbury for ice to be loaded through the circular hole in the front of the car on the roof. The man third from the left is William Parsons, fourth from the left is Paul Wimbrow, and fifth from the left is Willis Parker. The tall, older man in the left-hand group has been identified as Thomas Asbury Parsons. (Collection of James Jackson.)

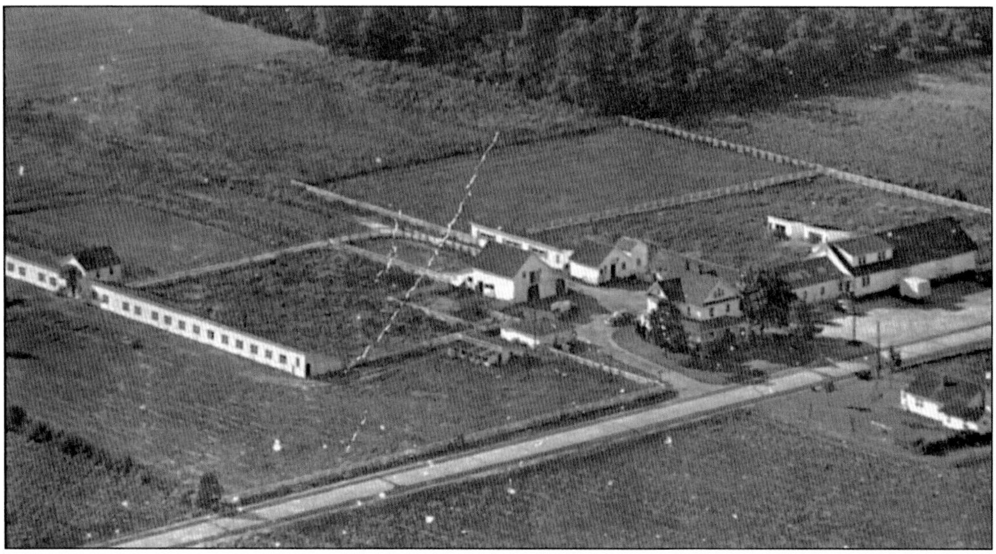

WALTER H. FARLOW & SONS HATCHERY. Walter H. Farlow and his sons, Essell and Otis, had this hatchery north of Pittsville on the Gumboro Road. Mr. Farlow started the hatchery in 1913, and this picture probably dates from the 1930s, before the broiler industry became completely integrated and hatcheries were separate operations. (Collection of James Jackson.)

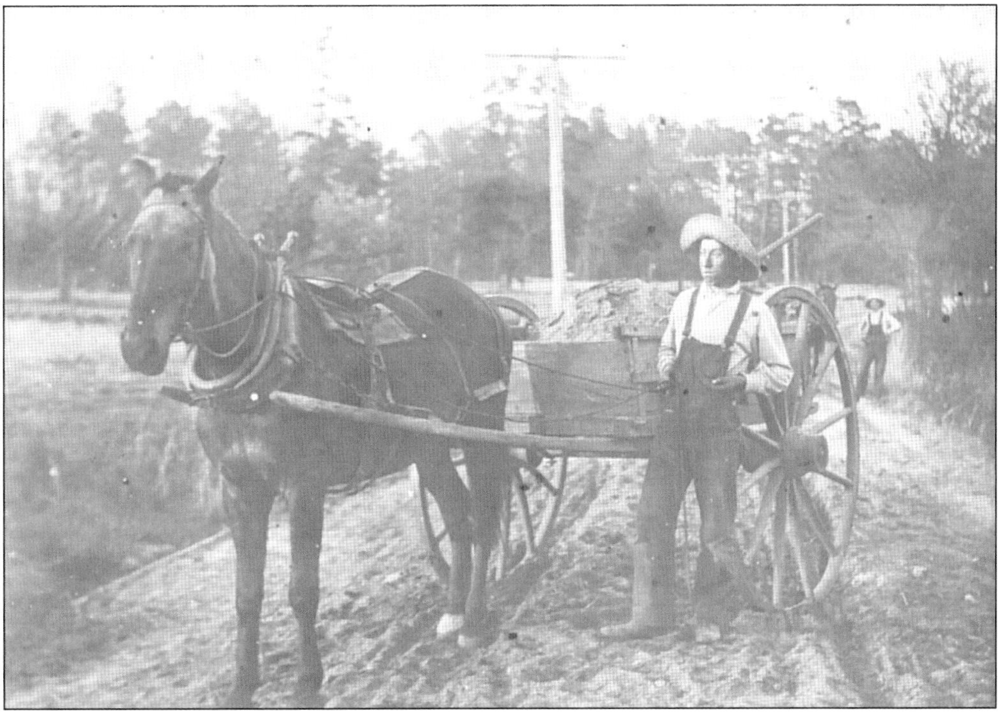

MAN WITH CART. This picture was taken in a rural area. The two-wheeled cart seems to be loaded with dirt and is probably a dump cart. The telephone poles tell us it is a main road. It is near Pittsville. (Collection of James Jackson.)

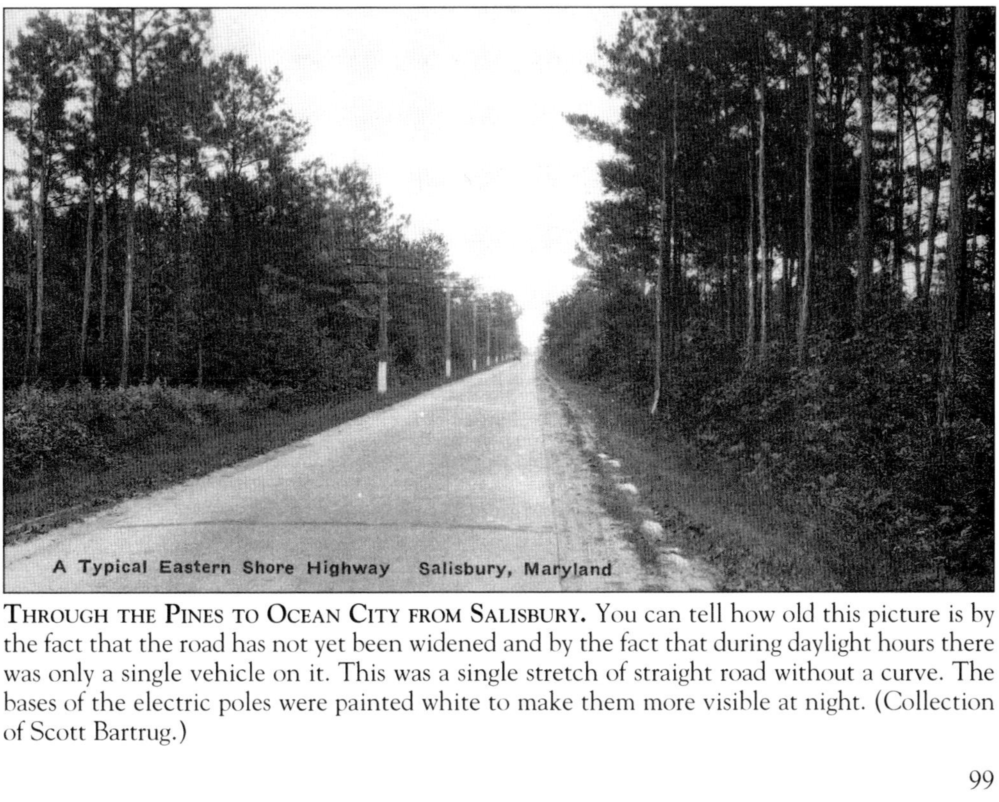

THROUGH THE PINES TO OCEAN CITY FROM SALISBURY. You can tell how old this picture is by the fact that the road has not yet been widened and by the fact that during daylight hours there was only a single vehicle on it. This was a single stretch of straight road without a curve. The bases of the electric poles were painted white to make them more visible at night. (Collection of Scott Bartrug.)

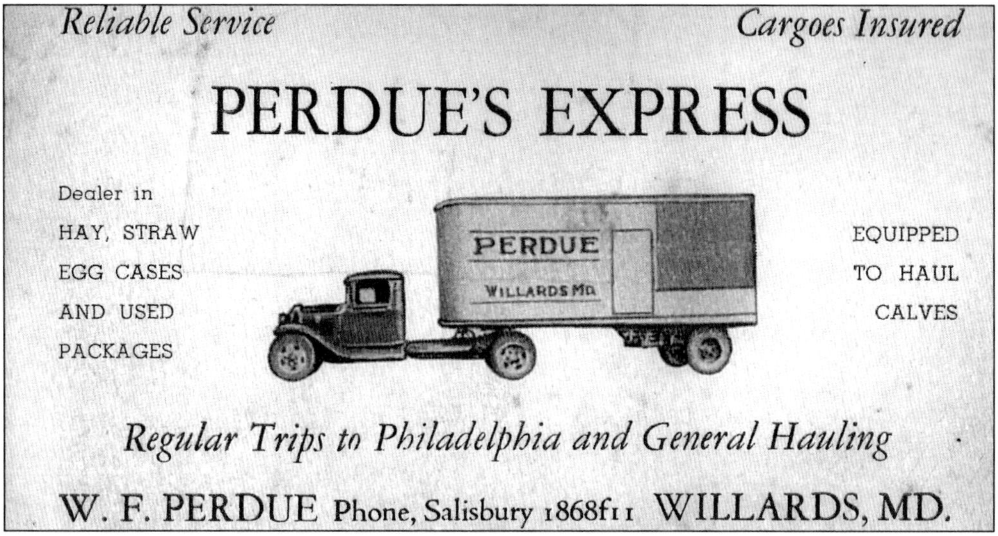

PERDUE'S EXPRESS. Walter F. Perdue made two round trips to Philadelphia from Willards each week. He hauled livestock and poultry north and whatever he could pick up in Philadelphia in return. Eventually he had two tractor-trailers. He lived between Willards and Powellville in a rural area and had a country party phone line. It had between ten and 15 people on the line, and had a wall phone with a crank. People on the line could call each other without going through the operator, who would come on the line after one very long ring and then connect you to the number you wanted.

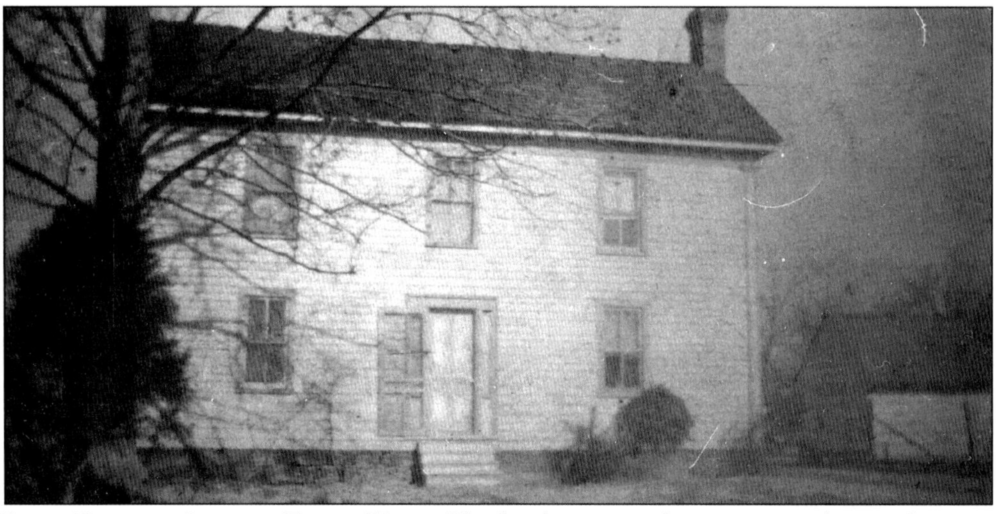

JUDGE BENJAMIN JOHNSON FAMILY HOME. The family graveyard may give us a better idea as to the age of the house and who built it more than anything else. The oldest stones in the graveyard are those of Benjamin and Catharine Johnson. Catharine was born on February 8, 1823, and her husband, Benjamin, was five years older. The windows and the front door are consistent with an 1840 building date. The two chimneys, one at each end of the house, undoubtedly had two fireplaces each, one up and one down.

This was the home of Benjamin's son Rufus and was the birthplace of Judge Benjamin A. Johnson and his sister Susan. The Johnson family lived there until 1916 when Rufus Johnson, Benjamin's son, died. The house was burned in the 1950s. It was located on the Johnson Road in Wango. (Collection of Mrs. John E. Taylor.)

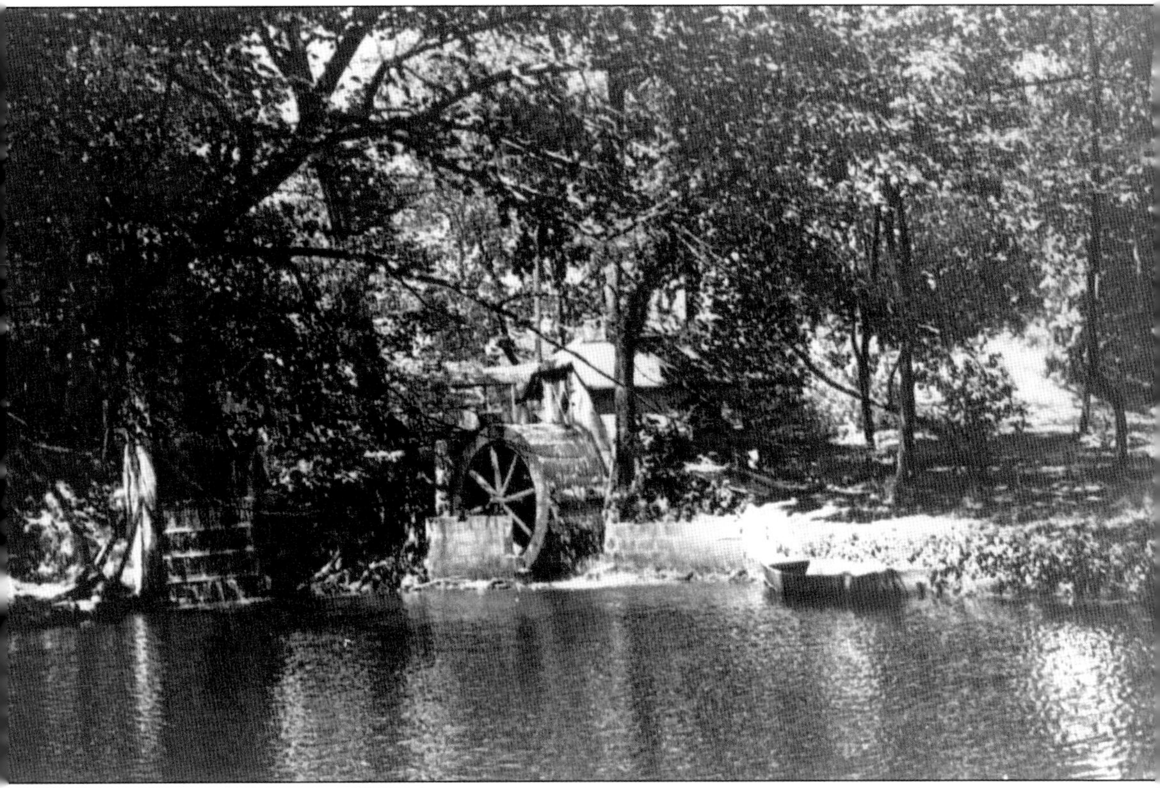

HINMAN PROPERTY NEAR PARKER'S POND. The wheel is not now attached to anything, but is for decorative purposes only. Mr. Thomas Hinman designed the wheels and installed them. Today they are no longer visible from the road.

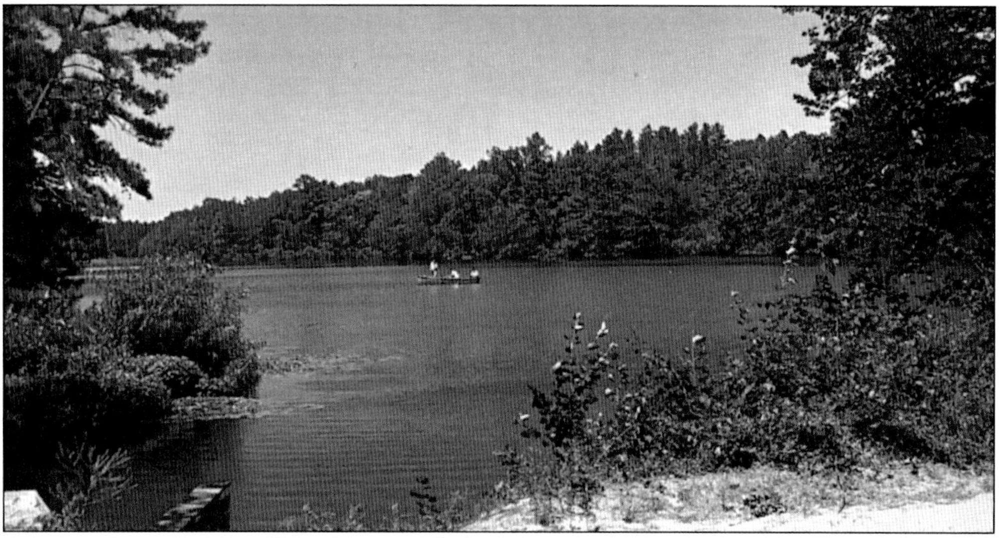

PARKER'S POND. This millpond once called Mangum's Mill Pond was acquired by Leon W. Parker in 1874. At that time he operated both saw- and gristmills. It is on the easterly branch of what later would become the east branch of the Wicomico River. The easterly side of the pond is now developed into a charming subdivision that is backed up to the Salisbury By-Pass on Route 13. It is located at the end of Shumaker Drive.

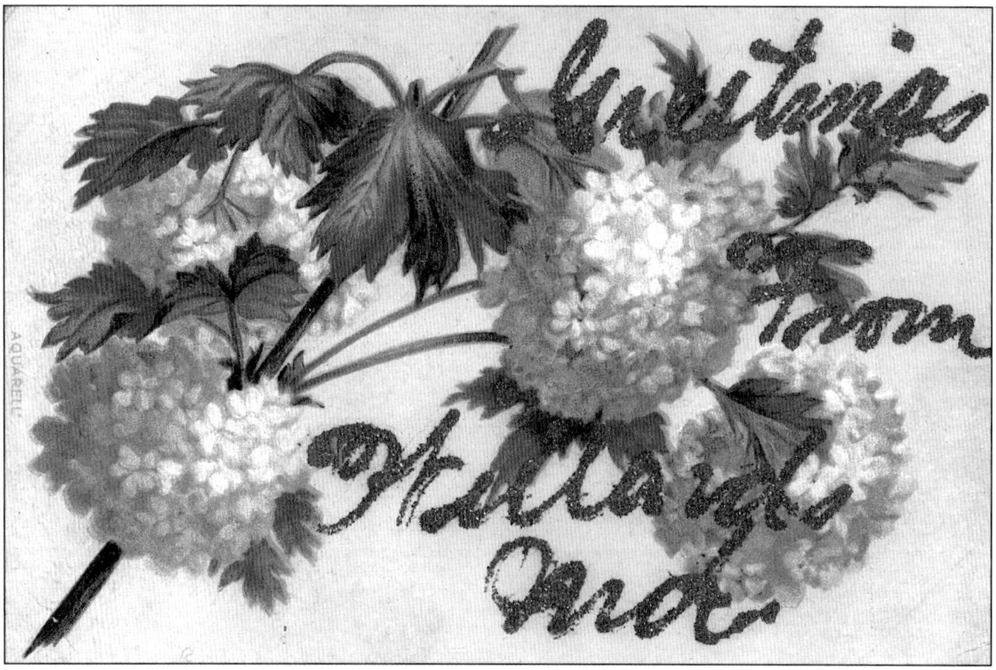

GREETINGS FROM WILLARDS, MARYLAND. This is an example of a card sold by one of the stores in town.

Eight

THE SOUTH SIDE

Fruitland began as Disharoon's Cross Roads, changed its name to Forktown when the Morrises moved in, and changed it again at the behest of the railroad. The Railroad Directors had planned to name it Phoenix, but they found that name already taken in Maryland. They left it up to Isaac H.A. Dulany, who was the storekeeper and postmaster. He successfully petitioned to name it Fruitland.

The Allen-Eden area is primarily rural. U.S. Route 13 cuts through its eastern edge, and the village of Allen sits on the edge of Passerdyke Creek, which forms part of the county line with Somerset. Few postcards have been made of this area.

Shad Point is an old community, containing the first subdivision of property divided into identical lots facing a street. It was also the site of a land patent called Cherry Hill. Siloam is the country neighborhood abutting it.

The Tony Tank mill was built in 1775. In accordance with law, the top of the dam formed a roadway for horses, oxen, and wagons. In 1838, the Camden Street Bridge was built across the river, and on the south end the road was extended to meet the road to Princess Anne. This doubled the traffic across Tony Tank and also doubled the business at the mill. The mill owners opened a store at the mill site and did good business. Isaac H.A. Dulany built a second store on adjoining property. This prosperity ended with the coming of the railroad to Princess Anne in 1867.

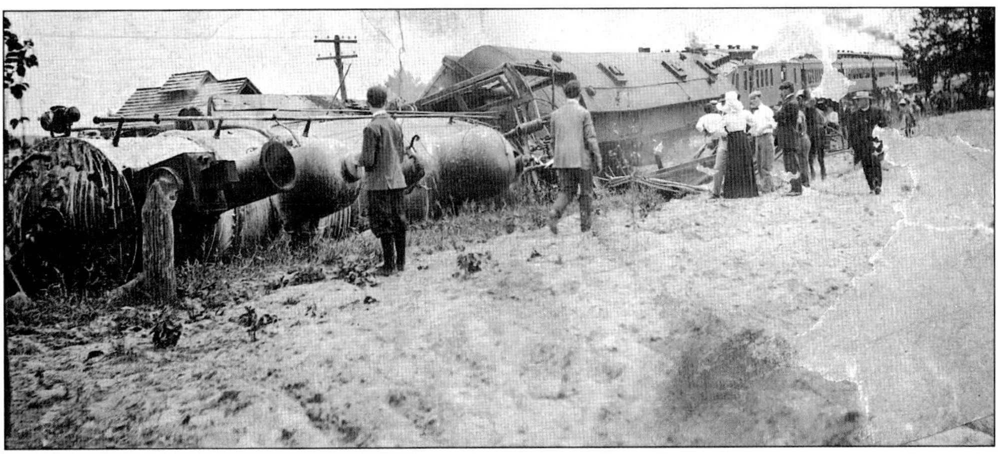

TRAIN WRECK AT FRUITLAND. This photo shows a number of spectators examining the train wreck that occurred on May 25, 1909, between trains belonging to the New York, Philadelphia and Norfolk Railroad, known locally as the "Nip'n N." Mr. Ned West, engineer of the northbound express, was killed in the crash. (Collection of Richard Carter.)

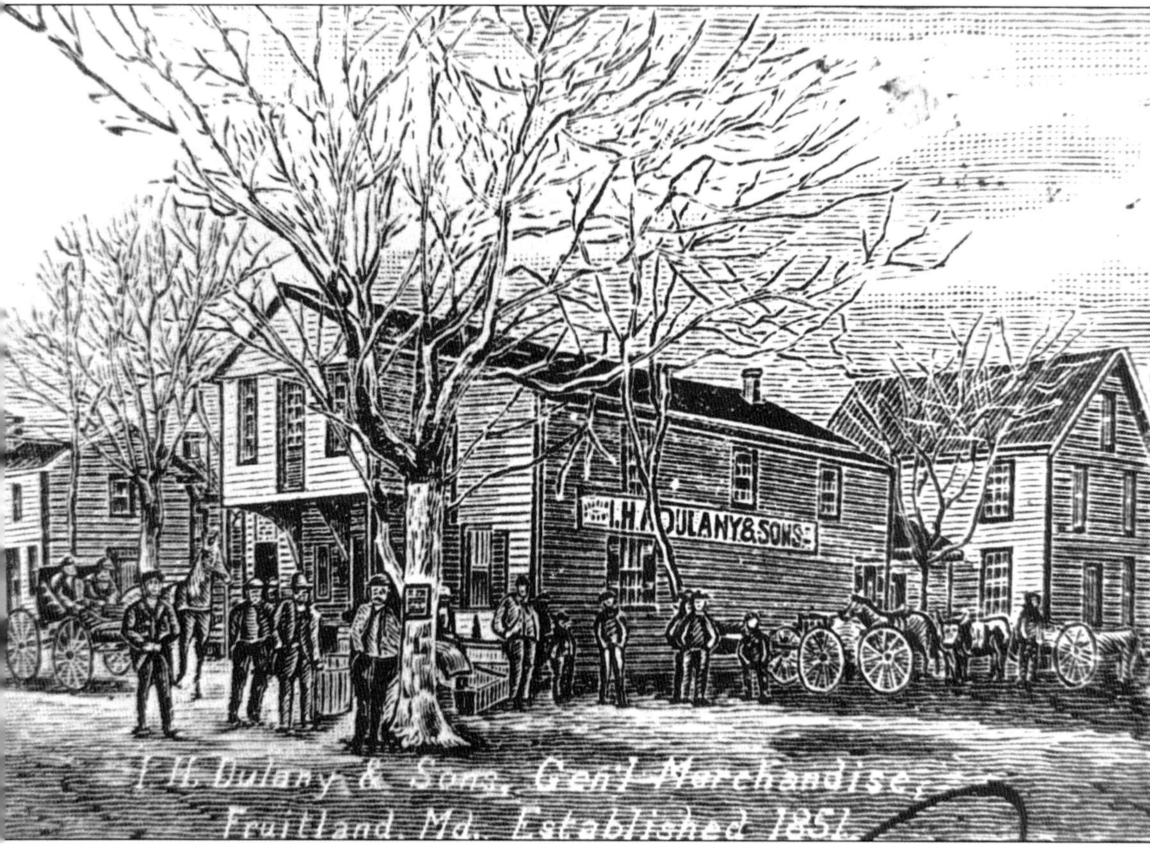

A DRAWING OF THE DULANY STORE IN FRUITLAND. Dulany had started on Camden Avenue between Tony Tank and Moore's Corner, but moved to Forktown when the railroad came through. He built this store there. This drawing was on his letterhead and was copied on a postcard at the 60th anniversary of the date his sons began to can tomatoes. You can see a stroke of the pen at the edge of the drawing. The company ceased the retail business and became a cannery and frozen food company. Ralph O. Dulany, Isaac's grandson, finally sold it. For a long time it was the principal employer in Fruitland.

LENA B. SAMPSON. Forktown had had a resident milliner since the 1840s. Jennie Cathell, Ralph Dulany's mother, was the proprietor of the shop before her marriage to John W. Dulany. She was succeeded by Lena B. Sampson, who advertised her spring opening in 1909. Cards to customers were the best way to advertise in a town with no newspaper. Lena went out of business about 1914.

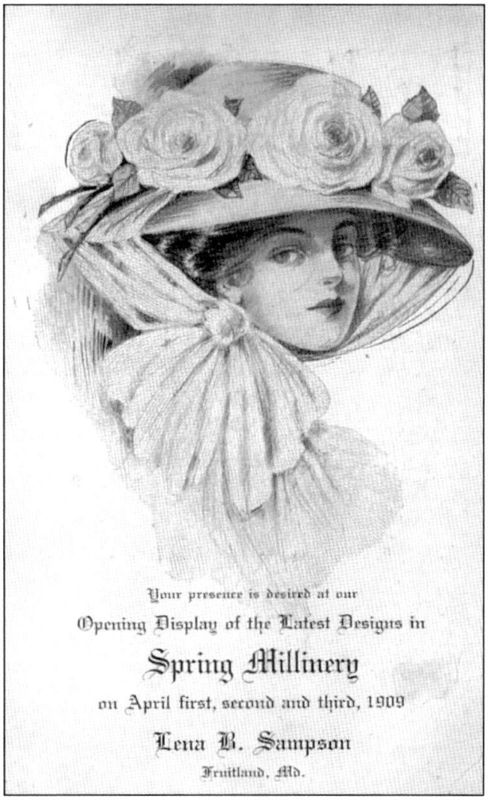

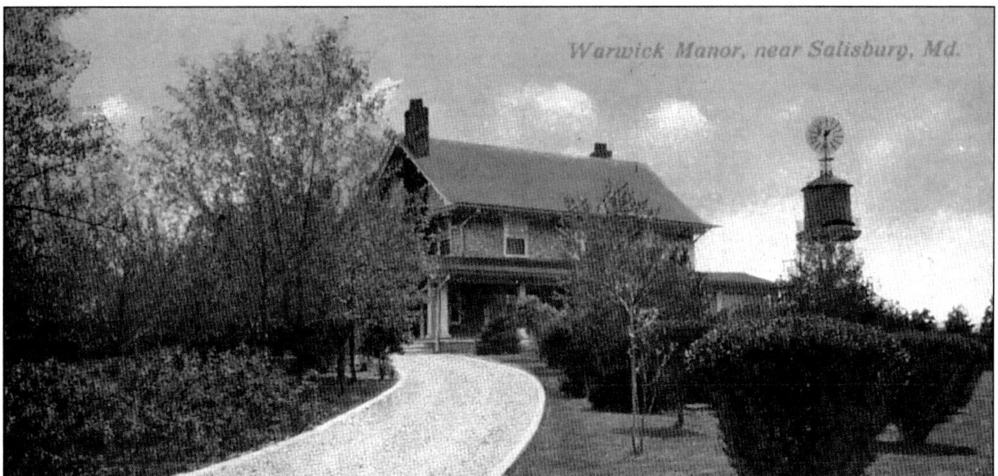

WARWICK MANOR. Thomas Clyde, heir to a steamship fortune, built Warwick Manor in 1906. He moved to Fruitland, probably on the recommendation of Mr. W.P. Presgrave, and built a race track nearly a mile long on which to train his horses. In 1908 the *Wicomico News* referred to it as the Clyde Club. He sold the estate in 1912 to William B. Tilghman Jr., who laid it out into lots. Caroline C. Rider bought the house and the lot next door. She married Col. Marion A. Humphreys, and he moved in with her. She was the mother of Mrs. William P. Jackson, and for many years it was their home. It is still a private residence, and is located at the corner of Camden Avenue and Cedar Lane.

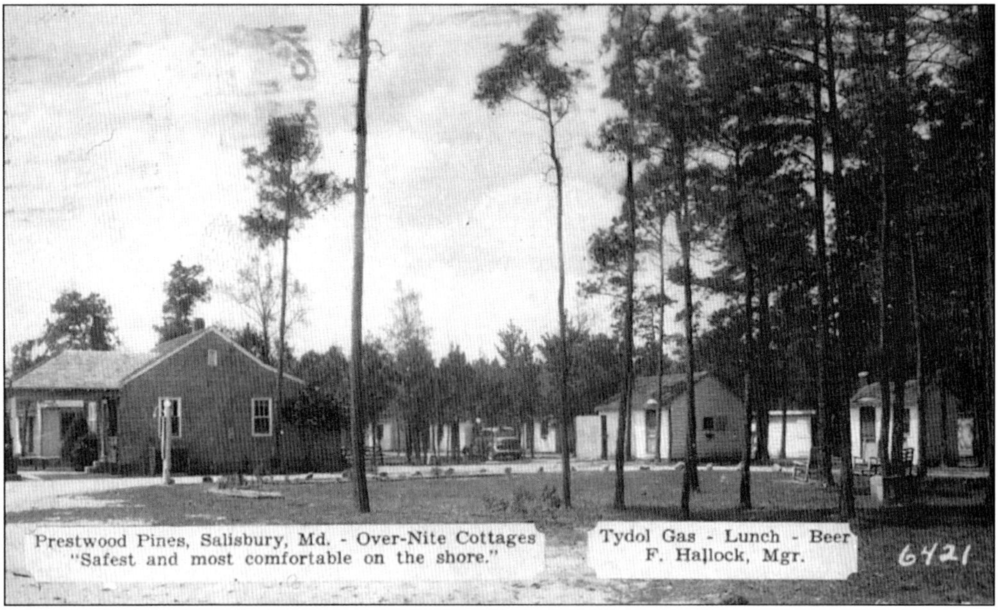

PRESTWOOD PINES. Prestwood Pines was known to the young men of the area as Twofers. This was because two cans of beer cost a quarter. Frank Hallock's was also the cheapest place to buy gasoline; he sold it six gallons for a dollar. Despite the address, "Salisbury, Maryland," on the card, it was in Fruitland on Camden Avenue. The cottages, which are visible behind the store, were frequently rented for an evening of romance.

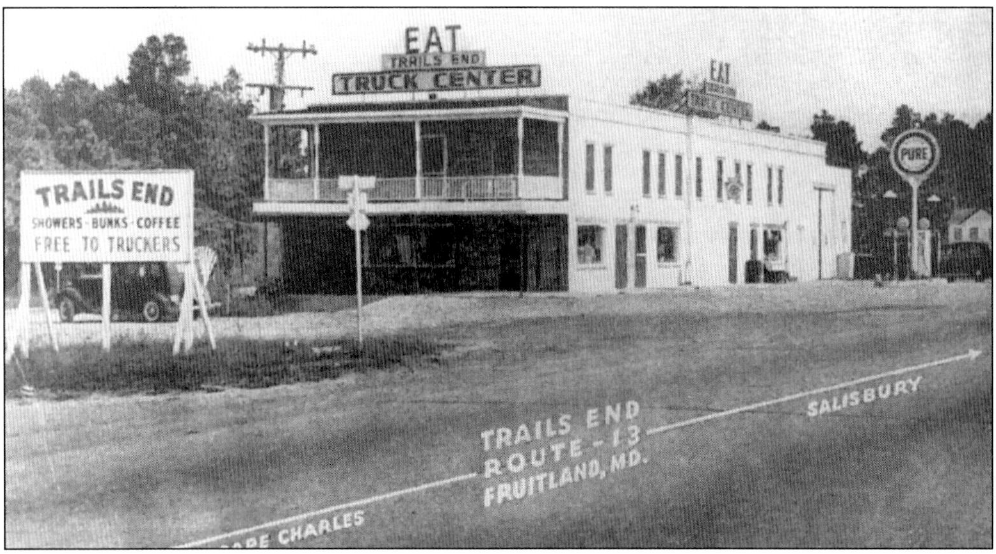

TRAILS END TRUCK CENTER. Trails End Truck Center was built in 1945 by Wilson and Sallie Tarr. At that time Route 13 south of Salisbury was a single-lane highway, but it had replaced the road through Allen. Trails End had a grocery store, a restaurant, an auto parts store, sold Purol gasoline, and had bunks and showers for truckers. The second floor contained two apartments for the owners and their son. The State of Maryland condemned the property to build the southbound lane of Route 13 and demolished it in 1954. It was located at the intersection of Route 13 and Camden Avenue. (Collection of Betty Webster.)

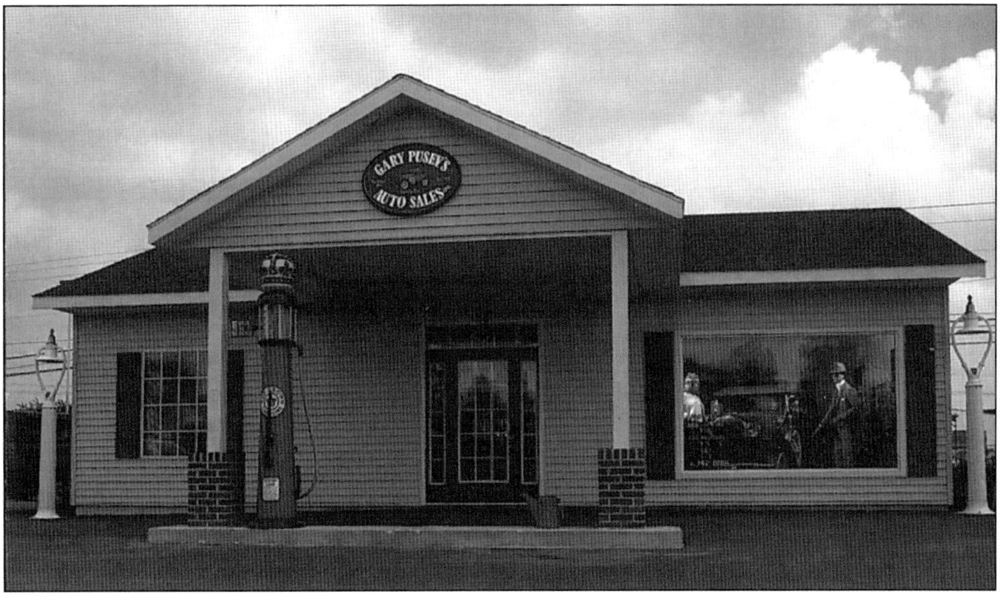

Gary Pusey's Quality Cars. This picture was made in 1988. The gas pump was obtained from Des Moines, Iowa, and the street lights from Broken Arrow, Oklahoma, shortly before publication of this card. The automobile in the showroom was replaced by a 1964 Galaxie 500 that belonged to Pusey's maternal grandmother. Pusey has been in the automobile business since May 1969. (Collection of Gene Wharton.)

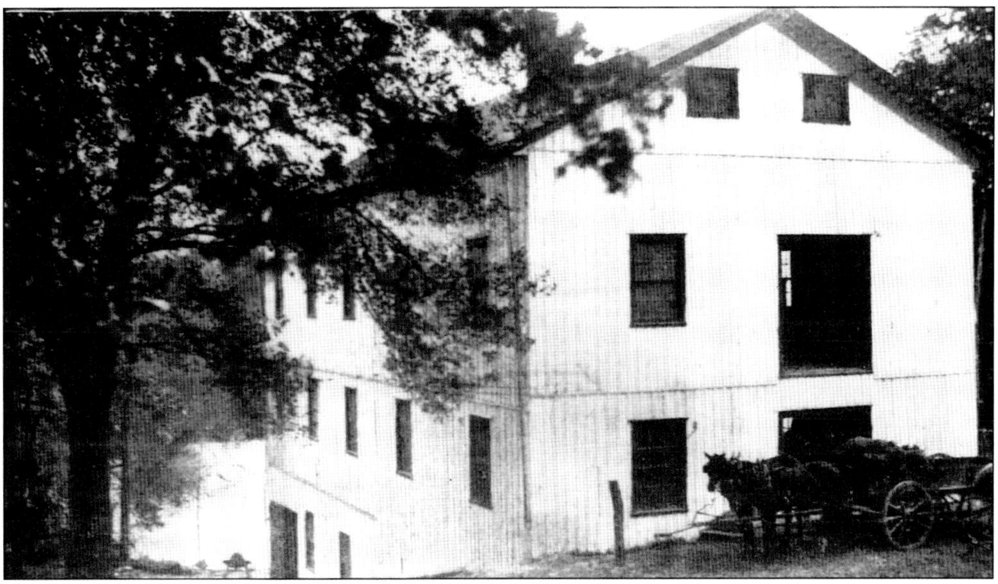

Idlewild Mills. This is a picture of the former mill at Allen. As you can see it is a three-level mill. The collection of the raw grain and corn and the delivery of the ground flour were made in front. The grinding stones were probably also on this level. The pond in the background is the boundary between Wicomico and Somerset Counties.

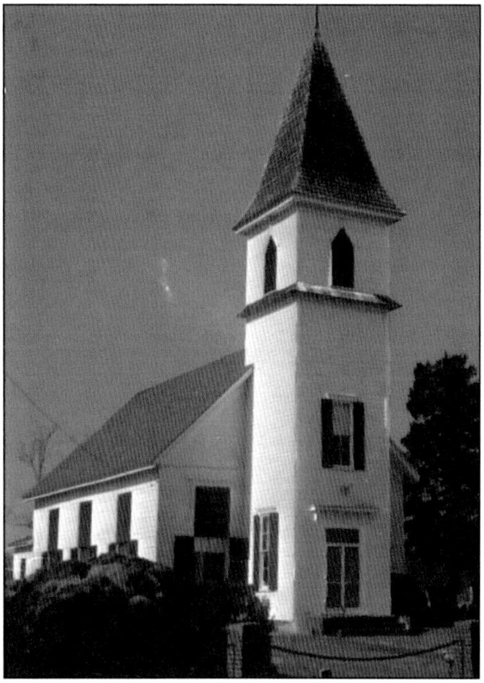

ALLEN UNITED METHODIST CHURCH. The congregation was founded in 1829 and the church was built in 1848. Its cemetery is the second oldest in Wicomico County in continuous use.

The original church had no steeple, vestibule, or choir space. A slave gallery was built over the front doors. The steeple and vestibule were added about 1883, and the church bell was added in 1894. The church was damaged by Hurricane Hazel and repairs and remodeling cost $10,000. The brick columns around the property were added in 1960. During the Civil War armed men slept in the church to keep northern sympathizers from taking it over, and in 1866 the church became affiliated with the M.E. Church South.

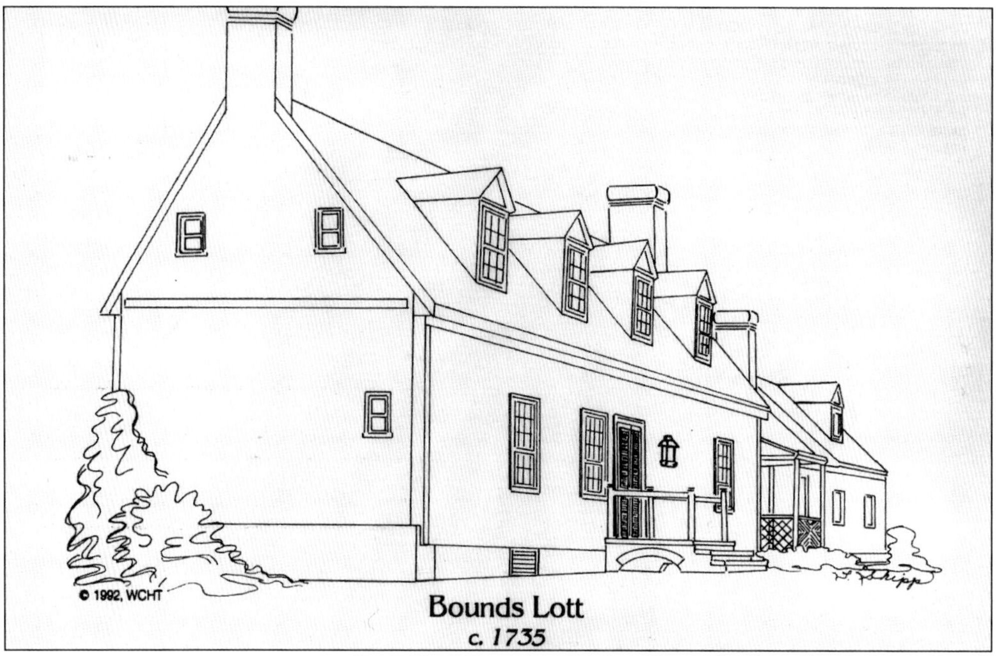

BOUNDS LOTT. This house is probably the oldest residence in Wicomico County. It was originally built about 1685 with two rooms and a loft. The original corner post can be seen in the house on one side of the present front door. The rest of the main house was added prior to 1740 containing two more rooms on the ground floor and one on the second floor, plus the hall and staircase. The bedroom wing on the first floor was from an old house near Delmar and was moved there by C. Robert Withey, its present owner, when he meticulously restored the original.

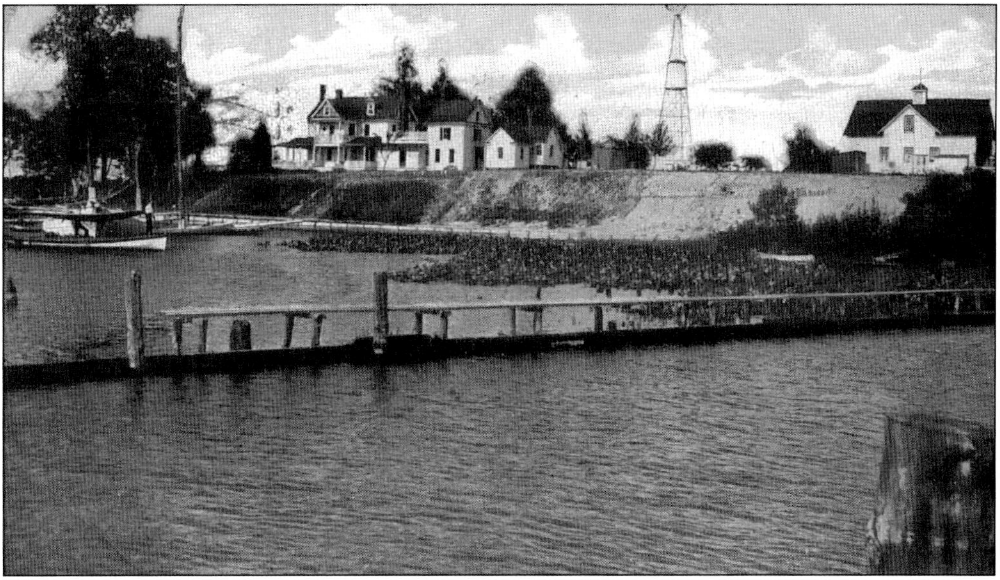

In the Suburbs. This house traces its history to 1830 when Samuel Somers, who then owned it, opened a public house to accommodate people who wished to use this new fast way of transportation called the steamboat. Salisbury harbor had silted up, and the coaches from Snow Hill also came to Shad Point.

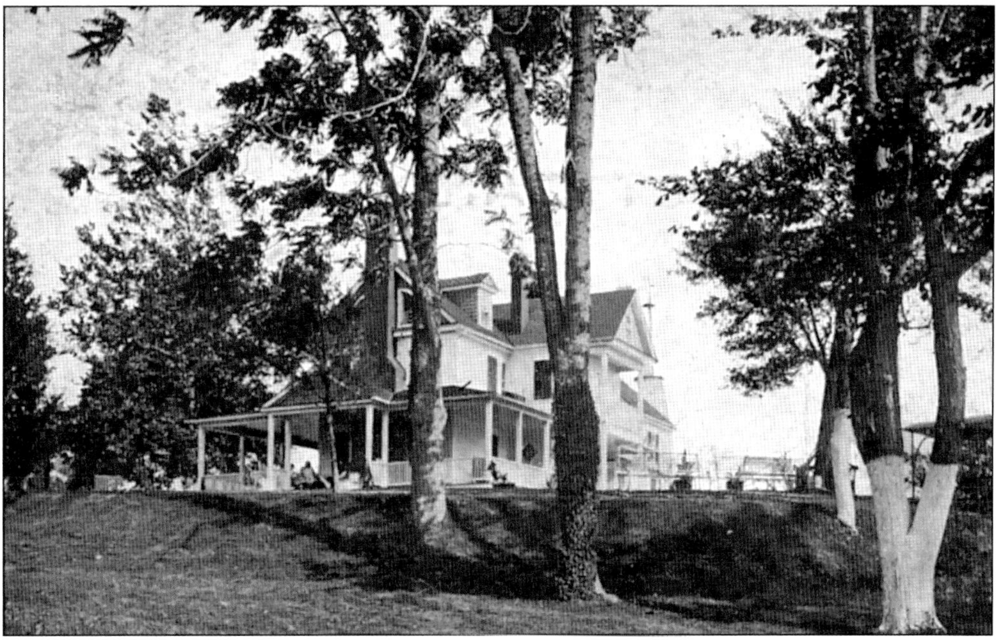

L.W. Gunby's Summer Home. After the years passed, L.W. Gunby, a grandson of Samuel, bought the house and remodeled it into his summer home. He bought a boat and chugged to and from his hardware store in Salisbury. After his death the property was sold to Symington-Wayne Corp., who converted it into their company offices, and for a while it was used as a regional office after its merger into Dresser Industries. Finally the house was torn down and the property sold to developers, who have named their high-priced development on the water—what else, Cherry Hill.

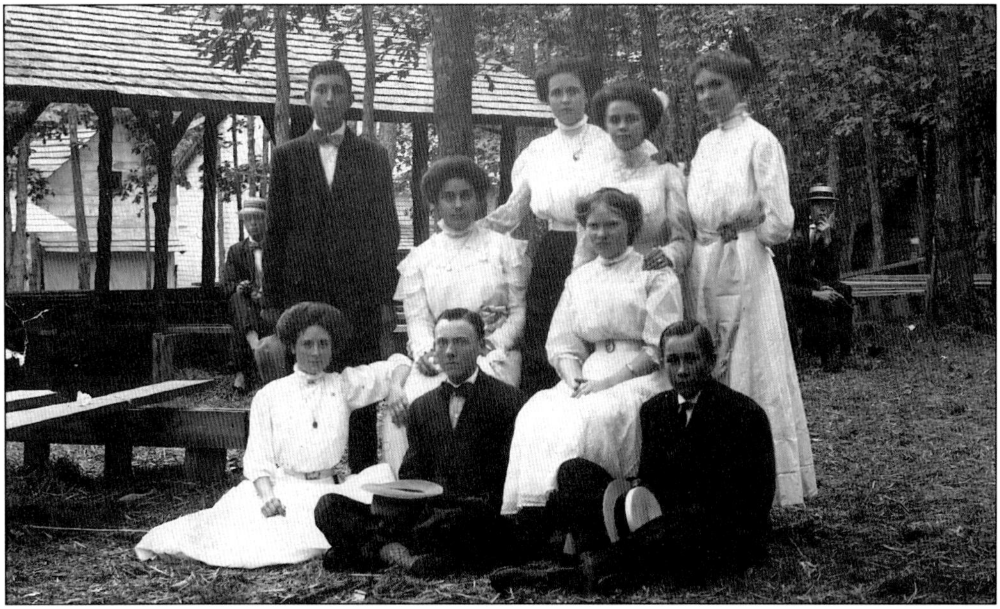

SILOAM CAMP MEETING. The Methodist Camp Meeting was as much a social occasion as a religious one. There was usually a circular walkway between the preaching and the tents. Around this the young people walked slowly, the males in one direction, the females in the other. The tents can be seen in the background at left. These were privately owned and occupied for the entire camp meeting session by the family of the owner. The people who can be identified are from left to right as follows: (seated) Maude Cathell, Powell A. Bounds, and Preston Bounds; (seated in the second row) Hilda Acworth Carey and Elizabeth Carey Atkinson; (standing) Stengel Dawson, Carrie Bounds, Ethelyn Vincent Ward, and Evelyn Dukes Carey. (Collection of Fruitland Historical Society.)

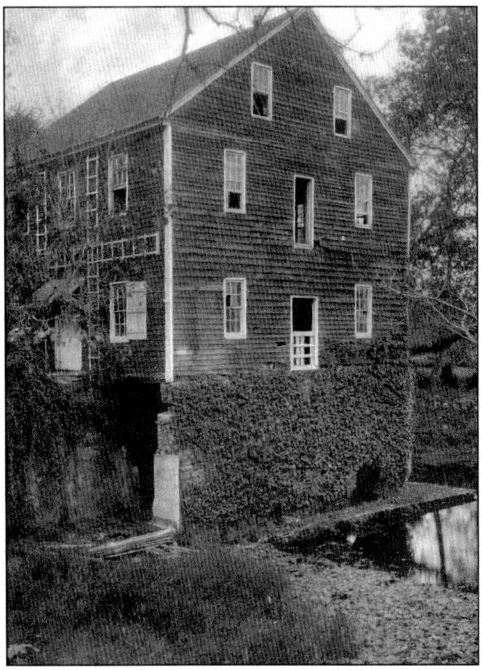

TONY TANK MILL. The mill was built about 1758 by William Adams and George Handy. It was subsequently acquired by Capt. Robert Dashiell, who became the richest merchant in Salisbury. The mill was last rebuilt and had new machinery installed while owned by W.D. Presgrave. Nothing is left of the mill now but the foundation.

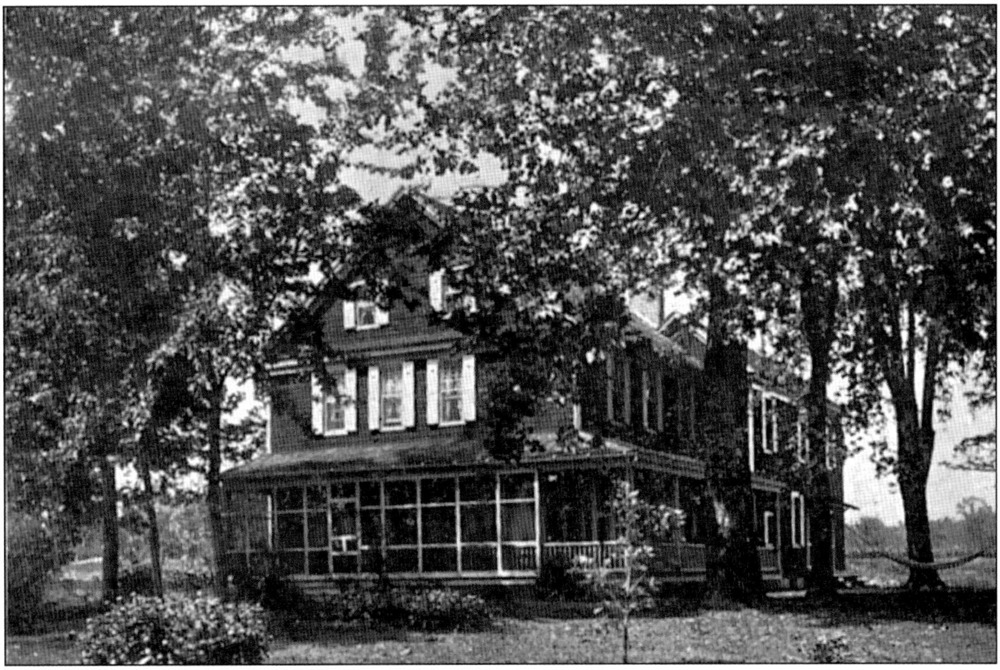

TONY TANK. This is how the mill owners' house looked before it was altered by W.D. Presgrave, who bought the property in 1905. Not only did he remodel the house but he also built a large stable on the north side of the creek at the corner of Rolling Road as well as several tenants' houses. He was a racing enthusiast, and it was the winter home for his horses.

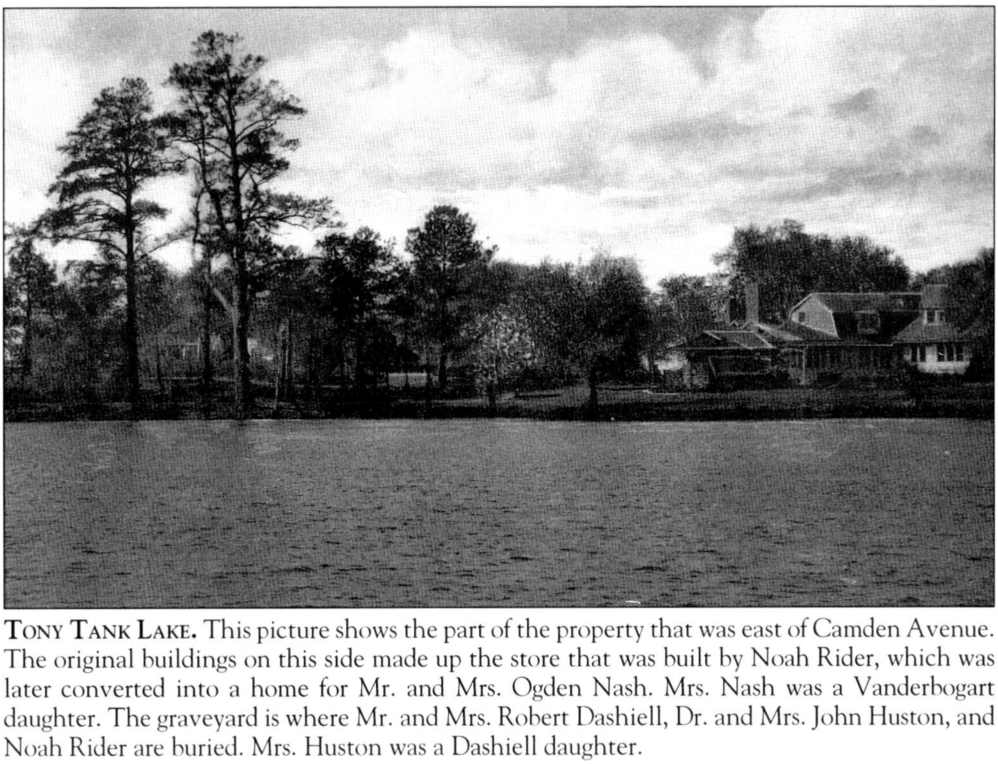

TONY TANK LAKE. This picture shows the part of the property that was east of Camden Avenue. The original buildings on this side made up the store that was built by Noah Rider, which was later converted into a home for Mr. and Mrs. Ogden Nash. Mrs. Nash was a Vanderbogart daughter. The graveyard is where Mr. and Mrs. Robert Dashiell, Dr. and Mrs. John Huston, and Noah Rider are buried. Mrs. Huston was a Dashiell daughter.

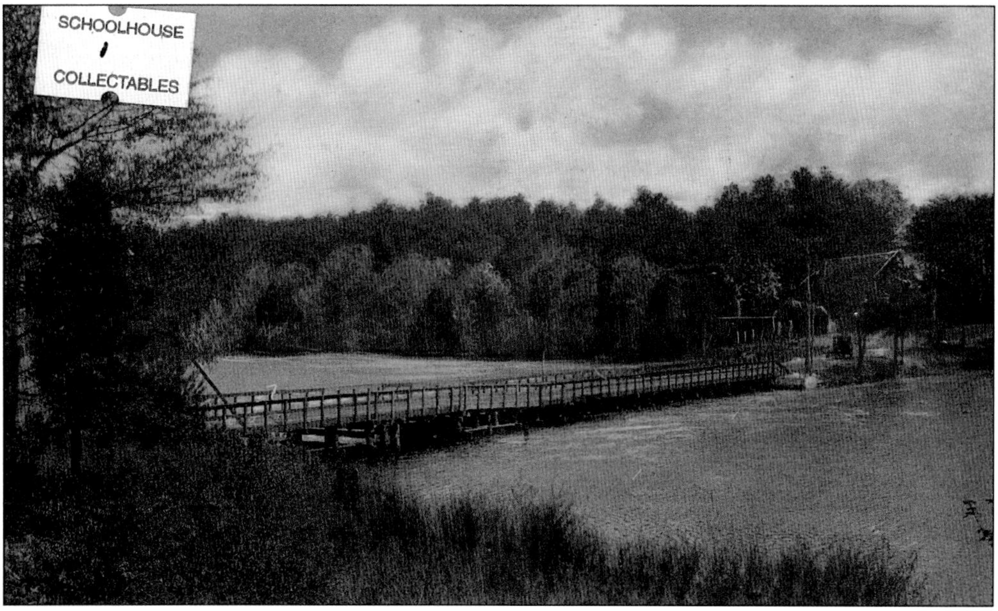

BRIDGE ON RIVERSIDE DRIVE. This picture is the first picture of the bridge built across Tony Tank at Riverside Drive. Mr. Presgrave violently opposed a stationary bridge here, and wanted a pivot bridge, but the county commissioners turned him down and built this in 1906. The stream was still tidal then. (Collection of James Jackson.)

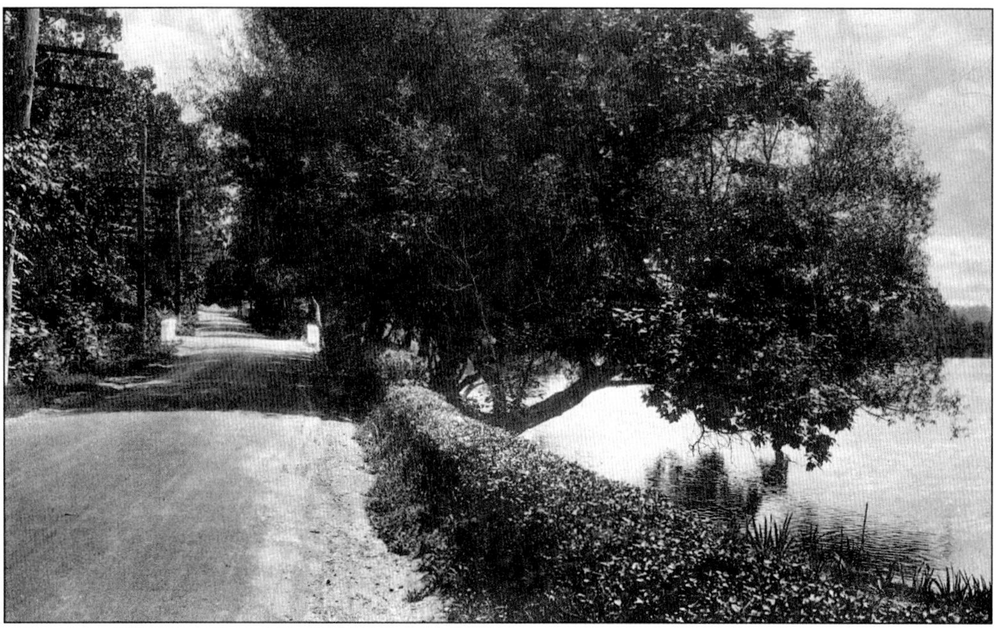

TONY TANK LAKE. This shows what the milldam looked like. Note the concrete abutments and see how narrow the road was then. The dam had washed away in many storms. This card was made after the last one since the road is paved, but the trees are still growing on the dam and the ivy still covers the approaches. (Collection of James Jackson.)

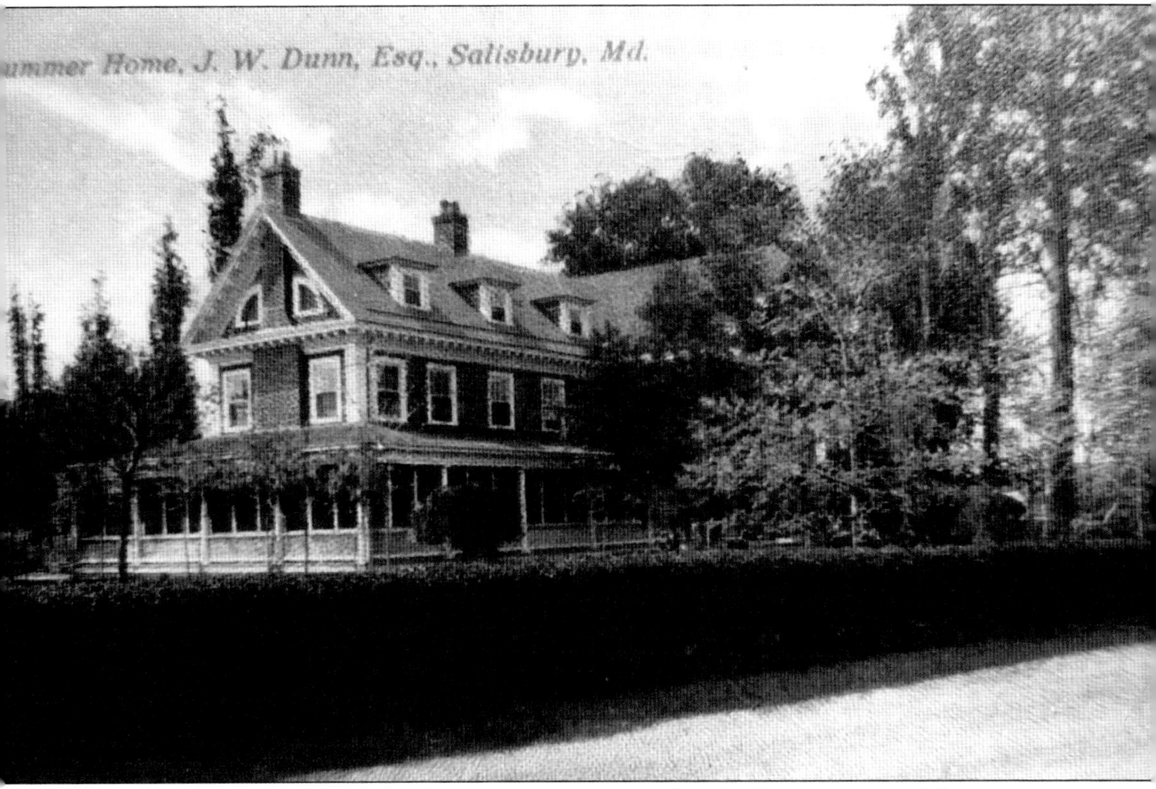

Summer Home of J.W. Dunn. This picture was taken after the Presgrave remodeling; a wing has been added. One wedding was held here at this time, in which a daughter married a local attorney, Arthur Everett Williams. Dunn sold the home because he was called back to New York due to the sudden death of a son. He sold it to Mrs. Margaret Vanderbogart, a daughter of Gov. Elihu E. Jackson, who lived there the rest of her life. The house is still referred to as the Vanderbogart Mansion.

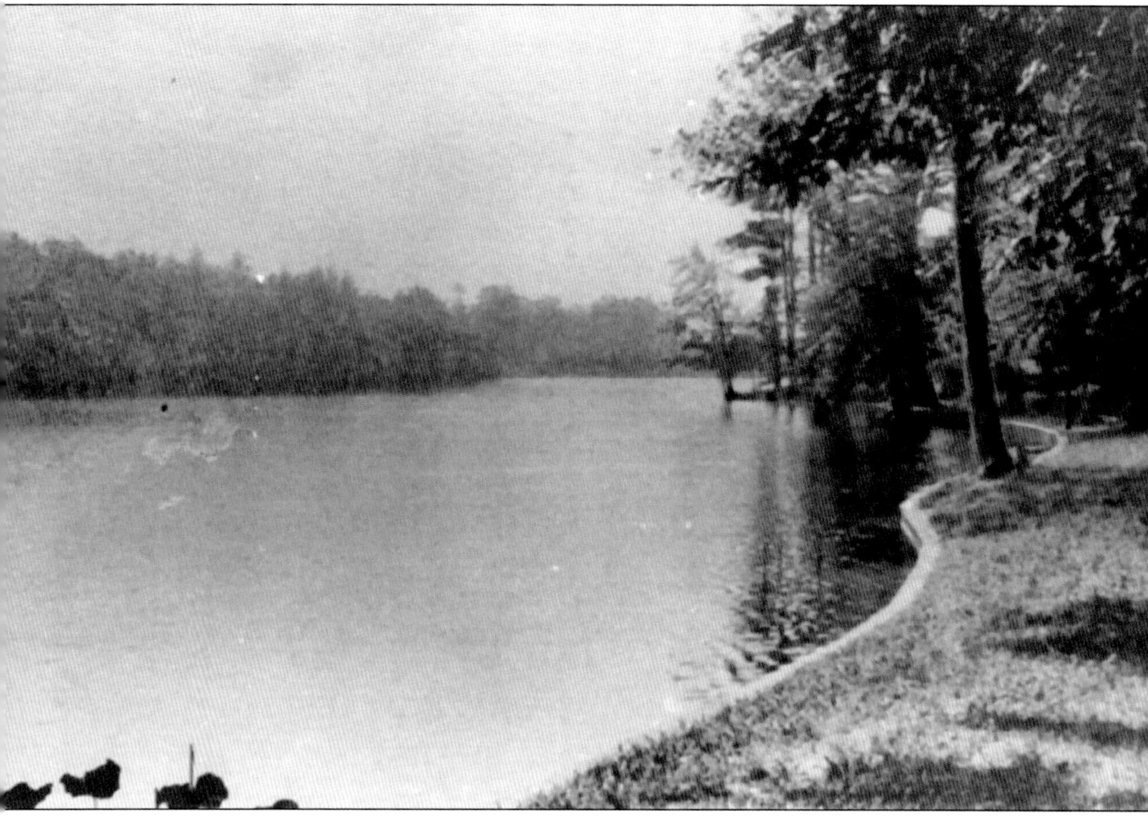

Tony Tank Lake. This picture shows what the south shore of the lake looked like before the Tony Tank development was built. It was entirely covered by trees.

Nine

Down on the Farm

Wicomico County is still comparatively rural, but with the advent of cars and trucks it has lost much of its rural flavor. This chapter celebrates that rural flavor.

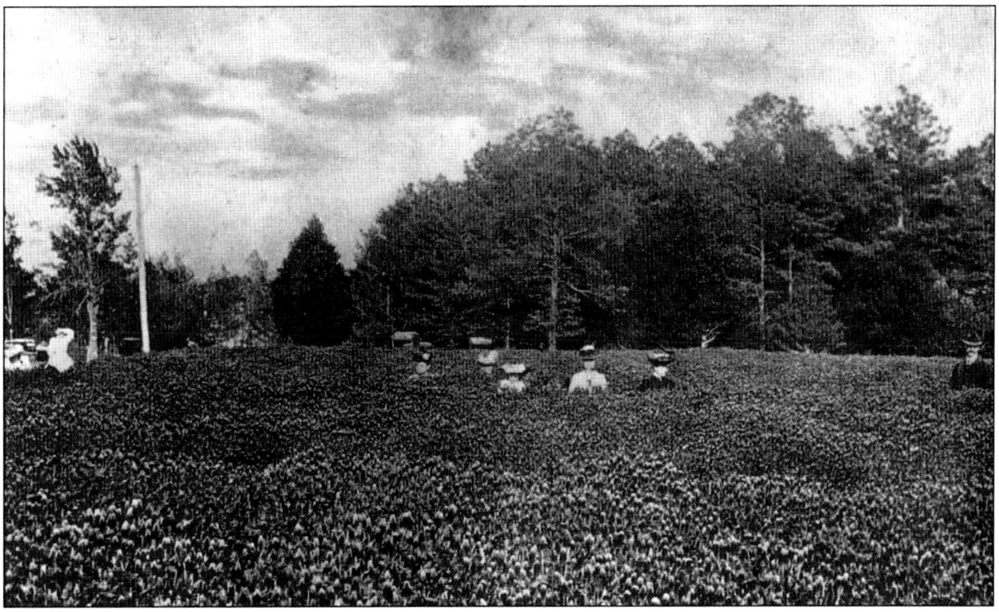

Clover Field. The card says this clover field was cut on May 10, and implies that growth since then has been phenomenal. The people in the middle of the field are up to their chests in clover, but note the woman at the left side of the picture.

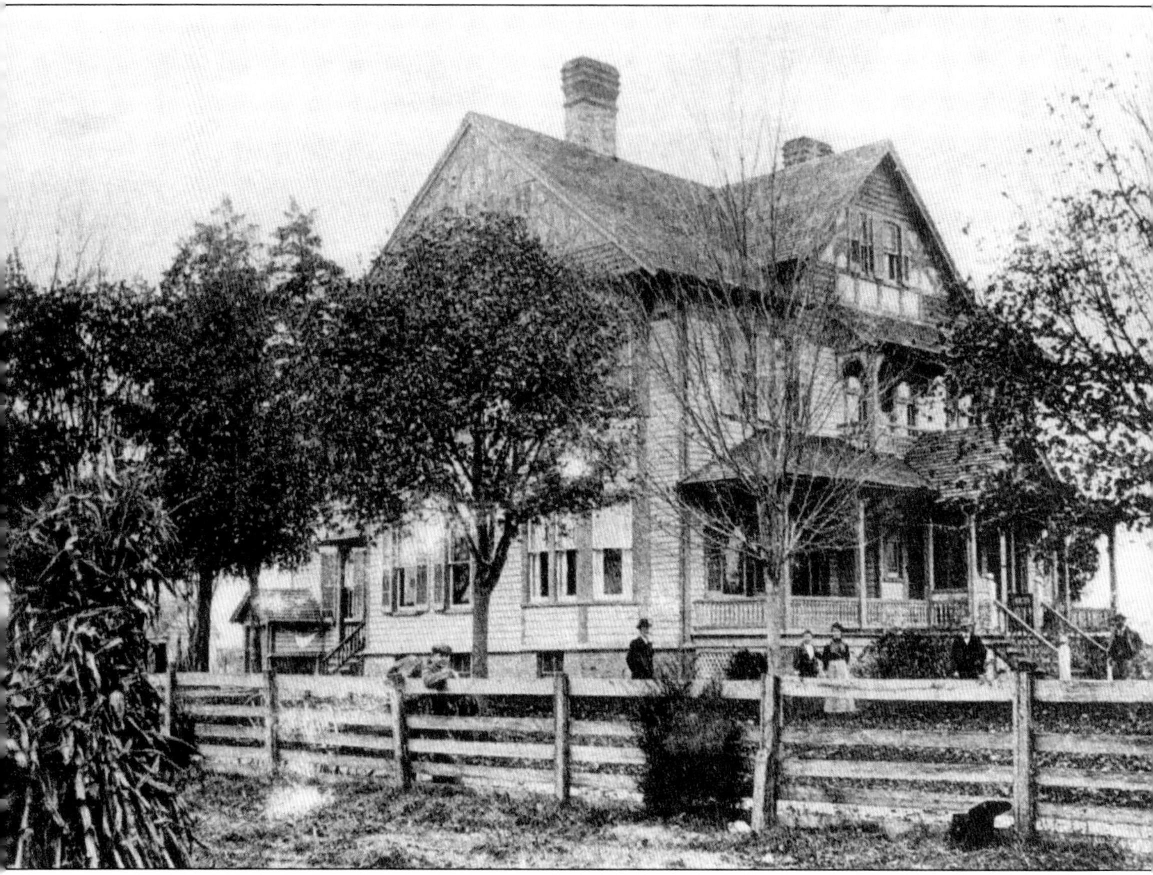

GRANT SEXTON'S DAIRY FARM. This house was indeed on Grant Sexton's Dairy Farm when this card was made, but it was the former home of General Humphrey Humphreys, who built the house on a farm that his wife inherited from her father. It has now been torn down, but was once the Wicomico Children's Home. It was located in the Fairfield Development on the Old Ocean City Road.

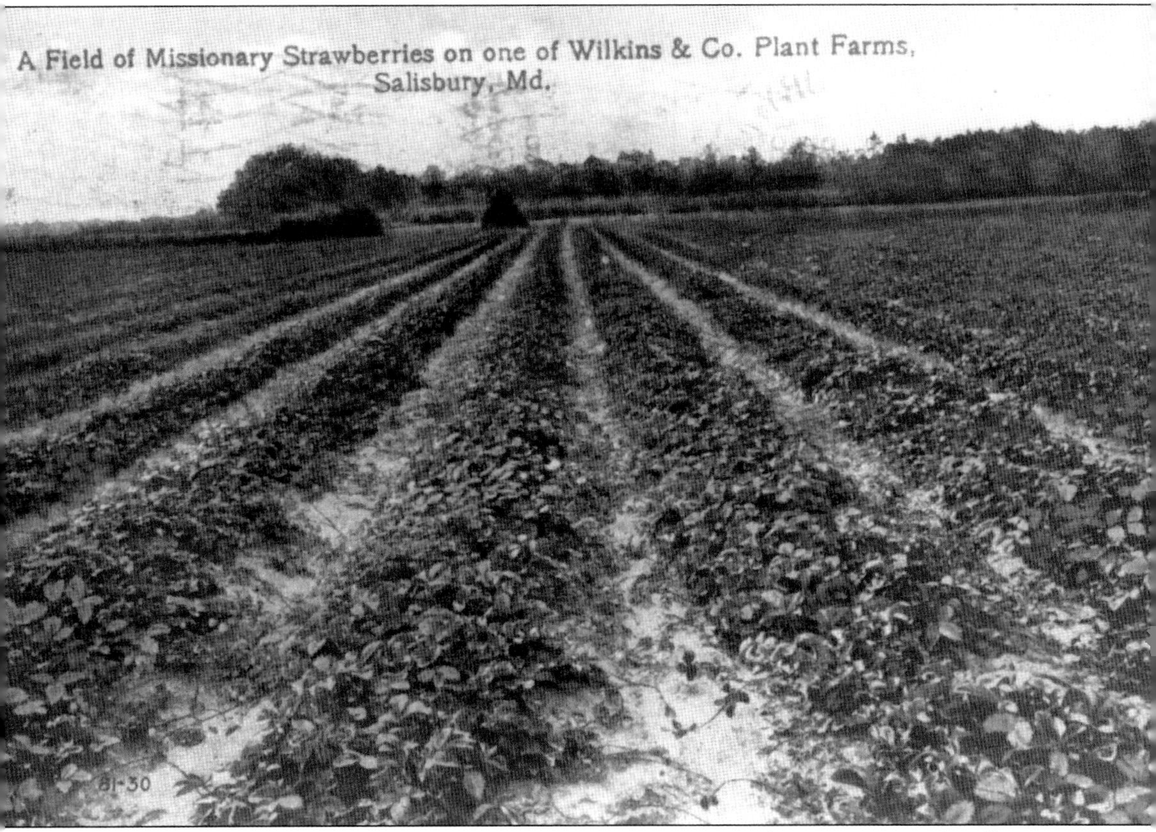

MISSIONARY STRAWBERRIES. Pictured is a field of Missionary strawberries on one of Wilkins & Co., Plant Farms in Salisbury, Maryland. Wilkins and Company was formed in January 1916 as a partnership between Ernest P. Downing, Charles E. Wilkins, Dallas H. Hearne, Arthur B. West, and Arthur H. Holloway, as a strawberry plant grower. Its first purchase was 66 acres of land in the Wango area.

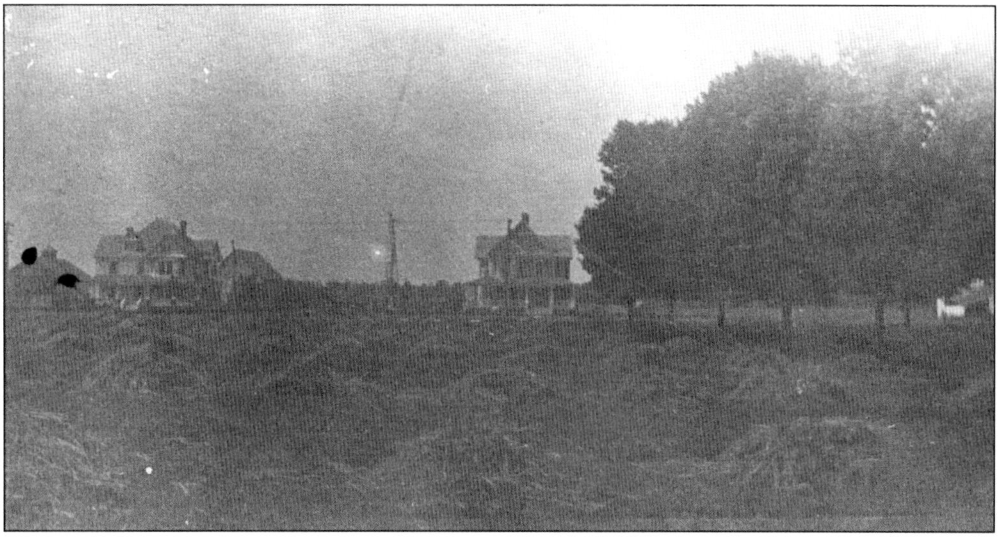

TWO HOUSES AND A HAY FIELD. These houses and the fields are on the East Side of Pemberton Drive, then known as the Anderson Road. (Collection of Gene Wharton.)

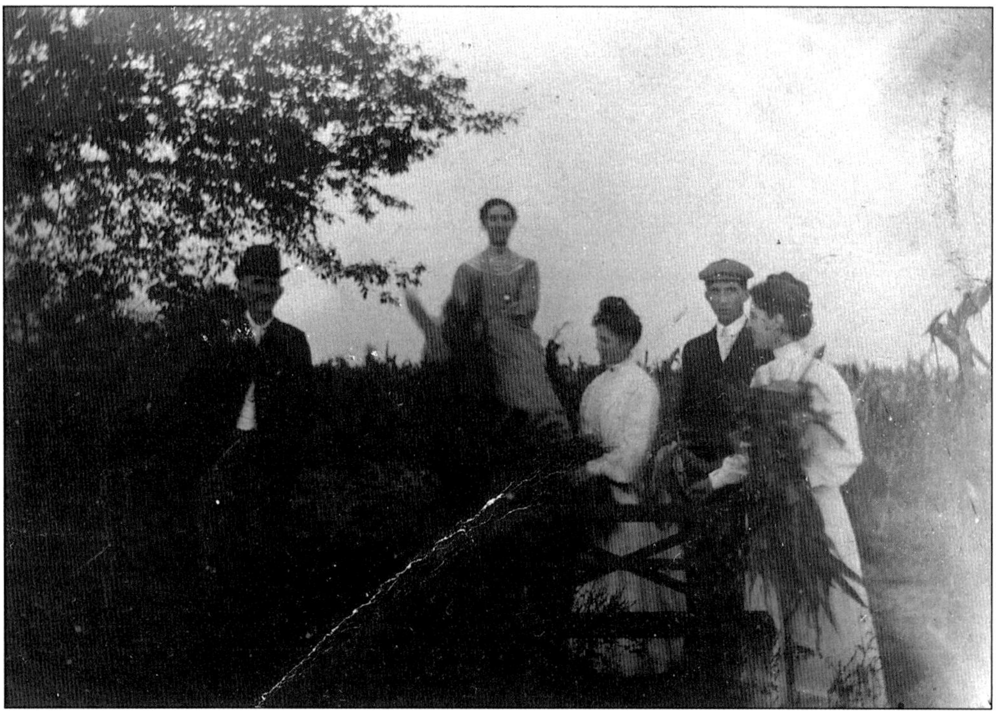

SORGHUM. This card was written from my mother to her brother, who was away at college. The beginning she refers to in her message was the growing of sorghum. It was grown for the molasses that was pressed from its stalks by a horse-powered mill. Today sorghum is widely grown for cattle feed.

Ten

Sleeping on the Highway

Before WW II, Highway 13 ran through the center of Delmar thence in a crooked line to Salisbury where it ran down Division Street to Camden Street went out Camden and turned right to Allen. In 1940 the southern half of the road was straightened and it ran in a line parallel to the railroad tracks south from the Somerset County line. Then the northern half was built through Salisbury north across the overhead bridge in a more or less straight line to a point on the eastern edge of Delmar where it met the Delaware highway.

Road building requires time: time to plan, time to acquire rights of way, and time to build once the money is available (the fight for funds can take years). And the building of a new highway can make or break the people on the old or new roads. This is the story of that change. The photographs in this chapter were taken of the hotels and motels that suffered.

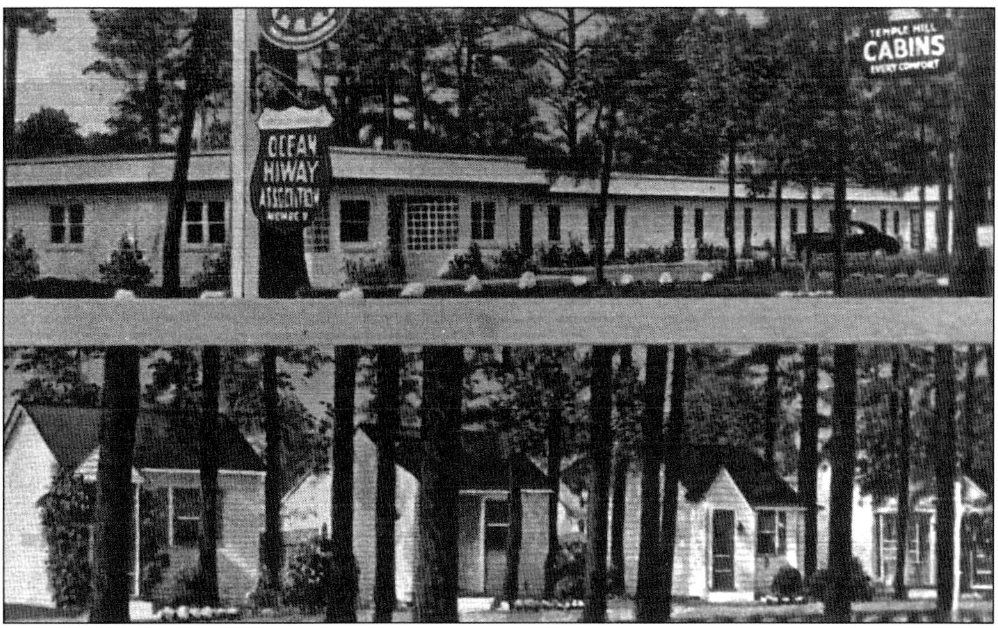

Temple Hill at Eden. This card shows both the guest cottages and the later-built motel. The Bergree Hotel Corporation bought the original land in 1952 and built this facility. When the State Roads Commission condemned the land for the second lane of the highway, it left the corporation with no road access, so they sold it for almost nothing to the adjoining property owner, who ran it for a while under a different name.

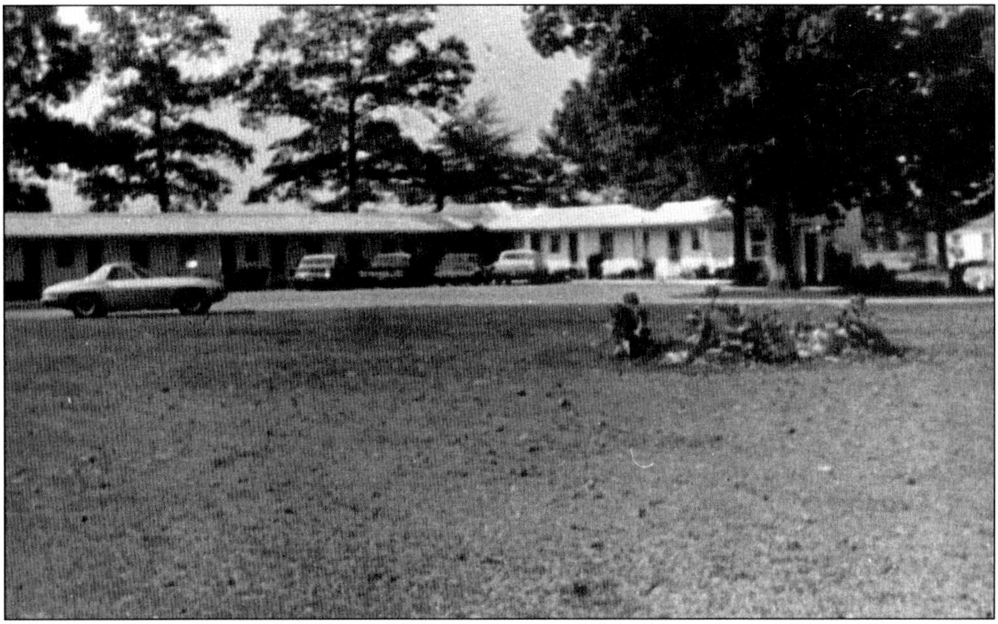

Oak Grove. This card shows the motel when it was under the second ownership. It was then called the Oak Grove, and access was through a side road to the closest intersection. (Collection of the late Hilda Fowler.)

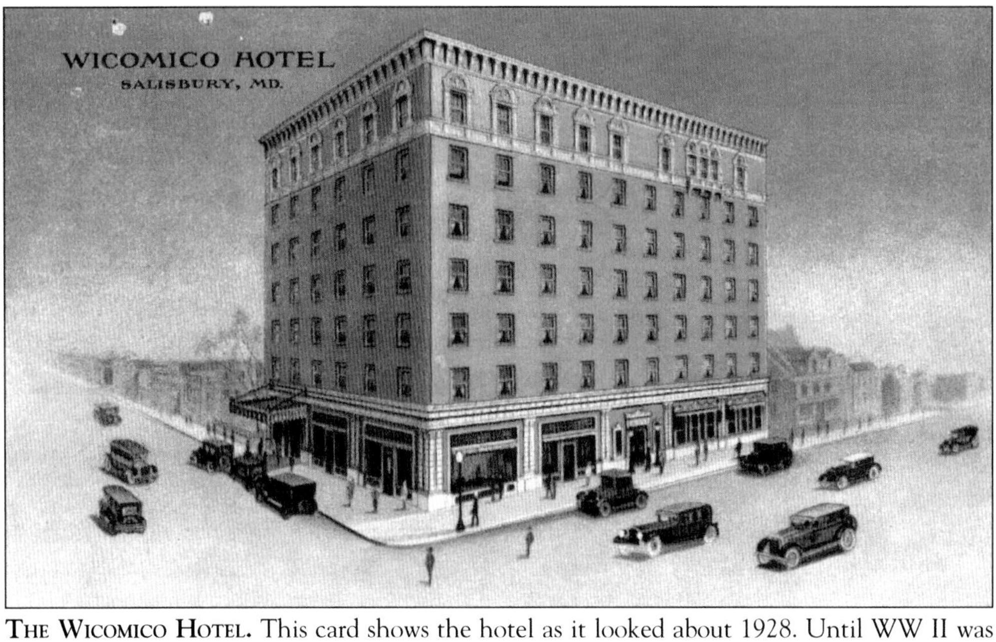

The Wicomico Hotel. This card shows the hotel as it looked about 1928. Until WW II was over and the second leg of the highway north was built, traffic had to pass the hotel. When that link was built, the hotel limped along for a few years, then was sold and changed to an office building. The reverse side of the card shows that the rate for a room with twin beds and bath was $6.

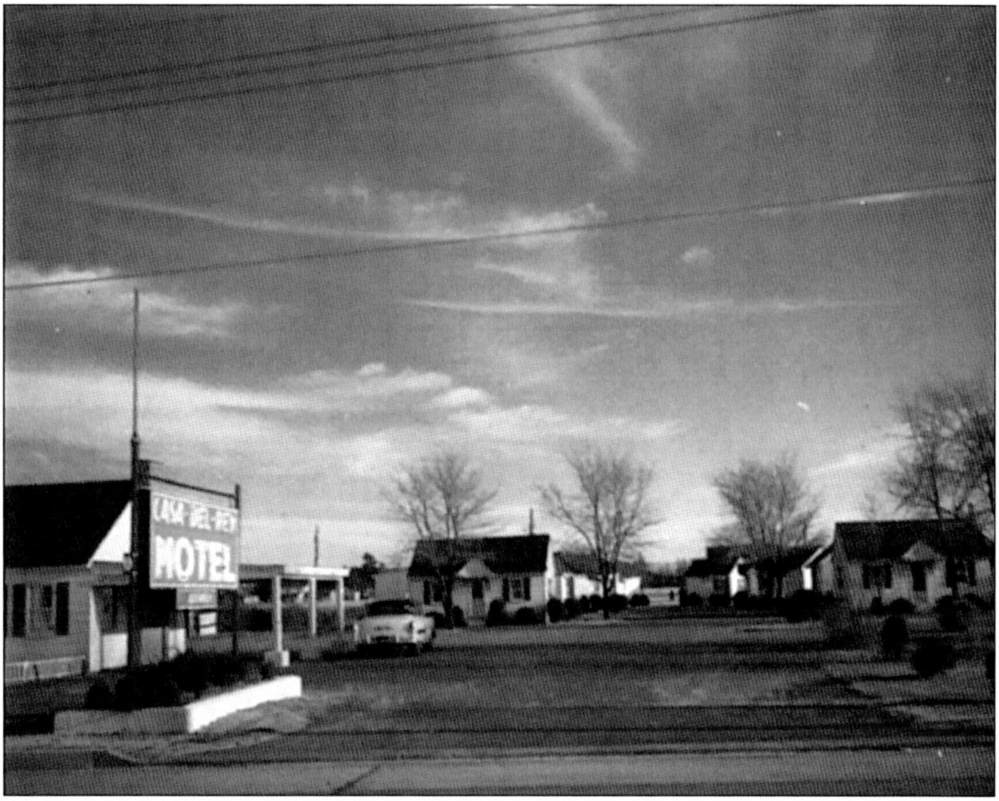

The Casa Del Rey. The Casa Del Rey Restaurant was leased to a man named Gottwald, who prepared delicious meals. My wife and I ate there on Friday nights for his sirloin tips over rice.

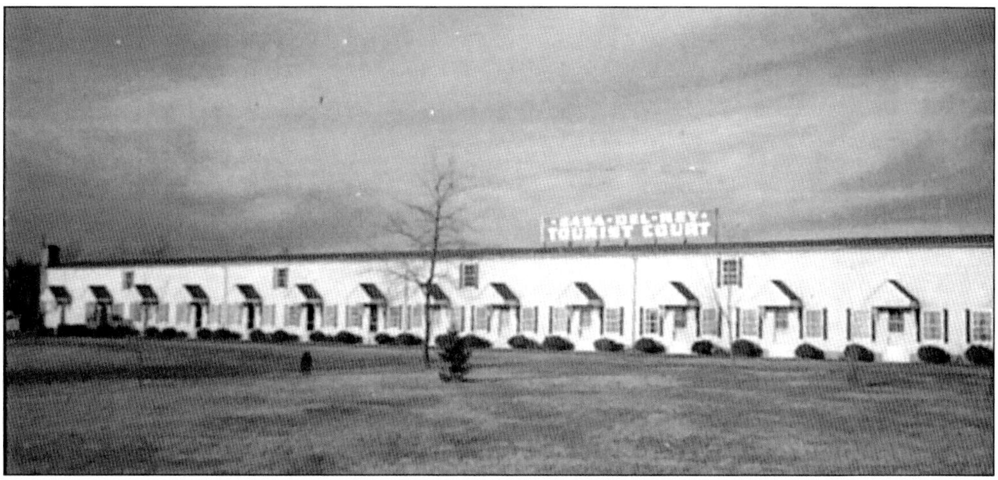

Casa del Rey. This was a case of opportunity bringing temporary success, but finally change passed it by. This motel had been a chicken house. When the highway went by, the owner remodeled the motel into 45 rooms with baths. When more modern motels were designed and built, who wanted to stay in an ex-chicken house?

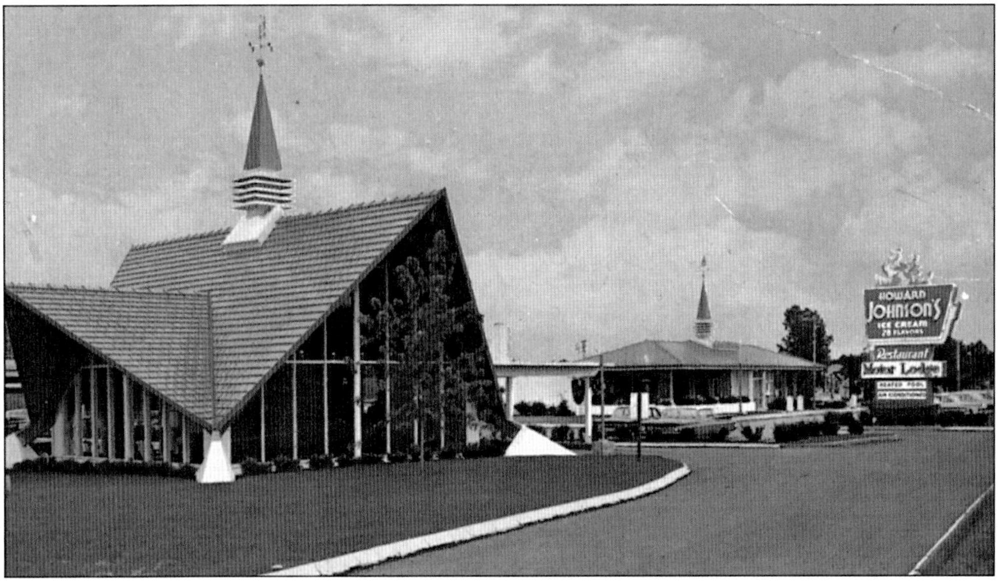

HOWARD JOHNSON MOTEL AND RESTAURANT. In 1958 when the Howard Johnson was built, the total cost of the project and the return made it attractive. But times change. Originally operated by State Senator and Mrs. Edgar L. Bennett, the restaurant is still in operation under the name Zia's.

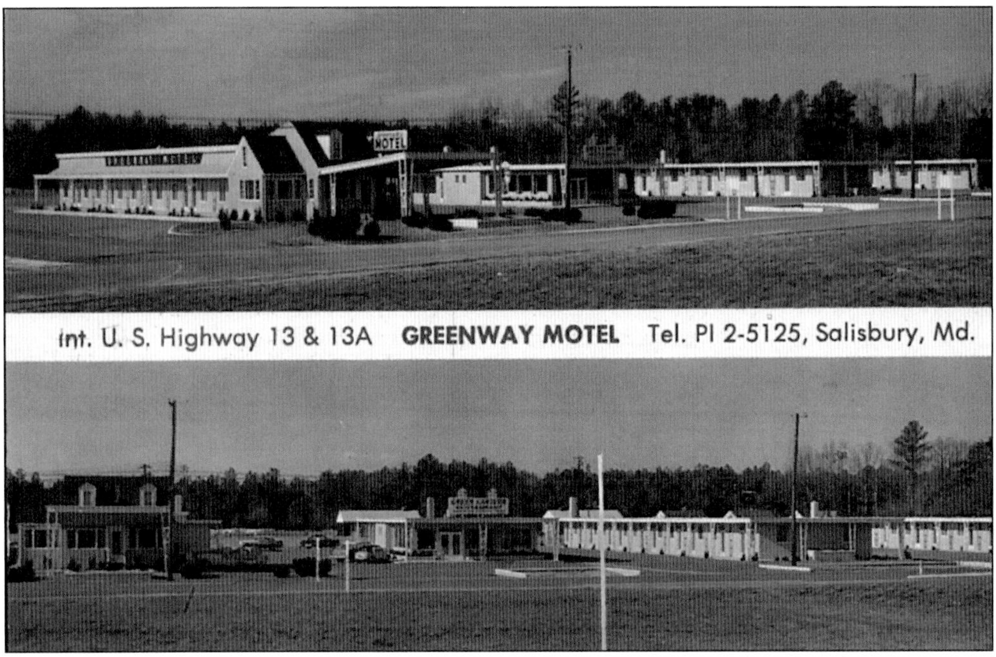

THE GREENWAY. The Greenway Motel started as a warehouse. It was bought about 1957 and converted into a motel, in which additional rooms were built and a pool was added. The Green Lantern Restaurant and Lounge was opened and offered live music and excellent food. The restaurant closed in the 1970s when the motel was closed and converted into two-room efficiency apartments. At the height of its glory the motel had a riding stable and a miniature golf course.

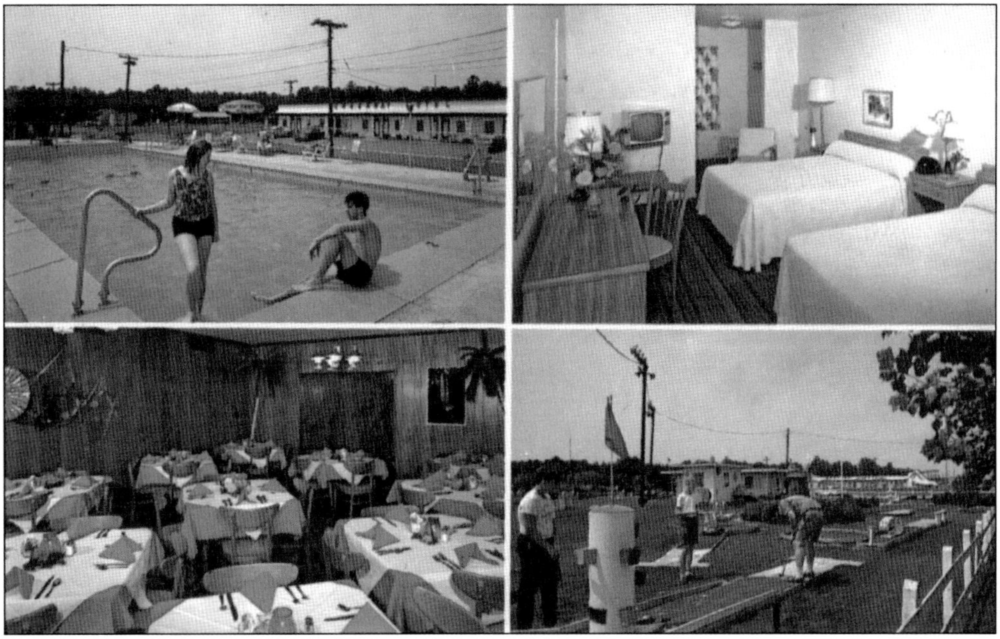

THE GREENWAY FACILITIES. This card shows the pool, restaurant, and golf course.

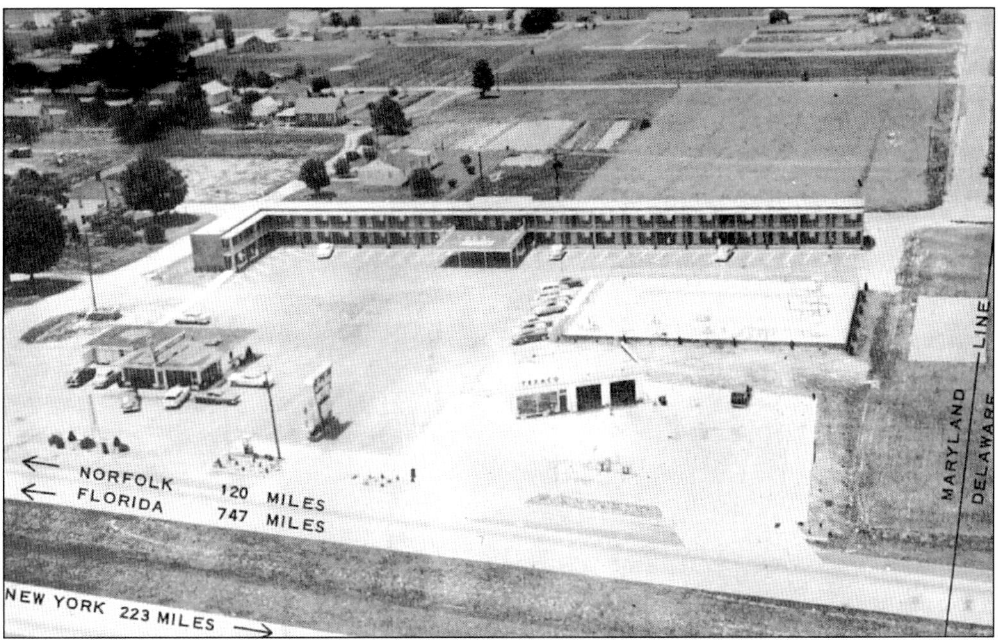

STATE LINE MOTEL. This motel was like Topsy, "It jus' growed." The restaurant was built first and was bought by Edward Wainwright at foreclosure sale. He had bought the adjoining property to State Street Extended in Delmar and started to build a motel. He built the Texaco Station first, then the pool, and the first motel units in 1959.

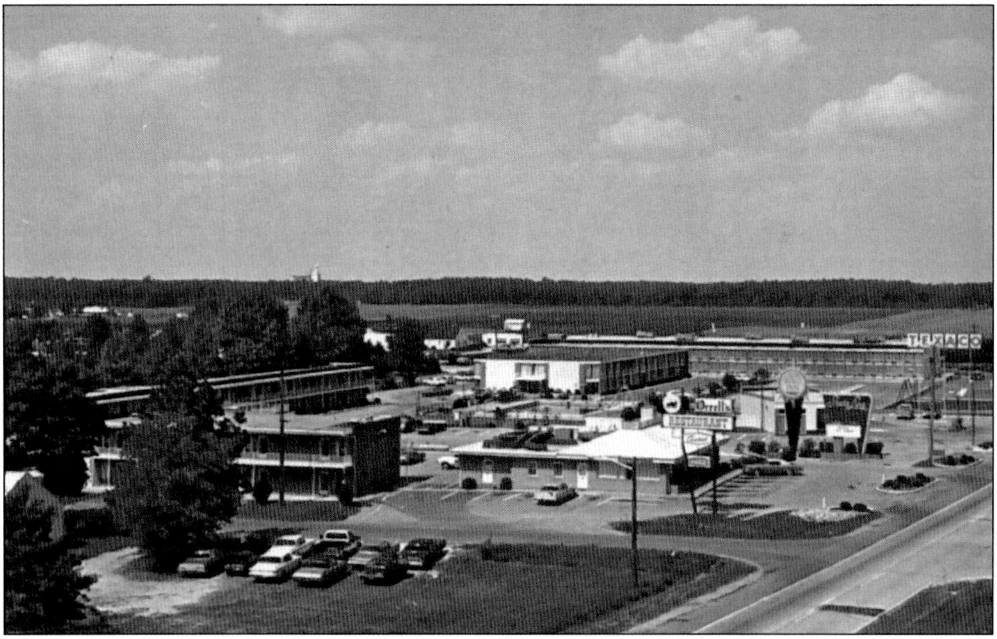

STATE LINE MOTEL AND CONVENTION CENTER. Mr. Wainwright kept building, adding a second building in 1964 and a Convention Hall in 1970. With the extra rooms he was able to attract large conventions to the area. The second building burned in 1973 and was not replaced. The Convention Center has had several owners since then but has maintained continuous operations.

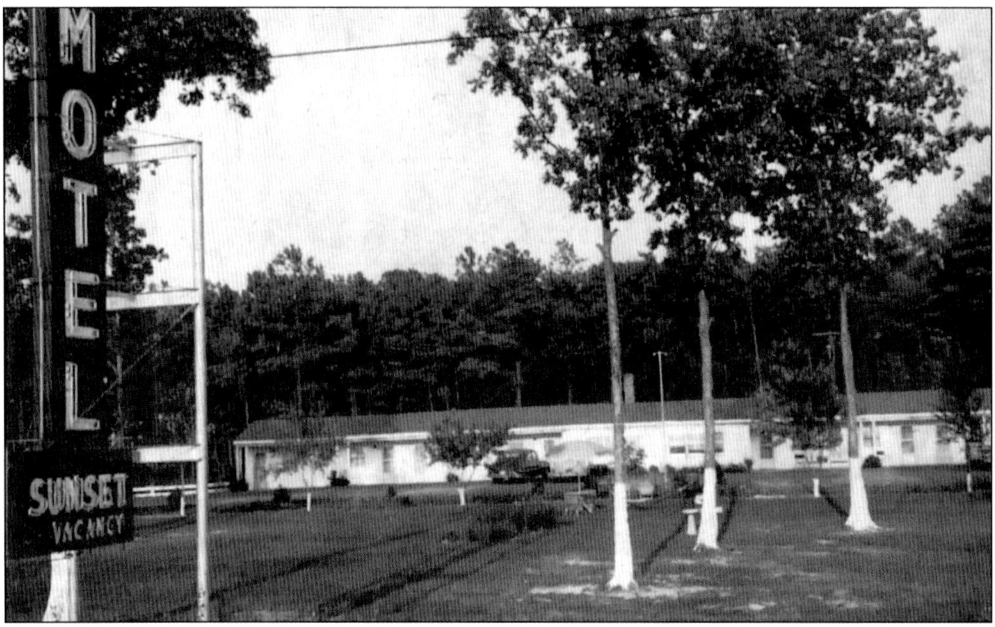

SUNSET MOTEL. This motel was built across the highway from the State Line by Mary Karakesh. At her death it was sold and has changed hands since, but it is still operating.

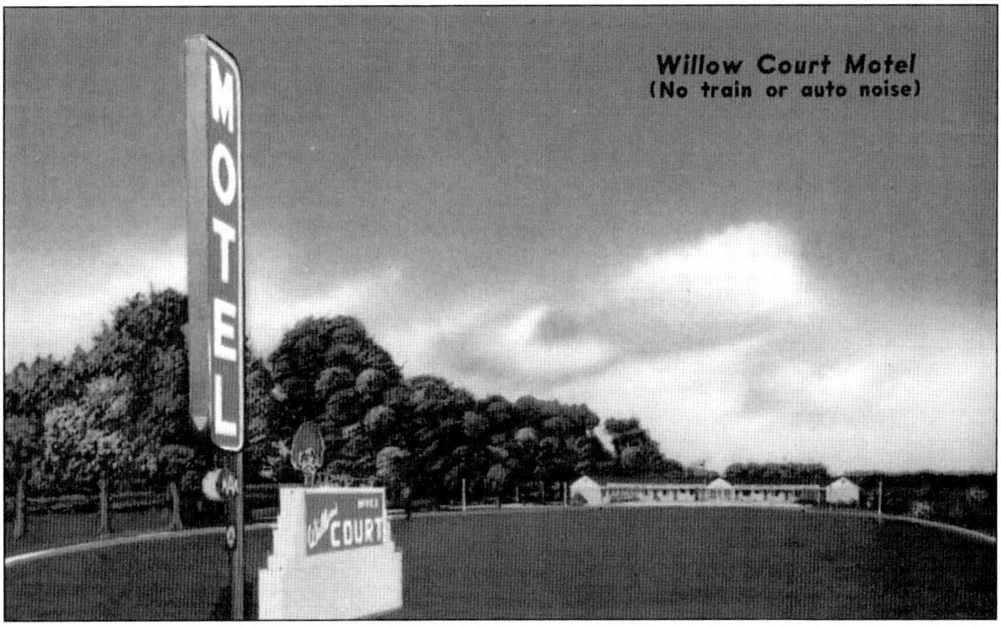

WILLOW COURT MOTEL. This motel was built in 1946 by Ellsworth D. Sherman. He called it Willow Court because of the line of willow trees that lined the driveway.

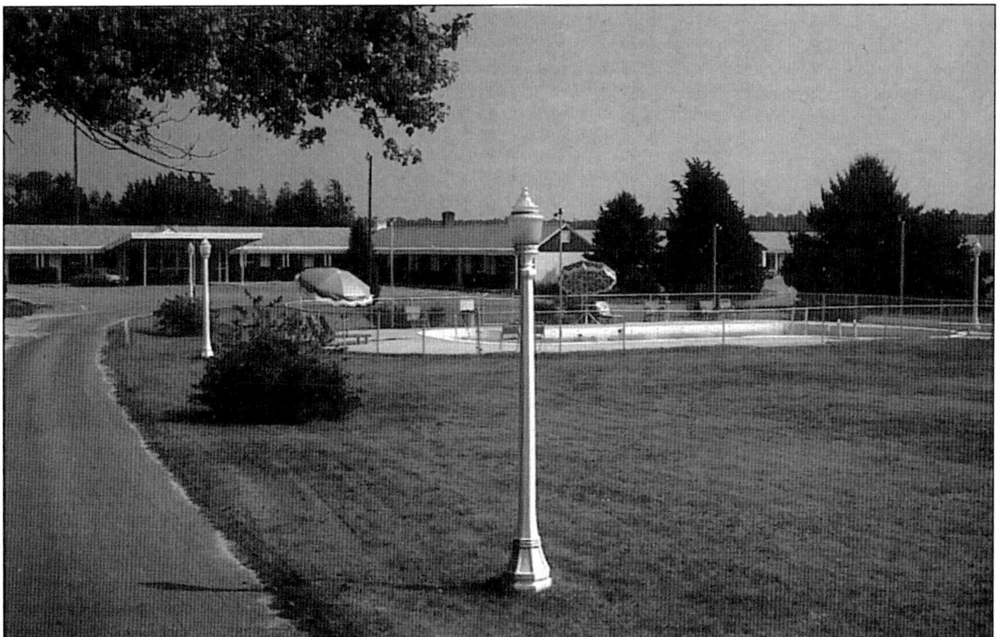

LORD SALISBURY MOTEL. Sherman doubled the size of the motel and changed its name to the Lord Salisbury. He sold it in 1973 to Salisbury Enterprises, a corporation that has run it ever since.

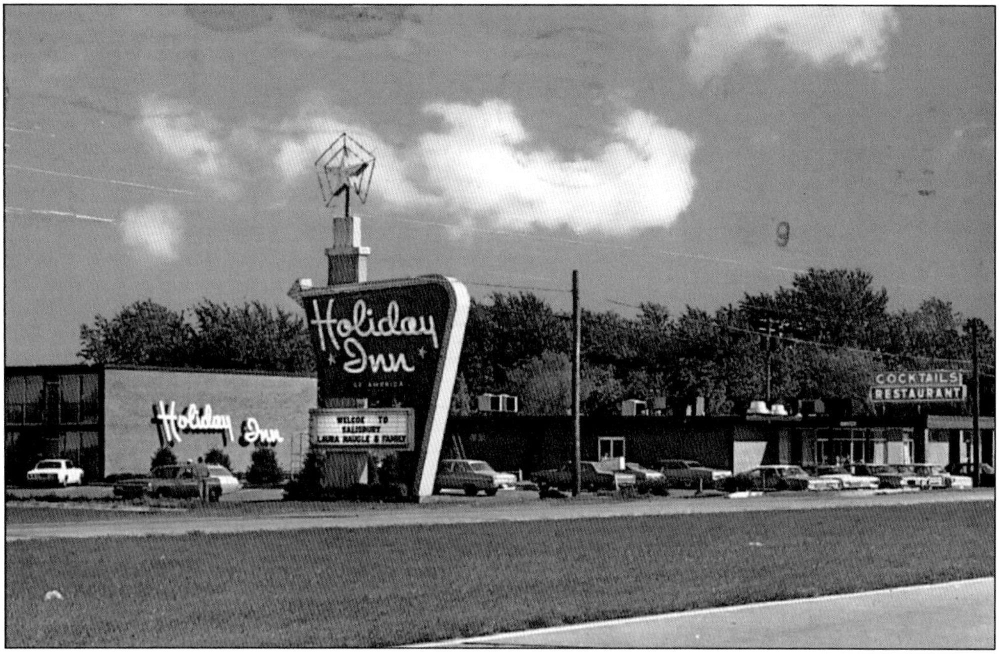

HOLIDAY INN. This motel changed its affiliation on January 1, 1998, and became a Howard Johnson, but there was no change in ownership. It was built in 1964 and offers meals and drinks. It also hosts moderate size meetings, as well as once being the host to a dinner theatre.

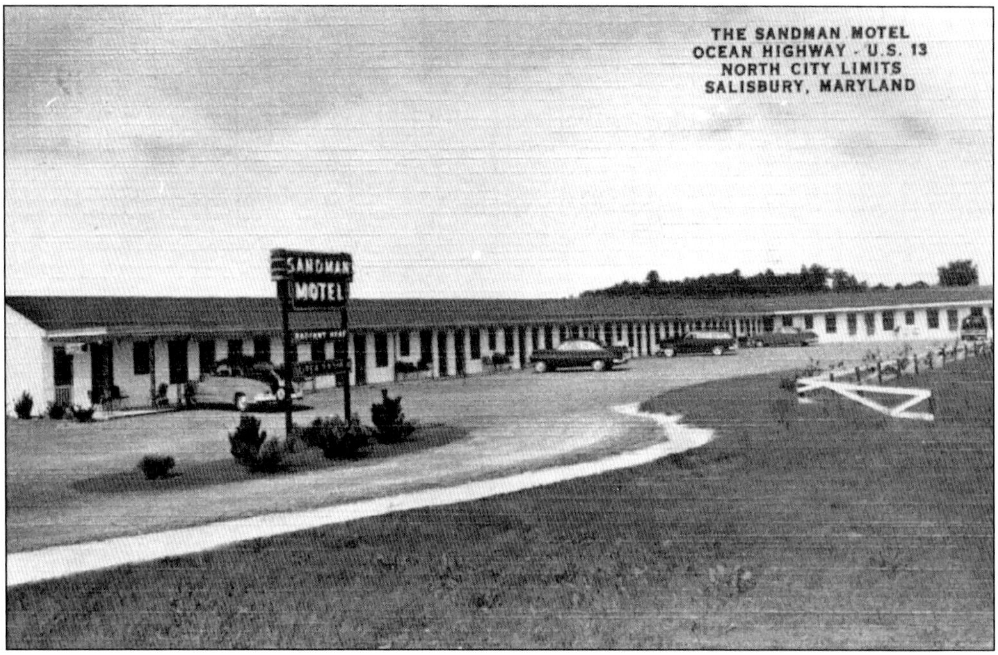

THE SANDMAN. The Sandman was built in 1950 on the West Side of Route 13 and on the north side of the overhead bridge. It was the first motel to advertise radiant heat. The picture shows only the original section. It had changed owners but still operated under the same name. (Collection of Gene Wharton.)

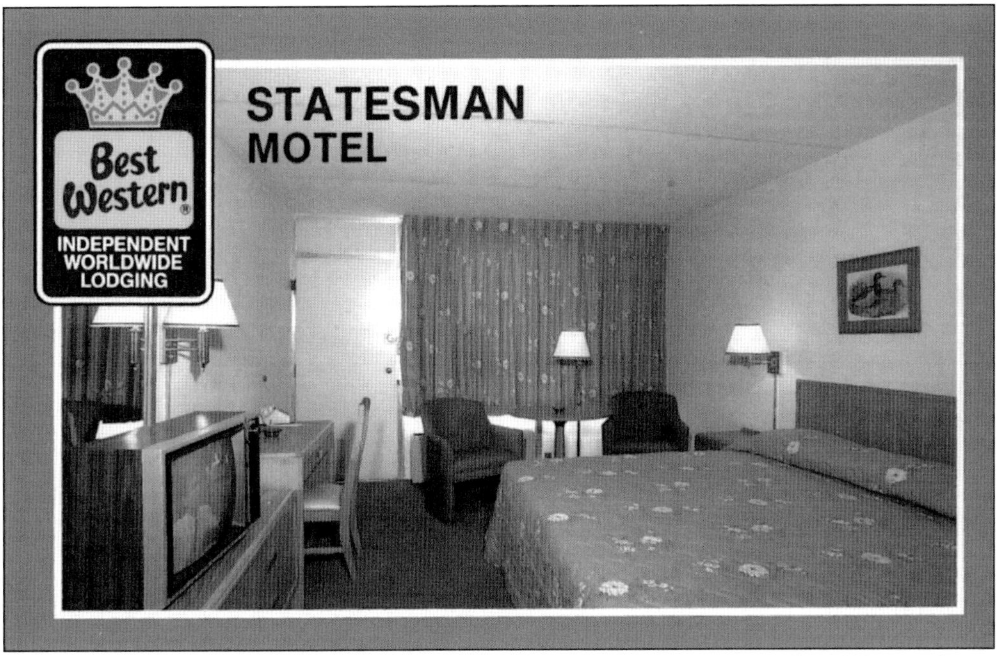

THE STATESMAN. This motel is in Salisbury at Baltimore Avenue. It was a Best Western but is now an Econo Lodge. The Statesman was started by Joseph Rodriquez 25 years ago but now has different ownership.

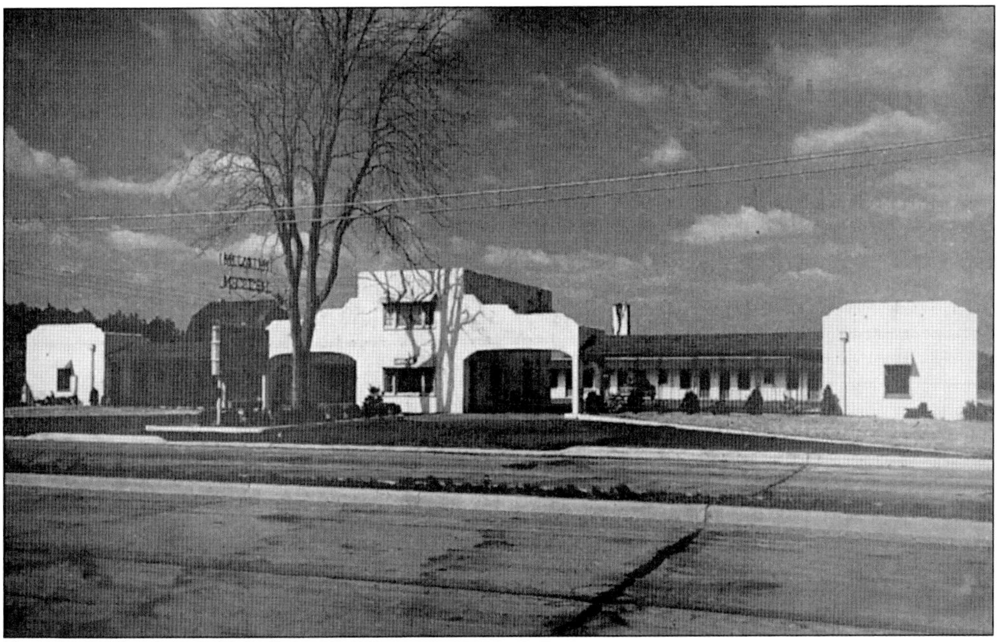

MIAMI MOTEL. The Pillsburys, who owned this motel during the 1950s and put out this card, were its third owners. It was purchased by the Larmar Corporation and was brick faced to spruce it up, then re-sold. Since then it has operated without incident and is the motel that has operated the longest in the Salisbury area.

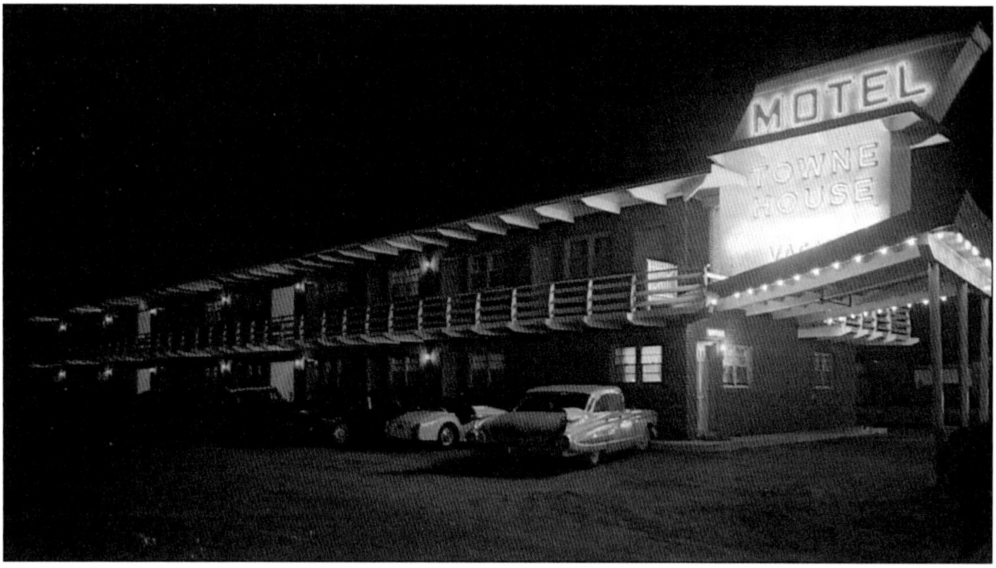

TOWNE HOUSE MOTEL. This motel is now the Thrift Travel Inn. It is distinguished as the first downtown motel in Salisbury and is located at Elizabeth Street and North Salisbury Boulevard. It is operated by Mr. and Mrs. Walter Bozman and offers a free continental breakfast as well as HBO.

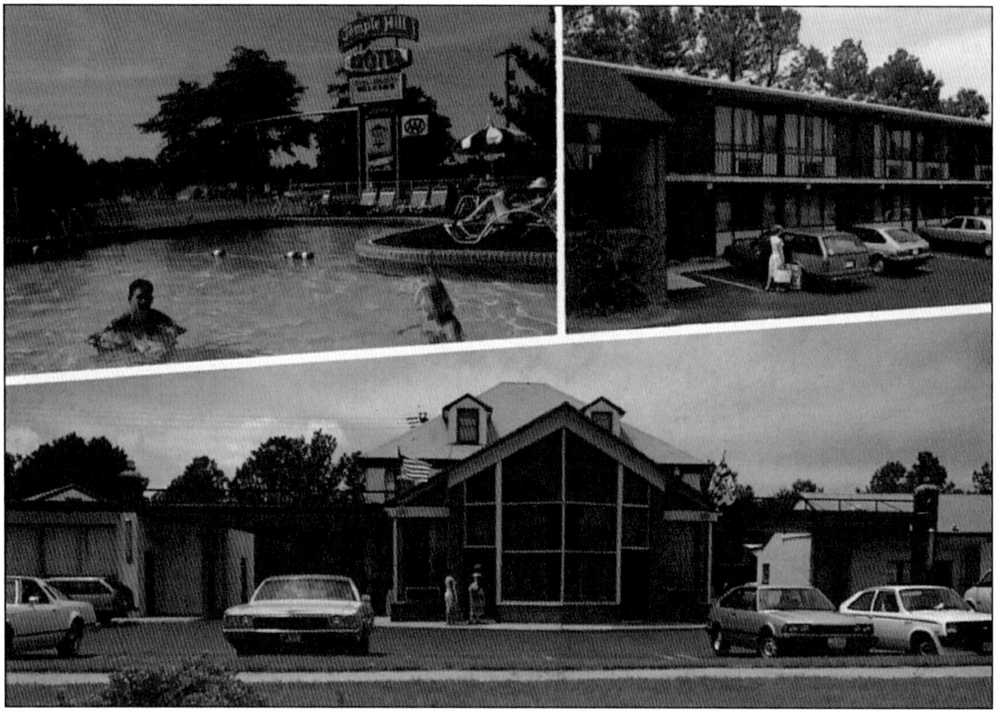

TEMPLE HILL MOTEL. The Bergree Hotel Corporation, when it lost its highway access, went to Elwood and Minnie Fleming and talked them into building and leasing to them a motel at the corner of Kay Avenue and South Salisbury Boulevard. When their lease ran out it was not renewed and was inherited by Mark Nelson from the Flemings. His daughter and her husband now run it.